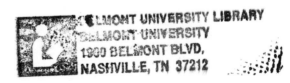

The Dirtfarmer's Son

Books by the same author

Gauguin's Paradise Lost
Scenario for an Artist's Apocalypse
Freud, Leonardo da Vinci, and the Vulture's Tail
Picasso's Brothel: Les Demoiselles d'Avignon
The Ara Pacis of Augustus and Mussolini
Little Sister: Tragedy of Young Love
The Youth of Cézanne and Zola
Cézanne and the Eternal Feminine
The Picnic and the Prostitute

Wayne Andersen

THE DIRTFARMER'S SON

ÉDITIONS FABRIART

GENEVA AND BOSTON

© 2003 Wayne Andersen

ISBN 0-9725573-9-3

Contents

Chapter

Foreword

For years I put off telling my life story, although impelled to write it. By what commanding necessity, I don't know. Maybe it's just that I will die one day and don't wish to leave my life in the darkness of its own grave. I had a friend, the New York sculptor, Herbert Ferber, who said one afternoon while with him at his Vermont retreat that he was about to cut down the trees he planted up there, resentful they'd live longer than he. He's dead now; the trees are alive and still growing. Unmindful of arboreal mortality he should have planted birch trees, not beeches. Made of sturdier stuff, a beech tree lives forever.

To write of one's life is not to relive it as one's self but to release it from imprisoning memory, talking it out before it too disappears. It was a life, after all, that I witnessed as the audience of my own performance, and I'm the only one who can narrate it for the only one listening at the moment, talking to myself as if I knew the person I'm offering as the myself who lived the story. I would like to write as an ethnographer, with the impassive intonations of a scholar, sturdy as a beech, as if writing up the life of someone else as concisely as I am able, like a coroner's report or a tree ring analysis. But the attentive reader would soon overwrite me, should I become evasive for the sake of unbending pride, finding me an author of an external existence, like a building without a door.

This book is far short of a life story. When page 250 came around and I was still fourteen years old, another 2000 pages would lie ahead of me should I be unable to stop. So this book stopped short at age fifteen when the Iowa kid was pupating into a California kid, and had begun pumping blood into his wing veins in preparation for flight. And then it occurred to me that I'd written less an autobiography than a history of a time and place as it impinged upon a youth over his formative years, the years that typical self-life historians dispatch with a few paragraphs, anxious to get themselves old enough to know what they were doing, to when adulthood puts the controls in one's own hands.

I've depended less on library and archive resources than a scholarly historian would, preferring to work with my own memory and that of my older sisters and cousins my age or older that still farm in northwestern Iowa. So this book is a delimited, partial history of Iowa during the 1920s to the early 1940s—the plight of farmers, the notorious Beer War, Milk War, Farmer's Rebellion, Penny Auctions, the early years of sinful Sioux City noted for its saloons and naughty women, politicians and police on the take, swing bands and jazz, the milieu in which I was born and almost grew up. From dirt farm to small town, to big Sioux City, to become—via California, New York, and Paris—a professor who taught at Columbia, Yale, and Harvard universities, and for twenty years at the Massachusetts Institute of Technology, not to mention becoming an author of many books and an architectural designer of mosques in Saudi Arabia.

I have written the unpolished simplicity of my childhood as it encountered the complexity that both aggrandized and eroded it, like a fast flowing river turning up rocks only to smooth them. The professional historian who may chance to read this book will recognize that I've pushed «the new history» to what may be its reasonable limit. Academic history books were once built on apocryphal events, like wars, and on notable people, like emperors, kings and queens, presidents, famous mobsters and artists, poets, and the like. There is a war in this book, the Milk War, that, to the extent of my research, had but one casualty, inadvertently shot. The First World War is mentioned a few times, but with no greater import within the scope of this text than foreclosures on farm mortgages claiming more Iowa victims than that war. While great events and famous people affect about everyone, it's the close environment and day-to-day grinding out of life that forms the unique character of individuals.

This book differs also from the structure of the new history to the extent that it blends with autobiography. I've restricted «history» to what affected my growing up years within a rural family that the 1930s Depression pushed into becoming a city family. When possible, I've resisted deploying generalizations and statistical averages that inform even the more recent historical studies, for there is no such person as a general or average person. The average is an abstraction. Real people, by the definition of reality, are not average. The average acreage of an Iowa farm doesn't tell us the size of anyone's farm. The average price of milk paid to a dairy farmer in, say, 1932, doesn't tell us what any single farmer received in total revenue. Still, I confess that the history of northwestern Iowa over the span of time I'm covering cannot require that a separate book for every individual be written. The best I can do with this single book is to mediate between standard history and absurdity.

And before being accused of distorting history by weighting my text with gray lead, so much about dirt and beer and social immoralities, while offering so little of the bright side of life, I will confess that indeed I have done that. But this book is not about everybody. It's about myself and the people, things, and events that fashioned the mold into which my youth was poured. To the extent of my capabilities as host of memories and scholar, and willingness to publicly undress, this book is a double of myself. Of my youth, yes, but because I'm writing as an adult, I cannot entirely hide my adulthood in its formative years, as if not responsible for how I remember and record those years. So let the more intimate passages graciously creep under you modesty and censorial repressions. You, too, were once a child. You know your secrets, some still embarrassing, others cherished. They are all fragments of your personal history, encapsulated in your name and proclaiming your reality.

There is no direct equivalent between reality and memory. One's reality in retrospect is largely filtered, censored, and adapted to one's sense of one's self as an adult, so no autobiographer can write the whole and unadulterated truth. And few academic historians will claim they write the absolute truth about the past. One fact stands out from my reading of history books devoted to Iowa. They all stop short of what might seem embarrassing. Oral historians avoid asking anything about the intimate life of individuals they interview. One contemporary interviewer of an older Iowan, on getting her to talk about automobiles in Iowa during the 1920s, cut off the subject when his subject recalled being on a drive with her boyfriend when he stopped in a secluded place off a country road and drew a flask of whiskey from the dashboard. No doubt wanting to hear what happened next, but fearing she might tell him, the investigator changed the subject, only to hear the woman say,

«C'mon now. We did the same things in cars back then that teenagers do today.» It's this and other sorts of censorship that pervade both history books and autobiographies. So when you come upon passages that get down to what would embarrass you to reveal about yourself, please just smile and pleasantly recall that either you had much the same experiences in your own contexts or you weren't conscious during your youth.

I have an American friend of considerable accomplishment, now living in Paris, who recently published his autobiography. When writing it, he omitted everything from his life that he didn't want his wife to know, so his follies and affairs were blanketed under layers of social morality and blissful fidelity. When his wife read the pre-published manuscript, she admonished him, saying, «What sort of man will people think I married and spent so many years with? a wimp?» She demanded that he put into it everything that would make it appear she'd had a real man in her life.

Some of my information may conflict with what others have acquired through academic research, but, as I said,. I depended on my memories and those of my extended family who grew up in the Sioux City area and were farmers and some of them still are. And I looked to newspapers and popular periodicals being read within a day or two of their issue. They tell what was believed at the time, by people of the time, which makes true history, not what others who were not of the time came to believe later. To you, the moon may look to be just gray rocks and gravel and dust, as the most recent scientific studies tell us it's made of, but once upon a time it was made of green cheese. Its grayness must have been mold.

Wayne Andersen
January 28, 2003

It's simply not true, as it says in the Bible,
that the meek shall inherit the earth.
In the Iowa of my youth, they got run off it.

Chapter 1

*Baby Boy Andersen: blue
eyes, blond hair, and a footprint
the shape of a rotten potato*

I was born in a farmhouse near Hinton, Iowa—to be precise, on July 7th, 1928, around three o'clock in the afternoon. All that I can recall about my birth is that, on feeling air all around me, I knew nothing of the external world. A lady from a neighboring farm, Elfrieda Meuche, acted as the midwife. She'd arrived on horseback, or maybe in a buggy, shortly after the call went out over the party line. A fleshy, plain-faced country girl, Elfrieda supported herself by scrubbing floors, hanging wallpaper, and delivering babies—human babies, calves, foals, or lambs, the procedure hardly differed among them any more than had the act that generated them. As deliveries went in that era of casual child rearing, surely she suspended me upside down by the ankles and smacked my tender butt to induce lung-expanding screams, and to make sure of my gender took a good look at my inert and defenseless penis. Life started that way for most of us, with a spanking and our privates made public.

I just said I was born on a farm—hand delivered. I've known this for a fact only for a few years. Over most of my life I've had to cope with the dreadful notion that I was born in Sioux City, in a hospital. Farm boys lose an aspect of pre-natal vitality when born in a city, like wild animals do if born in a zoo. So what I can't remember, but only imagine, got off to an erroneous start. My sister, Loretta, broke the thread that tied me to that thought in time to modify these opening paragraphs. «You weren't born in St. Joseph's Hospital,» she assured me from Ukiah, California, where she now lives. «That's where you had your appendix out when you were four.»

This timely information made sense also of something I remembered from about age four, but couldn't differentiate as to time and place. While in that hospital, I climbed down from my bed to retrieve a little balsa wood airplane I'd launched. The bed too high, I couldn't climb back up. Embarrassed, I hid under it. Apparently, an emergency call sounded throughout the ward to search for a missing patient, who wouldn't have gotten far, considering he had stiches in his belly and wore a flannel nightgown open at the back. In due time, a cleaning lady discovered me when her dust mop encountered an obstruction under the bed.

Loretta was twelve when I was born, a whiff of a girl while a farm worker in overalls, plow-boots and straw hat. «I was working in the field with Dad, cutting hay—he on the binder and me on the tractor—and when we came in you were in the basket,» she said, «and mother and Elfrieda were at the kitchen table drinking coffee, and supper was on the stove.»

I felt elated on hearing those words, so relieved to hear that I was born an authentic farmer. For farmers are basic. All of society fits within two poles, royalty and peasantry. The dirt farmer is as close to nature as royalty to highness. To be in between is like living in a zone rather than a place—low class to upper class, neither top nor bottom, fish nor fowl. I could philosophize endlessly on this construction that you might think fanciful, but I'd better wait until old enough in these pages to be mindful of what I say.

Other than my miraculous birth, Huey Long's election as governor of Louisiana, Herbert Hoover's re-election as United States President, Meyer Schapiro's first lecture on Impressionism at Columbia University (where thirty-three years later I took my doctorate), Mae West's debut on Broadway, the birth of Shirley Temple, and the invention of the computer at the Massachusetts Institute of Technology (where thirty-seven years later I became a professor) nothing all that momentous happened in 1928—not until 1929, when the Depression began, the Valentine's Day Massacre befell Chicago, and the anti-Prohibition movement got underway. And lest I neglect mentioning later in this story that Victorine Meurent, the Olympia of Paris' 1863 Salon des Refusés that set the art world on end, died about the moment I was born, in spite of its being said thirty years earlier that she'd taken to prostitution, drugs and alcohol, I will do so here. Such events come to mind spontaneously, without being called, and serve to ground me in reality, like Jesus in Christmas. Arbitrary dislocations come with the freedom of autobiography; from one's age of the moment one can move about in time and space, be most anywhere at any time, and associate with anyone, living, dead, imagined, or made up for the sake of the story.

I don't recall being born, of course, but the claustrophobia I suffer from still is said to be the supersensory vestige of a long wait in the dark and a difficult passage.

«Nonsense,» my mother said on hearing me say that years later when psychoanalysis of the 1950s offered an originating cause in infancy and early childhood for every neurosis and phobia. «You slipped out like a calf. The only difference was that it took over a year for you to stand up on your legs while a calf does it in a few minutes.»

I could only smile at her poke in the ribs, her exquisite way of nipping one's bubbles, and say, «Well, if I had been born a calf, you'd have been a cow and Dad would have castrated me before I was a year old.»

«Of course he would have,» she snapped back. «It would have kept you out of trouble. As it was, you weren't even circumcised.»

As a matter of fact, I wasn't given an official name either. When at the age of thirty-two in New York, about to sail to France and in need of a passport, I found myself lacking a birth certificate. I wrote to obtain one to the Woodbury County Clerk in Iowa, the county that embraced Sioux City and the hospital in which I thought I'd been born. The certificate arrived forthwith, but from Plymouth County where our farm was situated—my name: Baby Boy Andersen, blue eyes, blond hair, and a footprint the shape of a rotten potato. No wonder I'd suffered so many nicknames during childhood: Pete, Whitey, and Andy. I don't recall being called Wayne, maybe by schoolteachers. Most often my father called me Marius, his first son's name, saving him from cluttering his brain with yet another name, our extended family so huge—as many aunts dropping babies as our cows dropped calves. And after my fifth year, my mother often slipped and called me Harold, the name of my baby brother, the new focus of her attention. But such nominal transgressions need not be taken seriously. I've swallowed the first syllable of many a lover's name when in the company of one with a different name. So I hold no grudge.

Throughout my adult life I've not liked the name Wayne. In English it's a bit too pretty, and in other languages, too, it sounds feminine. At the age of twenty, after an exchange of letters with a literary intimate I'd not met in person—an Italian man, writing from Rome; me, from Hollywood—I received from him an ardent marriage proposal. Apparently my girlfriend at the time, Connie Fox, while on a bicycle trip throughout Europe, had told him about me but hadn't clarified my gender. Misled by my delicate name, and bedazzled no doubt by my letter-writing style, he took for granted that I was an enticingly passionate young woman, maybe a lusty movie starlet prone to Italian good looks and chest hair. Not wanting to embarrass him into impotency for hallucinations of making love mistakenly to a man, I wrote back, graciously declining his overture, saying I was engaged to a man and soon to be married. Surely desolated, he didn't write to me again. Maybe in grief he drowned himself in the Tiber.

In Germany, where I've spent some time, the natives cannot say Wayne, not having a W in their voice box, but rather Vain, which at times has sounded remarkably fitting. When living in Paris as a writer and itinerant intellectual, I usually introduced myself as «Wayne, *comme* John Wayne,» for everyone in France has seen his movies and overlaid masculinity on his name. Then I found myself addressed as Monsieur Wayne. In the Middle East, where I am known as a mosque designer and purveyor of taste and style, I am called Vesti, the middle name I share with my father and grandfather, and maybe all the way back to the middle name of Erik Bloodaxe and Harold Bluetooth, my ancient ancestral Vikings.

I was cruising through my final year of graduate studies at Columbia University in 1961 when that birth certificate arrived. For a couple of weeks I compelled my distrait fellow students to address me by my legal name, Baby Boy, evidenced by the certificate I carried rolled in my hand like a Roman magistrate. After the department chairman, Professor Rudolf Wittkower, had a sobering chat with me to adumbrate a bleak academic future with such a name, I decided to get registered as Vesti Andersen. But by then, in military, academic, and social security records, perhaps also in an FBI file (for in 1951, during the McCarthy era, I attended a single Marxist Student Union meeting in Los Angeles), I was officially Wayne Andersen, so the best I could do within reason was to have myself dubbed Wayne Vesti Andersen. The family name, ending with a «sen» to identify me as Danish, stayed with me. Because it starts with an A, that name has had greater import for my life than my blue eyes, blond hair, or that I wasn't circumcised. I'll get around eventually to saying why. I'll say a lot about myself as this text moves along, but being at heart a performer, I need a stage, a background, some props.

My father, Henry Vesti Andersen, an émigré at age fifteen, was born in Denmark on a farm north of Nyby, between the hamlets Gerndrup and Asbo, in 1889. That year, Paul Gauguin and Vincent van Gogh exhibited in the Café Volpini at Paris' World's Fair. My mother, Anna Marguerita Johanna Steinhagen, a broad and pillow-breasted woman (her parents immigrated from northern Germany), was born in Clinton, Iowa on November 3, 1895, about the time when, in Paris, the adventurous art dealer, Ambroise Vollard, was organizing the first Paul Cézanne exhibition. Henry and Anna Marguerita married on April 17th, 1912, at the height of Picasso's Cubism in Paris. By marrying an alien, my mother lost her United States citizenship under the controversial anti-alien Congressional Act of June 1936, meant to punish women who had wed non-Americans. Responding to women's protests, a remedial act of July 1940 repatriated her after she came to court and pledged allegiance to the flag. So between 1936, when I was eight, and 1940 when twelve, I had no nationality to speak of. My father didn't bother to get United States citizenship until September 1943, at the age of fifty-four, when affirmation of loyalty was required for World War II industry employment.

But the notion of not being an American didn't bother me if I thought about it at all, and I'm sure I didn't, because back then a child was known by the nationality of his father. As far as I was concerned, I was a Dane with the usual pride and prejudices—through osmosis made to dislike Germans, tolerate Norwegians, and spurn Swedes, not Swedish girls, of course, who are invariably beautiful, but Swedish men who are prone to excessive masturbation, are pale, white-haired and half-witted because their red blood cells drained out with their semen, or so I was told by my father. The expression, «Dumb Swede,» was up front on his tongue and he often said a Swede was a Dane with his brains knocked out. When he would occasionally tell a story in Danish, and then translate it—not to teach his children how to speak his language but to be entertaining—his favorite tales would open with the usual bias against Swedes. A limerick that works its simple poetry even in translation was, «Ten thousand Swedes went through the weeds, chased by one Norwegian.» And to demonstrate a grammatical difference between Danish and English that embarrassed Scandinavians when speaking English, he intoned such belly-convulsing phrases as: «Three times a day my wife threw the horse over the fence, some hay.»

Certifying me as a Dane is not that I'm more stubborn or smarter than an equivalent Swede, darker haired, or was less prone to masturbation, but that my name ends with «sen.» Throughout my entire life, I've encountered problems because of that birthmark. I'm not easily found in directories. Half the time my name in publications is misspelled. Often my records are lost—not lost, just not found. Recently an academic referee, hostile to a book manuscript that I'd submitted to Columbia University Press, spent a long paragraph pointing out gleefully that I'd misspelled the ancient Roman Tiberius Gracchus' family name—spelling it Gracchii. Yet, throughout his report he misspelled my name, ending it with «son». When called on his error in my rebuttal, he sloughed it off as a harmless slip, not aware that, whereas I had only made Tiberius into a plural person, he'd made me into a Swede.

My genetic makeup was a natural condition, like dogness is for a dog. The fact that my mother was German did not diminish my Danishness, for in those days a child's nationality was his father's. Everything in one's genes was from the father, we believed; one's mother was but an incubator—the quality of a calf depends on the bull. I did not think of myself as Danish, however, until I entered Sioux City's school system with its inconstant pupils of variable descent and different teachers at each grade level requiring pupils to be known to each other and to our new teachers. On the first day of class, we were told to stand one at a time at our seats and declare our name, nationality, and father's profession: «My name is Wayne Andersen. I'm Danish. My father's a farmer and runs a beer parlor.»

I don't recall any pupil saying, «I'm an American,» not even those who were second or third generation down from immigrant stock. So deeply imprinted was this identity that, at age thirty-three, on the first day of study in Paris at the Alliance Française, when the professor asked each student to give his or her name, nationality, and career choice, I said, *«Je m'appelle Wayne Andersen, et je suis Danois,»* at which point in my response the professor, sharp on accents, having taught students from many countries, interrupted with a shout, *«Danois! Vous-êtes Américain!»* I felt at that moment severely patriotic.

With Loretta out in the field driving a tractor, what were my other siblings doing at the moment of my birth? My sisters Bethel, Fern, and Esther were sent to a neighbor's house to return after the event and hear, «Surprise!» My brother Marius, mindful that births were strictly women's affairs, probably used my impending arrival as an excuse to saddle a horse, go into town, and shoot pool.

Pregnancies and deliveries were not talked about openly in those days. Nothing of sex and reproduction was explained to children. My mother was so ring-shaped on pork, potatoes, and butterfat that an added eight or nine pounds of fetus wouldn't balloon her. My father, whose vocabulary was not always laundry fresh, used the expression «in a family way» when referring to a woman's pregnant condition. Children were better prepared for what the Easter bunny delivered than what the stork was bearing over the countryside in its pouched beak, just the right size and shape to carry a baby. We were taught how to neatly prepare loose straw in a wood box on our screened-in porch—a nest for the bunny to lay gaily colored eggs in overnight, with no more thought as to how that bunny would get in through the hooked screen door than how fat Santa Claus would get down the chimney, since we didn't have one, only a metal flue from the kitchen stove. Few farmhouses had fire-places at the time; and fewer still had central heating. We children believed what we were told, and were never told more than we needed to know, or, as my mother would say, too much for our own good.

My parents' first child and first son, Marius, was conceived when my mother was sixteen and my father twenty-three. But no one's moral standards should be made to reflect on conditions back then when an unmarried thirty-year-old woman was an old maid. Fertility among rural people was a serious matter; no farm could grow beyond the subsistence level if a farming couple didn't produce children to help tend livestock and work the fields. It was not uncommon for a man to require proof of fertility before marriage; in days before that condition could be confirmed in laboratories, the only way to test the girl was to impregnate her. So a good many teenage farm girls were pregnant by the age of fifteen or sixteen, married or not. Just as many boys hadn't the faintest idea of how babies got into women's bellies. Some were at a total loss when envisioning the female anatomy, in spite of how many cows rear ends faced them in the milk barn, and a good many girls thought they were bleeding to death when their first period showed up as a stain on the backside of their skirt. At age eighteen in 1946, my cousin Norma Jean, who'd been courting eternal damnation by singing in dance clubs for over a year, said to her mother at an intimate moment, «Mother, I'm going to tell you a story but I don't know what it means: When the Virgin Mary became Mary, she was no longer a virgin. What's a virgin?»

«A virgin,» her mother replied, «is a woman who won't have anything to do with men.»

In fact, in the 1920s and 30s, Woodbury County, which billets Sioux City, and adjacent Plymouth County, where I was born, had the highest illegitimate birth rates in the state. One might credit that to licentiously wicked Sioux City, for nowhere in Iowa would be found a greater concentration of saloons and dance halls. In 1930, of roughly 45 illegitimate births per thousand in the two counties, the rate was found higher for urban girls than for country girls, disproving the plethora of «farmer's daughter» and «traveling salesman» stories that portrayed every farm girl as a simpleton pushover. Defenders of urban morality blamed the higher urban rate on erring farm girls coming to the city and getting pregnant, then coming again to the city to expel their illegitimate babies. But Sioux City was racked with moral problems not associated with the farmlands. The Sioux City *Journal* took up the issue in 1913, reporting that after nightfall the streets swarm with streetwalkers, among them young girls of tender years. «The preachers blame the police and the police blame the girls' parents, and chances are that both are more or less right. Whoever is at fault, there is no doubt that from a moral standpoint things in the city are in a regrettable condition.»[1] Street girls had been a social problem long before then, and would continue being long after. One year after my birth, a sociologist, writing in 1929, had this to say:

«Even granting some truth to the contention that farm girls migrate to the city, a series of other considerations compensate for the elevation of the urban rate. First, the innocent country girls who migrate to the city and become pregnant there naturally are to be regarded as urban, not rural victims. Second, if, to some extent, the city rate is elevated by the migration of sinful rural persons to the city, we must not forget that many country girls become pregnant in the rural areas owing to contact with city men—various urban salesmen, tourists, travelers, merchants, writers [writers!], leisure people, and so on. This may compensate for the elevation of the urban rate through migration. Third, the results of illegal sex life in the cities are concealed much more by the practice of birth control, and particularly by abortions, which are comparably more prevalent in cities than the country.»[2]

Aside from the fact that, to my knowledge, country girls were no more innocent than city girls, what this researcher missed was that the majority of pre-marital pregnancies in rural areas led to marriage. No self-respecting father would let man or boy escape the consequences of thinking he was casually spending his endowment. So incidents of pre-marital sex in the country were most likely much higher than the statistics submit.

Note: On visiting Sioux City during September 1998, I saw a large billboard downtown promoting the Marion Urgent Care Hospital, with nothing on the face of it but this admonition: «Don't worry, there's no poison ivy back there.»

I can't be sure that the city folk who sponsored this sign knew what that expression meant. My photographic memory finds it in a soft-porn men's magazine of the early 1940s depicting a man coaxing a country girl to go with him into the bushes, saying to her more less the same words, «Now don't worry, honey, there's no poison ivy back there.» Why would an urban hospital display that sign? That evening I called my sister Loretta, a farm girl, you will recall, from the 1930s, and told her what the sign said. Her response was as spontaneous as a scratched match head: «We also had to worry about stinging nettles.» Such dramas in bushes and grain fields were universal, whether in ancient Greek marsh reeds or Iowa cornfields. Nymphs and satyrs don't live in cities.

I was the sixth child, arriving when my mother was thirty-three and my father thirty-nine. Their last child, Nancy, came in 1938 when my mother was just shy of forty-three and I was ten. Over a twenty-five year span, Anna Marguerita tried every known method of contraception after the fifth child but still produced ten children, seven girls and three boys. She survived three of them: one daughter and two sons died rather young—Harold at age forty-two and Marius at fifty-two; heavy smokers and overweight, both suffered heart attacks. Esther, a militant Seventh Day Adventist and faithful to Shaklee vitamins and minerals, yielded to spinal cancer at age sixty. My father died in 1963 of pneumonia contracted in Oakland's Kaiser-Permanente Hospital, seventy-four and physically worn out. Surely his strong heart kept beating long after the rest of him was gone. My mother didn't wish to see any of her other children die. Peacefully, she passed away in her sleep in 1985 at age ninety, not ill or mentally discounted, just tired.

Chapter 2

The fecund torso of a
well-tilled earth goddess

The larger background of my Iowa youth is figuratively record-ed in the flow of the Floyd River downstream from farm-town Hinton—no more than a speck of a place on the county map—to small-town Leeds, to Sioux City and the Missouri. The Floyd River bears the name of Sergeant Charles Floyd, the only fatality of the Lewis and Clark exploration of the Louisiana Territory. In 1804, at an encampment on the Missouri where the Floyd River enters, he died not from a savage's arrow or tomahawk blow to the head but of a ruptured appendix. His grave, marked by the Floyd Monument, was the first reg-istered landmark in the United States.

Back when Thomas Jefferson sponsored the Lewis and Clark expedition, the position of the Missouri River was dead center on the United States map, with a symmetrical west and east. Only much later did the Mississippi take over that position as the nation's vertical equa-tor.

When I look at a United States map, Iowa stands out as one of the least misshapen states in the country, delineated top and bottom by lon-gitudinal lines, and at one's left and right by two mighty rivers on paral-lel though wriggling courses: the Missouri as the west border; the Mississippi, the right. Iowa's overall shape is rather wider than high, respecting the proportions of a framed landscape painting. A fertile and verdant undulating plain, not an acre of its terrain hostile: no moun-tains, no enraged rock-eroding rivers, some wetlands but no malodor-ous swamps, no landscape laid waste by erosive winds. The recumbent topography undulates quiescently like the fecund torso of a well-tilled earth goddess with her rolling belly, soft breasts and thighs under high and varied skies, gridded by roads in mile-square sections and quilted by patchwork fields of corn, alfalfa, soybeans, oats, and barley—an order-ly conceptual lattice, an expansive grid textured and densely populated by color-coded crops. Seventy-five percent of the Class A topsoil with-in the United States boundary covers Iowa's tiny chip of the globe's bedrock. Anyone taking leave of the state with dirt on their shoes or under their fingernails diminishes its thickness.

That covering is almost entirely agricultural, while the surfaces of most states of the Union, like those of the moon and Mars, were formed by geology. Even Iowa's most extraordinary landscape feature, the Loess Hills, that extend in bands on the east side of the Missouri from just above Sioux City to St. Joseph, Missouri, are benevolent. Sparsely treed and prairie-grass clad, these hills were created in the last Ice Age when quartz, high in silica, was ground down to silt and sus-pended in water, deposited and dried, not as fine as clay but finer than sand, and molded by rain and westerly winds into dunes.[3] Only one other place in world has such powder cake hills. That place is in China.

If seen from outer space, Sioux City would appear as having been mapped by natural agriculture and livestock before human life evolved. Buffaloes defined and settled its surface millennia before evolution pro-duced Clovis People or Paleo-Indians. Buffaloes knew which geological paths to follow, which lush prairies to graze in the concurrence of fresh water. They transformed the natural geological map into a buffalo-ter-ritory map of roads and waterways, cutting its grasses with their teeth, burying seeds with their trowel-like hoofs, fertilizing the ground with manure droppings as they grazed. Where the Big Sioux enters the Missouri, where pioneering people would fashion Sioux City, three deeply trod buffalo trails converged. The broadest and most worn trail started in the hills a few miles east of the city's northeast edge and coursed through the very place where the Union Stockyards would be built, presaging the route descendant beef-cattle would take to the slaughterhouses. From there, massive herds crossed the Floyd River at Half Moon Lake and moved along the Missouri to the mouth of the Big Sioux River. A second trail crossed the Floyd River near 12th Street, went over a slight hill near 8th and Jones, and continued north of Central High School, past the Cathedral and across the grassy tops of clay bluffs to the Big Sioux.

To avoid flies and mosquitoes that luxuriate in the low and moist flats, buffaloes and Indians favored dry high ground when traveling, while the colonizing settlers, encumbered by coaches and heavy supply wagons, entered Sioux City along the level baselines of bluffs and the dry flood lanes that typically border meandering rivers and streams— the Missouri, Big Sioux, and Floyd rivers, and Perry Creek. Before the advent of railroads, paddle-wheel steamboats moved up and down the Missouri bearing traders, immigrants, and cargo to the Port of Sioux City, back when geographical intuition promised a waterway to the Columbia River and thence to the Pacific and the Far East. All that remains of this trade is an old-lady riverboat, The Belle of Sioux City, now a popular casino tied up at Larson Park where the port once was, a symbol of Sioux City's remote notoriety as a drinking and gambling town.

Iowa's boundaries were established at the Territorial Convention of 1837, and admitted to the Union as a state by an Act of Congress on December 28th, 1846. Sioux City was platted in 1855, and for a few decades known as the gateway to the Northwest Territory. Three states converge at its western edge: Sioux City in Iowa, South Sioux City directly across the Missouri in Nebraska, and North Sioux City (Dakota City) in South Dakota. Theodore Bruguier, an educated Frenchman born in Canada in 1813, who fled a broken love affair, built the first house within the Sioux City zone. He spent a while in the Council Bluffs area, about 125 miles south of today's Sioux City, where a settlement was flourishing, then came up the Missouri in 1835 where he continued to trade with the Indians and the American Fur Company until settling at the mouth of the Big Sioux River (then called the Calumet River). Friendly with the local Indians with whom he traded and sometimes lived, he married a daughter of Chief War Eagle and gained great prestige among the tribes. His decision to settle where Sioux City was born is a famous piece of frontier lore. He said that one night alongside the Missouri he couldn't sleep, so he hiked to the top of a bluff and tried sleeping there high above mosquitoes. In a light sleep, he dreamed that he saw a place where three rivers came together. On awakening, the dream puzzled and stayed with him. He told War Eagle about it. The chief said, «I'll take you to it.» They hiked a ways down river. At the mouth of the Big Sioux where it joined the Missouri, War Eagle said,

13

«This is the place of your dream. Here you can make a great camp.» Bruguier built a log house there, and farmed an acreage that included what is now Sioux City's Riverside Park.[4]

The city's inhabitants multiplied rapidly for a few nineteenth-century decades, only to level off as the expansion of railroads demolished the Jeffersonian vision of an agrarian republic unified by connected river ways. Machine technology had intervened. Steam engines chugging on iron rails outpaced riverboats on water. Self-sufficient rail-serviced towns that became cities took shape further west. And even though every town in Iowa would eventually be no less than fifteen miles from a railroad, the major east-west lines would pass a hundred miles south of Sioux City through Council Bluffs, Iowa, and Omaha, on the west bank of the Missouri, in Nebraska.

Abraham Lincoln's romanticism was responsible for Sioux City's dashed hopes of remaining the gateway to the Northwest. One day in August 1859, when Iowa was only thirteen years into statehood, the fifty-year-old Lincoln stepped off a Missouri river steamboat to look over Council Bluffs, by then a thriving river town of 1,500 people. Its businessmen had their own thoughts about being the railway metropolis of the Midwest—another failed dream, for unlike many other states, Iowa would never have an industrial center the likes of Pittsburgh or Detroit, and no single port of entry such as Boston or New York or New Orleans. Council Bluffs was destined to remain a small town.[5]

At the time of his visiting Council Bluffs, Lincoln was not yet the United States president. He had served two terms in the Illinois legislature (his first election was in the same year that Iowa was granted statehood), one term in the United States Congress, and had recently lost a senatorial race. He hadn't stopped by at Council Bluffs for political campaigning but to inspect seventeen subdivision lots and ten acres of pastureland he'd accepted as security for a loan made to his campaign manager. Still, he did take an opportunity to give a speech. The town's *Weekly Nonpareil* announced the incident sarcastically: «The distinguished sucker has yielded to the earnest importunities of our citizens, without distinction of party, and will speak on the political issues of the day.» After the event, the same paper reported that Lincoln had given a masterful and unanswerable speech in which he applied the political scalpel to the Democratic carcass. The rival Council Bluffs paper, *The Bugle*, said that

Lincoln, with many excuses, as if conscious of the black Republican rostrum, announced his intention to speak about the Eternal Negro, and then reported in summary what Lincoln had told his audience, that this government cannot endure permanently the country being half slave and half free—the topic of his famous debate the year before with Stephen Douglas.

On this occasion, Lincoln met Grenville Dodge, a topographic engineer who had just returned from a railway-surveying trip to the West. Dodge recalled in his memoirs, «We sat down on a bench on the porch and Lincoln proceeded to ask all about the country we'd been through; in fact, he got from me the information I'd gathered for my employers.» At that time, the railroad did not extend further than Council Bluffs. The next segment, far to the west, was a 22-mile line in the Sacramento Valley of California. Lincoln made the decision then and there that the railway to link the East with the West would run through Council Bluffs and Omaha. So not only did Sioux City miss out on the continental railway route, squelching all hope of being a metropolis like Chicago, but the railroad brought a halt to river traffic and Sioux City would no longer be a river port.

When my parents married in the spring of 1912 and were farming near Battle Creek, Iowa, Sioux City's population was 50,000 (about the same as the population of the 42 bands of Sioux Indians fifty years earlier, before their number declined). In 1938, when my family moved off the farm and into the city, the population was 79,000. Since then it hasn't grown much. Today's count is only 86,000 at near zero growth—about the number of people a coliseum would hold for one of today's Super Bowl games. Post World War II economic recovery, more industrial than agrarian, overlooked Sioux City, and sexual reproduction remained uniformly offset by people dying or moving away.

Iowa can take credit for Herbert Hoover, Glenn Miller, John Wayne, and painters Grant Wood and Ray Parker. Robert Waller's *The Bridges of Madison County*—the story of a lonely Iowa farm wife and a passing stranger entangled in a fiery liaison, read by millions and visualized by a film made of it featuring Clint Eastwood and Meryl Streep—engendered for Iowa the sensual fame that Flaubert's *Madame Bovary* did for Rouen in nineteenth-century France. But the movie made of the United 232 airplane crash in 1987, and weekly ribbing on the David

Letterman show as «coming from its headquarters in downtown Sioux City» did a lot to create national awareness of the woebegone city that lends itself to caricature: its folk hero, a man stricken with appendicitis; its most famous historical building, the Corn Palace fashioned entirely of cornstalks and ears.; its civic anthem, Sioux City Sue. At this very moment, Sioux City is appealing the National Aeronautics Board's refusal to change its airport code: SUX.

Historians of Iowa tend to disparage Sioux City, either by speaking ill of it or ignoring its existence. The celebrated Bancroft Prize winner, Fulbright Professor at the University of Edinburgh and Grinnell College's Parker Professor of History, Joseph Wall, devoted only a portion of one sentence to Sioux City in his 1978 book, *Iowa: A Bicentennial History*. Wall discussed Grinnell College on eleven pages, and «college people» in the eastern towns: Iowa City, Grinnell, Cedar Falls, and Ames, but Sioux City's Morningside College, which gave the world the Friedman twins, «Dear Abby» and «Ann Landers,» is not mentioned. While not wanting to denigrate Wall's superb book, I must mention that, on detailing inventions by Iowans, he cites the invention of the fountain pen but ignores inventions identified with Sioux City: the first automobile trunk, the first monoplane without wing struts, and the first concrete street. He cites an inventor in Des Moines for inventing ladies cold cream added to face powder but not the genius in Sioux City who invented the soft and absorbent baby diaper. When he mentions men's clubs, he cites the Rotary, Kiwanis, and Lions, but not the Moose Club, the lower crust club to which people like my father belonged. Wall's only concession to Sioux City is that over the first decades of this century it became a meatpacking center, second only to Chicago. So his book is not a complete history of Iowa but rather history presented as statistics and in generalities that don't apply to any single individual. Sioux City is on the western edge of the state, the frontier side. Academics are concentrated on the eastern edge where scholars look east and are prone to identify themselves with cultured cities and well-bred institutions: Harvard, Yale, Princeton, and the Universities of London and Edinburgh.

Chapter 3

We were born to kill pests and varmints

Henry Vesti, my father, was one of five sons—Andrew, Mark, John, Henry, and Clem—of Mads Vesti Andersen, a Danish dairy farmer. Times were economically much tougher in the tired «old country» than in juvenile America that was growing, expanding westward, and short of labor. Denmark had no wilderness, no frontier, no room for sons to establish their own farms, and hardly the least chance to buy one other than from a widow with no sons.

Henry Vesti immigrated to the United States in 1904. His older brother John preceded him by two years. At the age of seventeen in 1902, Uncle John saw an ad in a Danish newspaper glorifying the New World of opportunity and offering passage from Copenhagen to Battle Creek, Iowa for a lump sum payment of twenty-seven dollars. John signed up. My father's passage was under similar terms. He never told his children much about it, while Uncle John had plenty to say.

«It wasn't no luxury cruise,» he said. Over the entire voyage he never saw the sky but was confined with a great number of others to the dark, dank, unsanitary hold. Meals were soup fished with a dipper from what today one would call a garbage can, and herring forked from a brine barrel. When at last they arrived at port they were transferred without rest to an immigrant train, packed in with little space to move about, each immigrant given a loaf of bread and a ring of bologna to last until they would reach Iowa three days later. Somewhere in Ohio, the train had to stop for a herd of cattle on the track. The immigrants saw a pond nearby. Not having had a chance to bathe in three weeks, their clothes and bodies stinking beyond anything they'd smelled on a Danish farm, they spilled out of the train and plunged into the pond, shoes off, some clothing on, and refused to reboard until they felt reasonably clean. When Uncle John reached Battle Creek, he knew not a soul and could not speak English. But while still at the train station, a man approached him, speaking German, which John could understand to the extent that Danish and German share throat sounds and cognates. The German asked if he would like a job on his farm. John agreed, no questions asked, and that evening he was doing the same farm chores he'd done in Denmark, earning $1.25 a day plus room and board. The amount seems trifling by today's currency, but around 1900 it was fair pay.

Uncle Andrew came over next. Then came my father in 1904. John helped him get a sequence of jobs as a farm hand. After a few passing years, he was hired onto a farm next to the Christopher and Louisa Steinhagen place. The Steinhagen's almost sixteen-year-old daughter, Anna Marguerita, who would become my mother, laid eyes on the handsome young Henry working the fields nearby and took every opportunity to run into him. Among farmers, this feline stalking and assailing was not uncommon. She was the aggressor, as girls are more often that men will admit, and she made no bones about bragging it up to her daughters. I'm not sure how long she knew my father before their marriage. With delight I imagine her wearing him down in the cornfields and haymow, and then nailing him for good.

With Uncle John's help the couple undertook sharecropping on a farmstead near Ida Grove where Danish blood was thick. That's where my oldest brother Marius was born. Farm economics took a terrible dip about that time, so two years later John set up my parents to run a small one-counter restaurant in Correctionville, across the street from his pool hall. At the back of this soup kitchen, two rooms served as living quarters, where in 1917 my oldest sister Loretta was born.

Loretta recalls our father's optimism during those harsh years when living in the mystic shadow of economic disaster. «As long as I have some water, I can make soup,» he said. After three years of serving soup, stew, meatloaf, and hot dogs, my parents leased a quality 240-acre farm near Kingsley—like Correctionville, a hamlet just a few miles outside of Sioux City. They farmed well and survived the plunge of produce prices and bank failures in 1921-22. That's when Calvin Coolidge's economics were creating wealth in the Eastern cities while the rural Midwest sunk into a mercifully short depression. Then, in

1924, a hog cholera epidemic blanketed the Kingsley area. My parents lost their brood sows and young pigs—killed, burned, and buried in the field. They recovered over the 1925 and 1926 years, when excellent crops from high-yielding Krug corn fetching good prices put some cash in the bank.[6] In the spring of 1927, a year before my birth, with their first five children and a load of equipment and implements in tow, they were able to relocate to a large leasehold of prime corn acreage fifteen miles north of Sioux City and four miles east of a milling hamlet and railroad junction called Hinton.

The Hinton farm's production was diversified, as were most midwestern farms before the onset of industrialized farming—half of the acres in grains, the other half devoted to meat, eggs, and dairy production. The 360-acre spread was larger than the average 150-acre family farm. We had ample fields of corn, oats, and alfalfa; a grazing pasture for milk cows, beef cattle feedlots and pig-lots, and space left over for potato and melon patches. The buildings were solid-built, plumb and square, and except for the white farmhouse, painted red. We had a horse barn, milk barn, hog house, cow shelter, silo, two chicken houses, a double corn crib, an oats granary, a machine shop, tool shed, cob house, smoke house, wash house, two-seater outhouse, and the smallest building of them all, a wren house. We had eight work horses, a team of mules, a thoroughbred gelding for riding, twenty-eight Holstein and Jersey milk cows, a small herd of Shorthorn beef cattle, twenty or so Duroc brood sows, a good service-boar, and in season, a rented bull. We had fifty or so Plymouth Rock laying hens for egg production, a few hundred White Leghorn fryers to eat or sell, ordinary white geese for holiday dinners and pillow stuffing, a nourishing vegetable garden with flower and herb borders, a rat terrier, two rangy herd dogs, a dozen or so barn cats to keep down mice, rats, and moles, pigeons in the cupola, sparrows nesting in the eves, swallows in the horse barn, yellow-jacket nests in the ground, and hornet nests where you least expect them. We had a 1925 Fordson tractor, and the year I was born, my father sold his Model-A Ford and bought a spanking new 1928 Chevrolet.

Our two-story high-gabled clapboard house and the barns, silo, and corncrib were built early in the century from Department of Agriculture plans that gave uniform architectural quality to midwestern farm buildings. With four oatmeal-papered bedrooms—two upstairs and two down—the house was roomy enough for a large family accustomed to sharing beds and night-pans. It was night-lighted with gas and kerosene lamps with brass bases and smoky glass lanterns, and heated in the winter by the wood-burning kitchen stove and a coal-burning potbelly in the dining room; warmth rose through convection grills to the second floor rooms. A giant maple tree that dropped thousands of whirly-gig seeds in early summer was in command of the house yard. A Dutch apple tree grew next to the house, blossoming flagrantly in the spring, and a few small pine trees at the base of the yard offered winter greenness. We lived well, all of us healthy and robust. In this era before penicillin was put to use we deftly survived the childhood diseases we were certain to catch: chicken pox, measles, whooping cough, strept throat, and scarlet fever.

We were born to kill pests and varmints, to mow down field crops in their prime and slaughter animals we raised. Butchering was what one had to get used to—a squealing pig or bellowing cow hoisted by a block-and-tackle rigged rope about its hind legs to a cross beam, a steel tub under its head, suffering a pig-sticker to its heart and butcher knife jabs to open its jugulars, so as it died in jerks its failing heart pumped out blood caught in the tub and made into blood sausage. Those of us not yet hardened would run with hands over ears to the wood lot or far out into the fields to avoid the horror. Yet the most delicate among us, sister Bethel, was efficient at killing chickens—each victim grabbed with a leg hook and held over a chicken-killing stump, crisscrossed with cuts and stained dark with old blood, the ax coming down smartly and the holder tossing the beheaded victim away, so as it flapped around with spurts from its writhing neck, making Jackson Pollack paintings on the ground, it wouldn't spatter our clothing. I recall at about the age of five trying the ax on one occasion, my arms not steady, my aim off the mark; only half the chicken's head came off. For years the horror of it haunted my dreams.

Our food came directly off the hoof and off the land. The vegetable garden was vast, the house yard ornamented with lilac bushes, peonies, and annuals planted every spring: snap dragons, petunias, four-o'clocks, marigolds, phlox, zinnias, and sweet peas on the fence—dependable blooms that define a peasant class domicile. Across the dirt road was an orchard of crab apples, cherries, plums, and a couple of black walnut trees. A butchered beef cow, fattened on rich timothy grass in the summer and fermented corn-stalk silage in the winter, got packaged and stored in the town's ice-locker. Corn-fed hogs were rendered into sausage, bacon, ham, and cured in the smoke house; the hog's head-meat made into headcheese, its knuckles jellied. Everything perishable but canable got sealed in Mason jars for winter cuisine—vegetables, fruit, and meat chunks for stew. White bread was baked weekly; the rising and heaving mountains of dough cut and patted into hillock loaves and brushed with salted bacon drippings to yield a toasty yellow crust (the fresh bread odor wafted all the way to the barn). Piles of potatoes hibernated like fat toads under the house without freezing. Carrots, turnips, rutabagas and parsnips, buried in sand-filled boxes, wintered in the dirt-walled storm cellar; and down there among the crickets, centipedes, millipedes, spiders, and sometimes a hibernating snake, were moldy, cobweb-cloaked wooden barrels and ceramic crocks of dill pickles and sauerkraut, and cases of bottled home-brew my father made for late-summer threshing days when troops of farmers moved from farm to farm, assisting with each other's harvest. This storm cellar was just a short distance from the house, its wood-plank roof mounded with dirt like a battle field bunker. My father fashioned wood benches down there, so when we were hustled from the house to safety from a threatening tornado we would have a place to sit other than on the creepy dirt floor. Shovels and an ax were on hand so we could chop our way out if the cave's door got layered over with wind-blown trees or timbers from a demised building nearby.

Just the staples were bought in town: flour, rice and beans, coffee, tea, sugar, salt—usually paid for by trading eggs with the Hinton grocery store or Siedschlag's Grocery and Meat store in nearby Leeds. We always had need for cash, especially during the late winter and over summer before grain and livestock went off to market. My mother sold live fryers, pullets and cockerels; my father sold milk and cream to the local dairies. During winter, when fieldwork slacked off, sister Loretta delivered freshly drawn milk at a discount to customers in Leeds, and my father and sister Bethel hauled dressed chickens to Sioux City to peddle at rich folks' doors for fifty cents apiece. At age five and six, I joined Bethel, and maybe Fern, to earn a few dollars trapping pocket gophers

21

with spring traps set deep in their mounded-over holes, ready to clamp down on a gophers front feet. Still alive when the wood shingle or cow-pie hole-covering was removed the next morning, those hapless victims had to be beaten to death with an iron stick and have their fat digging-feet cut off with a pocket knife, to be preserved in a tobacco can of salt and turned over to the county's bounty warden in exchange for five cents a gopher. Often I worked the traps by myself, and still hear the gophers' hissing pleas for mercy as their faces turned up and looked directly into my child eyes that could not yet see with compassion.

By Danish tradition we were Lutheran. Our white country church, Trinity Lutheran, with a gothic double-door, small peaked windows, plank floor, and oak pews, lay two miles to the northeast. To the side of it was a modest vicarage. This church was the focal point of women's social contact and young people's eyes for a future mate. Everything vital to one's avoidance of eternal damnation depended on Pastor Torgler's ministrations: baptism, marriage, communion, and forgiveness of sins. On dying, one got a funeral and a well-kept grassy churchyard plot for eternal rest. My mother belonged to the Ladies' Aid, and brother Marius and sister Loretta were active in the church-sponsored Walther League. Bethel sang in the choir. On occasion, Marius pumped the pipe organ's bellows. The pump room was a man-sized closet behind the organ; the pump handle about the length of a rowing oar. (On one occasion my cousin Clarence fell asleep while lying on his back pumping; the organ music slowly petered out. The pastor opened the pump room door, and out fell Clarence's legs. The solemn church air was corrugated by laughter).

We rarely missed a Sunday service, even during blizzards or through snow so deep in wind-drifts that the road disappeared for days. Our family-size sleigh, built by my father and dragged by four giant horses—Nancy and Queen, Princess and Dan—carried us merrily along, snuggled under blankets and with heated bricks under our feet. Those horses' ancestors probably hauled Hannibal's frostbitten elephants over the Alps.

By the 1920s, the church was less instrumental in organizing society that, in earlier years, when churches—especially Protestant churches—had little competition. By 1930, even in small rural towns, community clubs, women's clubs, and men's clubs, all being secular, supplanted a percentage of church socials. Because farmwomen didn't typically drive automobiles, and were tied down with home chores, the country church remained their social focus. Only when automobiles were prevalent, and women felt comfortable driving them, did secular social clubs in town draw women away from the church. Then the preachers began secularizing religion in competition with social clubs that permitted card playing, square dancing, and mild gambling, such as Bingo. Men's clubs had by then added bars and card tables to their meeting halls, and it was not unusual for members to view porno movies in a back room.

So it was wise of our country preacher to not credit God for everything that went right, like the ancient Greeks had done. He would remind farmers that they'd better not depend on the Lord to tend their fields and do their chores, but every sensible farmer knew, without being reminded, that any farm worked by the lord god alone would soon fall into a sorry state. The oft-told pleasantry on this subject was a story of a pastor new to his assigned rural parish, wanting to get acquainted with local farmers, who made the mistake of complimenting a farmer by saying, «You and God have certainly made a wonderful farm out of this land,» to which the farmer replied, «Yup, but you should'a seen the mess it was in when God was working it by himself.»

Once at a church social, when everybody had been seated for lunch, hungry and pious and waiting for the pastor to say grace, he yelled all of a sudden: «God helps those who help themselves!» and at that moment grabbed up a whole platter of fried chicken. On another occasion, just after he had folded his hands and everybody had done likewise, bowing their heads, he said jokingly, «Before I give thanks to the Lord for our daily bread, I want to thank all you nice ladies for the meat and potatoes.» He knew how to butter his congregation on both sides.

House-life centered on meals. Although we had many laying hens, eggs were gold coins for cash income and rarely on our plates. At breakfast we ate Cream of Wheat and oatmeal, bread and jelly, and drank the morning's fresh milk from green glass goblets. The noon meal, called dinner, always included meat, potatoes, and sundry vegetables, often as hearty soups and stews, but sometimes pancakes slathered in butter and sprinkled with white sugar crystals until snowed under.

Leftovers were saved for supper and the next day's school lunch, wrapped in yesterday's newspaper sheets and secured in a lunch pail. Supper was taken after the evening chores, usually bread and milk in a bowl, boiled rice with milk, sugar, and cinnamon, or cornbread doused with corn syrup. For desert, a bread, vanilla, or chocolate pudding. One worked better with a full stomach, but slept peacefully after a light meal.

The huge kitchen was furnished with a black, silver-trimmed wood burning stove, a cob box and wood box, a large table with ten to twelve chairs. Meals were had in the kitchen, except on Sundays or when guests came. In one corner was a water cabinet; on its top, a huge washbasin. The farm was not electrified, so the house had no water pump, no tap water: drinking and wash water was hauled in from the house yard well, pumped into a galvanized bucket and served up by a tin ladle. Kept handy on the washstand was a bar of homemade soap, a towel, and a large broad-toothed ivory-colored comb—items shared by all. Throughout the day the same wash water was used over and over until, reluctant to rub its muddiness on one's own face, someone of faint heart would dump it outside on the grass or snow and refresh the water. Affixed to the wall was a face mirror. From a nail hung a duel-purpose razor strap: a shaving aid for my father and brother, and like a picture of crucified Jesus hanging from nails, a reminder that we'd better behave ourselves or risk dying for our own sins. I don't recall that strap smacking anyone's butt, however. Our father was easy-going with his children; only on occasion did his temper flare. A box on the ear delivered by my mother was enough to keep us in line. And she had plenty of home remedies for unruly and obnoxious behavior: knowing that if a child picked its nose it meant he had worms was enough to keep one's hands under control; being locked for an hour of two in the windowless cob house—a squatter village for rats, with light coming only through a few warped boards and knotholes—would cure most any behavioral flaw.

The dining room was where the family gathered after supper had been taken in the kitchen, for it had the only gas lamp in the house. In this mixed-use room, family life was casual, even though the dining table was covered with a cloth crocheted by my mother's devoted and skillful hands, and the furniture polished to a reflective sheen. Circular doilies with floral centers and vining margins adorned side tables—knick-

24

knacks on them and on corner shelves: pink-cheeked porcelain ladies in hoop skirts, adorable cats and dogs, virtuous milk maidens in floral aprons and wooden shoes, a ceramic birdhouse with a ceramic bluebird on its perch, pottery of incised lines and painted flowers, mostly stamped «Made in China.»

In the harsh white light of the gas lamp, my mother crocheted from string balls in a bamboo tray that must also have come from China, or rocked the most recently arrived bundle of joy. School-age children did their homework, while little ones played on the floor: marbles and jacks, tidily-winks, tinker-toys, and stacks of wood blocks defying all principles of architecture; also coloring books, paper dolls, a wooden train of linked cars behind an engine, and assorted wind-up tin cars and trucks, a steam shovel operated with a crank. Our father, his mighty arms warmed in a cabled cardigan, helped the girls with homework and enjoyed playing Parcheesi and gin rummy with anyone able to count beyond ten.

Bedrooms were shared and often fought over as to who slept with whom, and on which side of the bed. When three people sleep together in the same bed, it's said in Iowa lore, the one next to the wall gets a wish, the one in the middle gets a golden slipper, and the one on the outside is for the rats and mice (I never understood what that aphorism meant, and still don't). The iron-frame beds had crocheted spreads or patchwork quilts over sheets without trim and goose-down pillows with embroidered flowers on the hems of white cases. On the floors were parti-colored rag rugs in which every garment my mother stitched was represented by remnants torn in strips and crocheted in outward spirals with her big wooden needle.

The parlor embodied the glory of the household furniture. The upright mahogany piano was polished weekly. Featured as well was a padded love seat with a knitted throw, a maple rocking chair polished to a bright shine, a mohair sofa with the customary Afghan folded over its back, and two or three fine chairs, all arranged on a Brussels rug, framed pictures on the floral-papered walls, one of Jesus, another of white birches leaning over and reflected in a placid stream. On a small walnut side-table, a book of holy homilies and a red-letter edition of the New Testament. The parlor was strictly mother's room, and not used except when the piano teacher gave lessons to sisters Loretta and Bethel or when either had to practice. But in the parlor the family celebrated Christmas Eve after we'd traveled on the family sleigh to the church for the early evening Children's' Program. While we were away, fat Santa somehow got down the skinny stove pipe and out of the hot stove to lay out gifts on a library table that never had a book on it except on Christmas Eve—the gifts not wrapped in expensive holiday paper but set in neat piles that Santa had labeled for each child.

The outhouse, with the traditional first-quarter moon cut into the door, was a ways from the house—the interior festooned with spider webs and curly skeins of sticky yellow fly paper that never ceased buzzing until the first hard freeze of winter, where last season's Montgomery Ward and Sears & Roebuck catalogue pages served as toilet reading and toilet paper (recycling is fundamental to farm life: jelly jars became drinking glasses, paper scraps kindled fires, emptied cans were flayed of their labels and used in the tool shed for storing nails, bolts, nuts, and washers). Over rainy or winter nights we used an enameled chamber pot in the house, called the slop jar, primed with water like a proper city toilet bowl and emptied mornings in the outhouse. Non-electrified farms were of course without electric water pumps and water heaters. The New Deal's Rural Electrification Act came along only in 1935 when I was seven, but it took several years for bathtubs and showers to show up in rural homes.[7] By the end of the 1930s, only about twenty percent of Iowa farmhouses had bathrooms. For bathing, my mother and sisters could sponge bathe at the sink cabinet when males were out in the fields. Saturday sit-up baths were taken in a galvanized metal tub with homemade soap in the shape of a turtle, fish, or rosette. («Prayer is the soul's soap,» I heard said about that time without having the faintest idea what the adage meant; but if soap could wash dirty words out of one's mouth, I would imagine that soaping one's entire body could wash away the more stainful sins). In winter the bath water was heated on the kitchen's big iron cook-stove. In summer, the tub was placed out on the lawn, where sunrays warmed the chilly pump water and we children could splash without mother's hysterics over splatter on her kitchen floor.

Once a week we changed clothes—underwear and socks more often. But the girls got a fresh apron every day for wearing to school, affording them pockets for pencils and crayons. Their aprons and billowy bloomers and white ankle-length sleepwear were made from decorative flour and chicken feed sacks. In those days, the sacks were finely woven and colorfully printed for recycling as clothing, especially as aprons, not just to keep one's dress from stove-top spattering, but for hitching up like a basket to hold cut flowers, orchard and garden pickings—cherries, plums, leafy greens, peas, and string-beans—and for broadcasting chicken feed and flapping to shoo off flies or a canary-stalking cat. For little bashful children, a mother's apron was good cover to hide under or for playing peek-a-boo.

My mother was a skilled dressmaker, her glossy black Singer sewing machine decorated with vining gold lines and driven by a foot-treadle. But men's and boy's clothes were store-bought long johns, shirts, and overalls. After morning chores on Sunday, everyone dressed in their finery: mother and the girls in pretty dresses and bonnets, the men and boys in suits, freshly ironed shirts, and Christmas-gift neckties. The condition of our clothing was mother's source of pride, which extended to how she laundered. By the time I came along, the wash-board days were behind her. No more boiling the fabrics in a metal tub on the kitchen cook-stove, or shaving soap bars with a knife and stirring up suds with a flat stick. She had a very noisy, gas motor-driven Maytag washing machine and a wringer that lusted after careless fingers and girls' dangling hairlocks. The machine, supplied with water heated on a wood stove in a wash shed, did most of the work. The hard well water had to be broken with lye, the resulting scum removed by skimming (soft rain-barrel water, collected from roof gutters, was reserved for the girls to wash their hair). Fels Naphtha, White Laundry, Blue Barrel— then as today soap companies did their best to convince women to change brands, so all of them had to be tried and compared, the coupons redeemed at the general store. Bluing was added to the rinse water to make whites whiter. A woman was judged back then by the appearance of her laundry, hung out on clotheslines visible from the road—the whites pure white, towels hung with towels, sheets with sheets, underwear with underwear, socks with socks—every article in its proper place was a sign of domestic order and good housekeeping.

Chapter 4

*The cycles of the sun and moon
are about all a farmer can depend on
to keep the globe from wobbling*

Afarmer's world doesn't require a lot to be a complete globe and an integrated social body: the farm itself, a church, a school, a few neighbors on the party line with whom to exchange news and gossip, and respond to emergencies; a nearby town outfitted with a granary, general store, feed store, meeting hall, beer parlor, dance hall, pool hall, and softball diamond. We had most of that in Hinton but the bigger town of Leeds was just a few miles further away, edging towards big Sioux City. Everything else in the world existed as radio waves or in newspapers and *National Geographic* and *Life* magazines, in the *World Book* and *Book of Knowledge*. By the mid-twenties most farm homes had battery-powered radios that cut into reading time. Farmers didn't have much time to read anyway, other than a daily or weekly newspaper and a magazine or two, such as the *Saturday Evening Post, Copper's Weekly, Wallace's Farmer*, journals from the Farm Bureau that disseminated knowledge of scientific agricultural methods, and religious brochures mailed out by churches.

Our school was a mile-and-a-half hike by the roads—just a mile as the crow flies, but crows don't have to cope with barbed wire fences, a creek to cross, farm dogs, and glandular bulls pastured with aromatic heifers in heat. We learned to get through those barbed wire fences really fast. The school was a genuine one-room schoolhouse with a single teacher, Miss Manz, for kindergarten through the eighth grade. She was an «old maid,» which didn't mean she had to be old: married women were not allowed to teach at country schools, and besides, any unmarried woman beyond her twenties was considered an old maid. The classroom had two coat closets, a big pot-bellied stove in the front corner, a line-up of duplex desks with inkwells and pencil drawers, and a black-board stretched across the front wall. Centered at the front was Miss Manz's desk; facing her were two five- or six-foot-long recitation tables. Only when pupils were seated at those tables did pedagogical communication pass from teacher to child: instruction, stories, drilling in reading and arithmetic. Others worked at desktop assignments while trying to ignore what was going on at the front. If a pupil needed the toilet, which was an outhouse, a raised arm with one finger up signaled a need to urinate, two fingers to do a number two, meriting a few minutes more absence from the classroom. In a no-nonsense school with thirty to forty pupils and rarely more than six at any grade level, any lapse in proper behavior—whispering, gum-chewing, spitball-throwing, note-passing—caused one to be marched to the cloakroom for a sound spanking («sound» meant hard enough to produce sounds: a yell or audible crying). But only the little ones got spanked. It wouldn't do for a twenty-two-year-old city-bred female teacher to lay a burly sixth grade farm boy over her knee.

The quality of education in country schools throughout the Midwest was generally poor and not uniform. Ours was superior by chance. It could just as well have been mediocre, awful, or worse. With one teacher to a school, teaching quality didn't average out as it does in an urban school with many teachers, some highly competent, others so-so, still others hopeless.

Rural one-room schools were white—not red like the «little red school house» in New York City—and the interiors were plain. The annual salary for a one-room school teacher was less than for an urban elementary school teacher, and each rural teacher was also the school's doorperson, janitor, stove stoker, lawn mower, snow shoveler, and school nurse. In 1933, the year I entered school, Iowa's median salary for a country teacher was $730, while an urban teacher's median was $1,085 at the elementary level and $1,452 at the high school level. Most of the one-room school teachers were young and unmarried, many were just high school graduates with minimal teacher training, scoring so low in testing for teaching certificates that they had to settle for a country-school position where living conditions for a single woman were difficult and socially restrictive. Lacking automobiles or carriages, the teachers were obliged to room and board at a nearby farm. Most bided their time at a one-room school until a job in the city opened up. To impress urban school boards as to their competence, pupils' grades and attendance records were often inflated, adding to the myth that the one-room country school was at the core of proper education.

As early as 1880, it was determined that Iowa had the highest literacy rate in the United States. Expressed as the illiteracy rate when a new national rating was published in 1920, Iowa had the lowest percentage of illiterates, just 1.1 percent. In 1930, the rate was even lower, 0.8 percent, meaning about everyone could read and write, in spite of the fact that Iowa's population then was nine percent foreign-born, 25 percent of foreign-born parents, and that 45 percent of the total lived on farms or in farmland hamlets. Still, what did these percentages mean? Historian Joseph Wall wrote a few years ago that one of the most devastating blows dealt to educational reformers in Iowa was the 1880 census revelation that Iowa had the lowest rate of illiteracy in the nation. For the next sixty years (up to 1940, when I was twelve), Iowa school boards remained smugly content believing and promoting that dubious fact, impervious to the hundred-year-old observation of Amos Currier—once dean of the State University of Iowa's School of Education—that an ability to read and write had been a high sign of personal distinction one thousand years ago, but greater things were needed to justify boasting about it in modern times.[8]

A survey of books owned by Iowa farm families conducted in 1925, shortly before I joined the population, reported that books were to be found in 80 percent of the homes—an average of 33 books for tenant farmers and 57 for farm owners. In some farm homes, a collection of children's books from doting parents and grandparents may have distorted the statistics, offsetting the count of novels by such popular authors as Jack London, Mark Twain, James Fennimore Cooper, Jules Verne, Charles Dickens, and Zane Gray. Other than pre-school nursery tales, most books bought by farm families were adventure stories for the men and boys; for young women, novelettes featuring heroic nurses and pioneer teachers. Every child in my family beyond the age of three received a book for Christmas. The Christmas gift slogan was, «Something to wear, something to read, something to play with.» As for playing, farm children at most any school age had little need for toys—

so much all around them to play with. The rural environment was varied and expansive: equipment to fantasize on, trees to climb, creeks to explore, real live pets: kittens, puppies, calves, lambs, baby chickens, ducklings, turtles.

As Mark Twain wisely said, «There are lies, damn lies, and statistics.» What accounted for Iowa's low illiteracy rate was not the quality of its education system, but its demographics. Iowa had no remnants of illiterate slave families, as did the southern states, no masses of impoverished and undereducated sharecroppers and fieldworkers as in Arkansas or the Kansas and Oklahoma dust bowls, no residual railroad coolies and migrant fruit pickers as in California, no coal mines with boy labor, or assembly line sweat shops with girl labor, as in Pennsylvania, Indiana, and New York. Iowa was populated largely with Protestant whites from British and northern European stock, Germans and Scandinavians. Moreover, far removed from the long-established eastern educational system based on European traditions, with Greek, Latin, Philosophy, Theology, and abstract mathematics given highest priority, Iowa's educational policy fit the special needs of inland agricultural people: reading, writing, and just plain arithmetic.

The 1920s was the decade of psychology, especially child psychology and sociology. Sigmund Freud's focus on infancy and youth had entered into the curricula of colleges, and pedagogical theories of Montessori and John Dewey were promoting that children were not just immature adults who would grow up like pollywogs becoming frogs and maggots becoming flies. Children were becoming recognized as a discrete and special population, looked upon by manufacturers as a lucrative market for clothing, educational toys, and books. British writers and illustrators had dominated literature for the very young for two centuries. Publishers in the United States were belatedly coming to see that American infants were being raised vicariously in an English nursery. Profits could be made from texts written especially for children: hired writers were inducted by publishers to turn out formulaic stories: Nancy Drew, The Bobbsey Twins, The Hardy Boys, Tom Swift.[9]

While upholding the preeminence of the Anglo-Saxon race, books for children began to emphasize frontier virtues and the Great American Dream. Much earlier, Little Black Sambo had been transformed from a dark-skinned East Indian boy into an African-type

Southern Black. Soon the exotic lands of India and Africa, favored by British authors of children's literature, would give way to the Western plains of American pioneers, rowdy cowboys, and vengeful Indians on the warpath. The 1920s and '30s were also decades when national awareness of America was changing from that of a strictly agricultural nation to an urban and industrialized one as well. Farmers were being set in contrast to city dwellers: the country mouse, city mouse syndrome was fast becoming the most uncomfortably felt polarity of American culture—virtuous farmlands and immoral cities; farm life as peaceful and elementary, city life as stressful and violent.

I've had to compare my memories of a rural childhood in the 1930s with what I've read by sociologists investigating the rural child as a sort of baseline pig, as it was with Comparative Anatomy back then, just as the study of human evolution is founded on the primitive mind, and comparative agriculture on the feral animal and uncultivated land. Without having to think beyond preconceptions, academic researchers could reflexively say that in rural communities life was uncomplicated while urban life was complex, for they had not been raised on a farm and were conditioned to look upon farmers as more physical than mental, living simpler, more routine lives than, say, a bank clerk, mortician, fireman, or pharmacist. Every set of statistics I've come upon concerning farmers was cut on that bias.

Farm life, as I recall it, was everything but simple—so much to learn, so many skills to master. A farmer worked his land but also managed it. Yes, our labors of the day and month were dictated by seasonal changes, by the tilt of the earth towards the sun, the growth rate of crops, the gestation periods of livestock, by seeding time and harvesting time, by what had to be done at the proper time—over which one's intellect had no more control than over the stock market or tomorrow's news. A farmer cannot act upon his seasonal and climatic environment, but if he plows at half-moon and plants at full moon, it means he has two weeks to prepare the field, the phases of the moon pushing him along, like clothiers in tune with seasonal fashions. The moon, itself, had no effect, but offered an orderly and uniform sequence for performing tasks. The cycles of the sun and moon, and advice from *The Farmer's Almanac* and *Wallace's Weekly* were about all a farmer could depend on to keep his piece of the earth in reasonably good order and the globe from wobbling.

We were born farmers, which doesn't mean we were born with a mushy cerebellum and diminished brain cells. At the age of six we could read our own books and help work the farm; we were taught how to milk a four-teated cow while seated on a one-legged stool holding a two-gallon bucket between our knees. About twenty sequential steps are involved in harnessing a workhorse and attaching it to the tongue and trees of a wagon or field machine. By their first teenage year, muscular Marius and lithesome Loretta, who called herself the hired man, had become daylight-to-sundown field workers with two- and four-horse teams pulling a cultivator one day, a mowing machine or hay wagon the next day. My sisters were not simple farm maidens wearing pinafores and lace bonnets, skipping along a cow path carrying milk pails decorated with painted daisies. By the age of eight or nine Bethel and Fern did some of the milking, even in the dead of winter when frigid nights fall quickly, milk freezes in the baby's bottle, and one dresses for school the next morning still in the dark.

At age seventeen, Loretta was a deadly pitcher for the Hinton Farm Girl's baseball team, their homemade white uniforms trimmed in red. The teams credited their success to practicing with the Hinton men's team, made up mostly of the girls' brothers and cousins who played as hard as they worked and gave no quarter to the fairer sex. Loretta identified with men when out working the fields while remaining a supple woman of flashy beauty—a shapely and dangerous vixen for any insecure, quailing man to woo. Come Saturday night, exuding femininity, hair permed and upper lip painted a Cupid's bow, it took a self-assured man to ask this luscious sylph to dance. And while Loretta worked with my father and brother, the next oldest, Bethel, a shy and serious girl, as gentle in demeanor as her features were lovely, was made mother's helper for housekeeping, chicken and garden tending, canning and bread baking.

Fern and Esther, like myself but older, were old enough to start milking but too young to do field work other than delivering lunches and water jugs to workers in the fields. Yet we did as much to help with barn and garden chores as kids our tender age could do: herd cows along the road, shovel manure from the trough running the length of the milk shed directly behind the cows when in their stations, clean the horse barn's stalls, tote milk cans to the water tank where, in the freshly pumped well water, the cows' body-temperature milk would cool and await pickup by the dairy truck. We gathered eggs, weeded, picked potato bugs and caterpillars off garden plants and dropped them into handheld cans of kerosene. We learned that difficult tasks are only those one can't yet perform, and we made games out of work. Unlike city kids, we didn't have tricycles, bicycles, scooters, or roller skates, since farmlands don't have sidewalks. Dirt roads, furrowed deeply by tires after rainstorms and criss-crossed by erratic runnels, were not cycling paths. As the saying went in those days, «Choose your rut carefully, you're gonna be in it for a long time.» By age three, I had a red metal wagon to haul around, but wagons are as natural to farmers as pouches to kangaroos. When pulling it along, loaded with most anything, no one, not even myself, could tell if I was playing or working.

Child psychologists during the 1920s and '30s compared rural children to those raised in urban centers, but old biases colored their findings even before they were drawn. The commonplace assumption was that farm children tended to be dull, non-intellectual, and enumerative, rather than expressive of feelings or opinions, reflecting a flat, tedious life. If farm children are enumerative, it's because arithmetic is a farmer's day-to-day mental tool. Acres are counted as to yields: how many bushels of corn will an acre yield; how many bushels of corn would be needed to bring one pig to market weight times the number of pigs needed to provide a certain amount of revenue with a couple left over for the smoke house? When winter-feeding cattle, how many tons of corn silage would be equivalent to feeding one ton of hay; how many pullets (females that have not yet laid eggs) would be needed to generate how many laying hens to a hen house; how many bushels of seed-oats to sow an acre; how many potato hills will yield enough to feed the family over winter? We used to joke about the mathematics farm children had to learn. I still remember this one: If it takes a day-and-a-half for a chicken-and-a-half to lay an egg-and-a-half, how many days does it take a rooster sitting on a brass doorknob to hatch out a hardware store? Only a smart farmer can answer that one. Such problems are too complex for the urbanized brain, and I've lived in cities too long to remember even the first step of the solution.

It's said that Eskimos have distinct words to describe many types of snow. Some people think that is an indication of intelligence. Well, city kids think every fly they see is just a fly, not knowing it's a bluebottle, while the farm kid sees house flies, too, but also greenbottles, horn flies, stable flies, horse flies, heel flies, black flies, and bot flies, and can tell the difference between a wasp and a hornet, a milk snake and a copperhead, can distinguish a millipede from a centipede without having to count the legs. Still, it would take a dictionary addict like myself to know that a two-winged fly is a midge, and that a bayonet fly is a bloodthirsty carnivore.

Analyses conditioned by biases and presumptive notions are not entirely unlike those that underlay studies of black children and chimpanzees—the scoring more accurately reflects the tests than they do the responses. Consider, for example, a quotation selected to typify a monotonous rural life—a nine-year-old boy asked to say what he did over the day before: «In the morning I done chores. Then went to school. When school was out I went home changed clothes, done chores. Then I went to bed.» Among many urban children today, the equivalent would be, «In the morning I watched TV. Then went to school. When school was out I went home and changed clothes, watched TV. Then I went to bed.»

Not a very inspiring day for either boy. The psychologist who cited the farm boy's text said of it, This routine of a day is typical of that described by a majority of the rural children. On giving an account of another farm boy of the same age who responded to the question, «What did you do today?» the researcher failed to see the profound wisdom of his response: «The same as yesterday.» The boy had refused to chop up life into incremental days. His answer acknowledges the dull silliness of the investigator's question, as if «How many cows did you milk today?» should be answered any more elaborately by a farmer than saying, «The same number I milked yesterday.» It would be indeed asinine for any researcher to assume that a farmer would count his cows every day, like a schoolteacher taking attendance.

Few researchers in 1930 would have known how to deal with such brilliant responses as this one by a fourteen-year-old dirt-farming boy, asked to describe two days in a row: «The sun looked very red this morning, and did not show itself until about an hour after sunrise, for it was cloudy in the east. Last night there was a round ring around the moon. These signs are good for unsettled weather.» Describing the next day, the boy continued, «The two signs that I'd seen have come true. Today it is raining very hard. It started raining before 7:00 this morning, and it rained all day. The morning was very beautiful as the frost was about a half-inch thick on every tree bough, grass blade, and fence wire. The evergreen trees in our yard looked more beautiful than the prettiest Christmas tree. The house yard looked as if it had not enough room for everything, as the frost made everything look much bigger than it really was.»[10]

Armed with such writings, sociology researchers were nonetheless drawn by convention to conclude their investigation saying, «These people were not given to introspection or to the consideration of subjective experiences. They were equally inarticulate concerning the colorful panorama of sky and hillside, of valleys and watercourses spread about them.» It is true, of course, that when a farmer sees a flooded field, he sees a loss of crop, a season's small profit margin drowned; he doesn't see what the romancing city dweller does: a mirroring flat sheet of sky reflecting clouds over the rough surface of the bare earth, the sky-god looking at himself in a mirror.

Ignored among the documents the sociologists had in hand was this descriptive text by a fourteen-year-old farm boy in the late 1920s: «The moon was almost full overhead. The sky was clear, making it almost as light as day, but I had not gone far when the clouds were racing across the sky making it darker. The night was, or rather seemed to be, weird, as the snow was crunching beneath my feet and the dogs for miles around were barking as if something had been cornered, but mostly because I was alone in the great big world it seemed. Finally, I started for home; the dogs still barking, and it seemed as weird as ever. What a relief it was when I got home! I went to bed, and turned over once or twice before morning came». The same boy wrote, after seeing a movie about Abraham Lincoln: «The show seemed to draw one into it, and it seemed funny to see the world of today when I came out of the theater.»

«Life was unhurried for these rural children,» reads a 1930 Iowa Child Welfare Research Station report. «The greatest educative forces to which they were subjected were the natural phenomena about them, and nature turns the pages of her records but slowly.» Whoever contrived this conclusion had never seen how fast nature can turn a page when lightening strikes a hay-filled barn, when a hail storm wipes out a farm's corn crop in fifteen minutes, when a tidal wall of flood water crashes down the Floyd River, erasing field crops and engorging livestock that moments before had been peacefully grazing.

Too often only the practical side of rural life is considered. «Sometimes the sheer joy of physical labor well done seems reason enough for living on a farm,» the report continues. The researchers failed to commensurately compare this farmer's motivation with an urban dweller's, such as, «The sheer joy of selling insurance policies every day seems reason enough for living in town,» or «The sheer joy of sitting on my butt all day in the office seems reason enough for living in the city.» In 1954, at age twenty-six, while driving across Nebraska in early July en route from the West Coast to New York, I empathized with a farmer I saw out in a cornfield on his tractor, cultivating. It was a very hot day, the temperature in the high nineties. I had my car windows open, and my bare left arm was getting horribly sunburned. I detoured up the Missouri River route from Council Bluffs to visit my farming relatives in Hinton. During an evening after chores, out on the breezy screened porch chewing the fat with cousin Clarence, I remarked about feeling sorry for that farmer on an open tractor under a scorching sun. Clarence's response brought me back to reality. «When I'm out in the field in hot sun, I look at cars going by on the highway and thank God that I'm on a tractor and feeling cool in the open air.»

Even scholarly researchers tend to romanticize farm life, as do former farmers when reflecting on a rural childhood and wanting to preserve only its pleasantness. The lives of artists, rock stars, gangsters, and farmers elicit imaginative envisioning more readily than do the routine lives of butchers, bakers, and candlestick makers. My argument with the sociology studies I've cited is not that their data was in every case inaccurate but that their prejudicial analyses reflexively portrayed country children as dull, unimaginative, excessively practical, and socially disadvantaged. When studying urban children, a different set of biases was typically applied. While dumbness and crudity were baselines for farm children, with imaginative and highly intelligent farm children noted as exceptions, in cities, intelligent children formed the baseline and exceptions were dummies—like saying that a forty-degree-Fahrenheit day at the North Pole is a very hot day; while at the equator it would be a very cold day. This kind of prejudice would also hold true when studying trained animals: the trainer who shows off a horse with a straw hat on its head that's able to count up to ten by pawing the ground and push a baby buggy with its nose has only taught an intelligent animal to act like a stupid human being.

The narrow confines of rural life during my youth did place limitations, however. Both school and home suffered from the closeness with which the lives of neighbors were interwoven, and one was usually out of touch with newer trends in social thinking. While the country school, with individual attention paid to every child, was advantageous for young children, it did not guarantee an education beyond the intellectually fundamental years, and rarely did rural children who finished the eighth grade in a one-room school look ahead to college or anticipate any profession other than farming. It wasn't exceptional that neither of my parents, even after their conversion from farmers to urban dwellers, attended my junior high school graduation or even the class play in which I starred. Education didn't mean much to them—just get a job, get married, and raise kids. Neither parent attended my baccalaureate graduation from the University of California, though they lived near the campus. When I tried to get my father to allow my youngest sister to go to college, as she was the last chance among seven of his daughters to do so, he grew angry and said, «The only reason girls go to college is to find a man to marry.» «Better than finding one in a bar,» I said to myself in response. When in 1964, I called my mother from New York to tell her I'd been granted my Ph.D., her response was, «Now don't let that go to your head,» and when I told her in I'd been appointed full professor at MIT, she responded reflexively, «Talk's cheap. It takes money to buy whiskey.» She was cautious to not let either of her children make themselves more prominent than the others.

She once said to me when I was was in my early twenties, «You'll never amount to anything. You've got too many irons in the fire, you talk too much, and you can't stay put.» Yes, I've always had too many irons in the fire, but I made a life out of not staying put and being well paid to talk. She wrote many letters to me over the years. I saved them, cherished them. She had less schooling than even the average farm girl of her generation, yet not once in her letters would one find a misspelled word or faulty grammar. And her rich deployment of witty say-ings would make a useful dictionary of unconventional language, with the title, «Madder Than a Wet Hen.»

One needs such mothers for putting final touches on one's upbringing. During a discussion of mothers with a writer friend, telling him what I just told you, he recalled being with his mother at her deathbed-side, grief-stricken, not knowing what to say, and saying, «Mother, I don't know to who I'll be able to turn when you're gone.» To which his mother responded, her voice failing, «*To whom*, David, not *to who*.» And at that moment, she died.

Chapter 5

I want to put salt on a
rabbit's tail so when it stops
to lick it off I can catch it

L oretta, my oldest sister you will recall, says that from my first day of walking I tagged her around the farmyard like a jabbering gosling attached to a goose, that I was hyperactive, reckless, and often a pest. Now, thinking about it, I'm sure that whatever was hyper-anything about me was probably not a chemical imbalance in my brain but directly her influence. She taught me to walk before I'd mastered creeping by repeatedly standing me up flat against a wall in military posture and backing away, saying, «C'mon, c'mon.» Thanks to the abundance of calcium in milk-fed farm babies, I'm not bow-legged as a result of having been prematurely bipedal. Because the wall kept me from falling backwards, I had to fall forwards. Perhaps from this training emerged my tendency later on to stand belligerently upright, back to the wall, when better sense would have me retreat on all fours. When I contracted pneumonia at eighteen months of age, probably from walking in naught but diapers out a careless door into harsh weather, Loretta nursed me back to hyperactive health. At age three, not wanting her out of my sight for a moment, I climbed atop an oil barrel to watch her feed hogs. The barrel rolled over, I fell to the ground, breaking an arm. This break was just the first one. Before I was eleven, I broke an arm three or four more times, maybe because in learning to walk away from the wall I fell so often that bone-breaking falls off anything—barrel, bike, walls—came naturally. A farm-bred cousin, Corletta, eight years older than I, recently said, «You ran around so crazily you were always falling over some stupid little thing, like a fallen tree branch or a tin can.»

One remembers from infancy and early youth most of one's painful experiences. Happiness is easily forgotten while pain lingers like ravens on doorways. I once read a story told by the Gestalt psychologist, Max Wertheimer, of a little boy seated on the hearth before a fire in a fireplace, his father in a chair nearby. The boy blurted out suddenly, «Father, I see fire-angels dancing on the logs.» His father cuffed him smartly on the ear. The boy cried out, «Why did you hit me?» The father replied, «So you will never forget having seen those angels.» Had I not had enough hurtful experiences on the Hinton farm to set up contrasts, I might not be able to recall much of anything.

Perhaps one's most efficacious motivation for growing up is to move beyond the displeasure of childhood, leaving the painful in the past, repressing shame and guilt by growing upward, like plants from their soiled roots. Every motion in the universe obeys a repulsive force, and nothing in a child's life, not even a petty crime, is immaterial to forcing adulthood on juvenility. In his *Confessions*, St. Augustine suffers guilt as a grown man over having swiped ripe pears from a neighbor's orchard when a mere boy, his transgression augmented sensually by recollection of the verboten fruit's luscious sweet taste. His adult guilt over this adolescent misdemeanor is no less weighty than had he, as a grown man, swiped a neighbor's wife from her husband's bed and relished her too. In one's governing psyche, taking a neighbor man's fruit can transpose over time into an act of adultery, just as a boy's shameless indifference to killing rabbits or ground squirrels can develop as indifference to slaughtering humans. More effectively than laws, shame and guilt safeguard humans from abusing each other. Shame is one's personal, internal police force, and guilt is well-deserved punishment. My mother's handy remonstrance to transfer her discipline to her children's self-discipline (a protracted changing of the guard) was «Shame on you!»

And one remembers deceptions in the form of kidding that induce embarrassment and stain one's consciousness like burns do skin—reminders not to repeat embarrassing acts. To be made a fool of when young helps condition one not to make a fool of oneself when adult. Cousin Corletta confirmed a recollection that stayed indelible in my mind from age six, and in hers as well for over fifty years: «There is one thing that still sticks in my mind about you,» she once said to me. «Do you remember when out at the farm you'd see a rabbit in the field or wherever and run to catch it? I can't remember whether it was my dad, or your dad, or someone else, who told you to put salt on the rabbit's tail, then you could easily catch it. So the next time you saw a rabbit you ran to the house and asked for a saltshaker. When asked what you wanted it for, you said, I want to put salt on a rabbit's tail so when it stops to lick it off I can catch it.» At the expense of my need to trust adults, a good laugh was bought for all. It was not on Corletta's dad's farm but my Uncle Henry Casch's that this happened. Armed with both a salt shaker and a coffee can filled with salt I'd chipped from a block of cowlick out in a pasture, I chased rabbit after rabbit along the hedge-rows, yet returned to the house distraught and empty handed, like the proverbial Chinese boy told to go to the stream and catch fish with a soup spoon. Trying his best but failing to catch one, he was unmercifully teased for being so foolishly trustful. Had I not been smart enough a couple of years later, I would have gone to the river fishing with garden peas as bait and a baseball bat, because I'd been told by my older brother Marius that the easiest way to catch fish was to sprinkle peas along the water's edge. When I asked what I was to do with the bat, he said, «Well, when a fish comes ashore to take a pee, you hit him over the head with it.»

Such joshing was not necessarily heartless. Ribbing and clowning around children was commonplace. Being teased is not without redeeming value to a child's education and conceptual development. It sets off a chain reaction, drawing attention to one's self and helping to circumscribe a strong ego; it also helps a child differentiate between fact and fiction, such as learning that no fish swims backward to keep the dust out of its eyes, that not every bird perched on a fence rail, with its mug on one side and its wump on the other, is a mugwump rather than a meadow lark or thrush, or that chickens don't cross the road for any reason other than to get on the other side.

Being teased can compress the self into smallness and render it explosive. An excessively teased child becomes hair-triggered. I suspect that at a very young age I warded off teasing by staying one step ahead of it—not by acting cool as if unaffected, but by being a show-off and mastering cuteness and cleverness as a defense. Cute children, like cute animals, are less subject to brutality than the not-so-cute. By acting cute, one can get away with most anything. Bethel says my first drunk-act—which wasn't an act! —came at age three when I would regularly deploy cute tactics to draw attention to myself and fend off being teased. A couple of harvesters, while resting on our lawn and drinking Dad's home brew before returning to the fields, thought it might be amusing to offer me a bottle of beer. «A typical three-year-old would have spit out the first taste, and been teased for it, but not you!» Bethel said when disclosing this incident some years later. «The more everyone laughed, the more motivated you were to guzzle and show off while teetering. Mother was evidently in the house; had she seen the goings-on she would have had a fit.» Now that I can reflect soberly on this, I'm mindful that what adults don't fully realize is that when little children play they do not play at being children but at being adults. Only grown-ups perform child's play. Rarely is life more serious than when one is a child. Insecure adults tend to fall back on childhood cuteness when their fragile egos are threatened.

I'm aware that over time I molded in my adult mind the whole ball of wax concerning farm life as idyllic, when in fact the sort of life I knew as a child was not like that at all—not like one reads about in Laura Wilder's *Little House on the Prairie* series, Louisa May Alcott's *Little Women* and *Little Men*, or sees in sentimental pictures by Grant Wood and Grandma Moses, or hears from aged city-dwellers raised on a farm who've washed out every black spot of memory—an operation common to mythifications and laundered biographies. While planning this book, I read a few life stories written by people my age who were farm-born and raised in Iowa, Nebraska, or the Dakotas. Their closely woven webs of daily life on the farm differ only slightly from what I've written thus far; farm lives are as invariable as coal miners' or fishermen's. But the antipodal side of their multiplication of bliss is a string of intermissions, of the typically left out: «Heavens! I wouldn't dare write about that!» Romantic pillow stuffing cushions hardships. Not one of these authors suffered more than poverty, foul weather, or the embarrassment of being quarantined with measles or scarlet fever. All had adoring, god-fearing parents, uncles and aunts, friends and neighbors. As a child, not one of them cursed, lied, cheated, stole, peeked through a window or under a sleeping sister's blanket, masturbated, tormented an animal, were sexually molested, stepped barefoot in pig-shit, or had a dirty thought in their head.

Throughout my adult life, I too have protected my farm and small town youth from aspersion by veiling it with romantic notions reflecting not what it was but what myth says it should have been—the mythical total defined by salubrious happiness that remains in the sieve after the woes and miseries have passed into the deep well of the mercifully forgotten. Yet idyllic farm life exists only in the poetic mind as relief from reality's harsh narratives, just as visions of eternal life in Heaven (the City of God, *not* God's farm!) relieve us from our ration of hell on earth by offering hope for a life hereafter of eternal joy. But the age of pastoral rapture never existed, not even in ancient Greece or the paradise of Genesis, which operate in myth like zero in mathematics—a toggle switch between plus and minus, ecstasy and agony. The psychology of agriculture came into our minds as punishment for Adam and Eve's sin: the Garden of Eden, wherein nourishment was freely given and reproduction by the word was replaced by cursed lands of thorns and thistles on which mankind was to toil for his daily bread, and in pain were women to bring forth children. Yahweh says, «In the sweat of your face you shall eat of the land 'til you return to the ground, for you are dirt and to dirt you will return.» And even after this wholesale condemnation to an earthly life of tillage, herding, and food gathering, he still found disfavor in farmer Cain's offering of grain from the dirt of his field.

Farm life as mean and dirty, which often I have denied, was forced upon my reminiscences when I realized how desperately one needs to remember a happy childhood. While interrogating my sensory anamnesis, I peeled away layers of memory to get down to the truth about our physical existence as a rural family—all the way down to hog and cattle-yard manure odors after a rainfall; the stifling smell of horse stalls not cleaned over the winter but layered with today's fresh straw over yesterday's bedding, brewing a winter's flow of urine into acidic mats two feet thick before spring cleaning; the sensation of fresh chicken and goose shit squeezing up through one's summer-time barefoot toes, the stink of the outhouse and the omnipresent dirty diaper pail; the slop buckets, hog-dip, fly spray, and rancid axle grease, mouse turds in the out-buildings' floor corners, cobwebs in the ceiling corners, runny cow shit splashing in the trough below the cows' filthy ass-ends and onto our pant legs and shoes while milking—and sometimes in the milk pail if one couldn't get off the one-legged stool adroitly enough. Manure was on the ground all around us and the odor of it infused every breath. Spring thaws were long mud seasons, summer downpours were drenching. When wet, every body-haired animal stunk.

Yet, the house and everything in it was tidy and clean—hardly a fly-spot on the inside of window glass and never a speck of dust. Sometimes a spider or fly would crawl its fatal way through a window screen crack, and a few explorer-ants from under the threshold would scurry around the kitchen tasting everything they bumped into, but insects and mice would starve to death if they hung around too long. Out of filial piety and a wish not to calumniate my childhood, I am urged to connect that sanitive state to the natural contrast of harsh work and slaughters with the gentleness of farmers towards children, livestock, and pets. But a voice within me says, «No, the lines of your early youth etched on your brain were not scripted that way at all—not gentle, not unstained, but defiled and brutish. Life was not a bed of flowers but of briars, cockleburs, blisters and rusty nails, guilty hands and guilty eyes. You only acted brave but you were not; you were shy, anxious, and frightened.»

One doesn't learn to be brave on the sort of farm that typified those of my youth but to conquer fear, just as one doesn't learn to be intelligent but to overcome ignorance. For every inch one grew one had to overcome a measure of fear. I'm not thinking of goblins, boogie-men, and trolls under bridges that frighten city kids in story books, but real creatures such as wandering gypsies along our country roads, hoboes, kidnappers, child molesters, and territorial dogs that in a setting of grasses, woods, and grazing animals regress down the evolutionary chain to being wolves and jackals. In the barns, stock pens, and pastures were inhuman beasts: sows, boars, and bulls. In the farmyard and out in the fields roamed an array of apathetic machinery with whirring drive belts, toothed gears, cutting blades, and a hundred places for hands or feet or whole bodies to be snagged, crushed or ground up. Statistics piled up each year, counting farm children deaths by machinery, falls, and ill-mannered animals. Stories of a child falling into the hopper of a threshing machine and coming out as hamburger, or falling off the seat of a disk harrow and being sliced like bologna by the blades, were not made up just to be scary. The most terrifying threat of punishment for misbehavior was being run through a buzz-saw, and the most heartless teasing of a little child was for the child to hear, «I'm going to eat you up»—the terror faced by Little Red Riding Hood on a path through a wood. Fear of being eaten was promulgated in children's minds through bedtime horror stories: *Hanzel and Gretel, The Three Little Pigs, The Troll and the Billy Goat*—all of the victims in such stories are farm and hamlet children, sometimes baby animals representing children. The Grim Reaper, after all, carries a farmer's sickle, not a briefcase, and the deadly sins ride horses across farmland, not down a city street.

A neighbor lost a dog to the threshing machine (somewhere someone's breakfast cereal had a strange taste). Nothing quite that awful happened on our farm, only to neighbors. Once, when loading hay into the barn loft, the rigging deployed to hoist the sling-laden wagonload of hay up to the loft door got stuck. My father climbed up to free it—leaned too far out the loft's door, fell forty feet, landing on the hay wagon's sideboards, breaking a side of ribs. And he lost a finger and a half to a saw, and a toe to a horse-drawn disk harrow when he'd raised the assembly to make an adjustment and the team suddenly jerked forward. The assembly dropped, a disk blade cleanly took off the left front edge of his right shoe, a toe with it. He picked up the toe, tucked it into his back pocket, unhitched the horses, drove them to the barn, unharnessed them, put them in their stall, and tossed a pitchfork of hay into their manger. By the time he got up to the house he'd forgotten the incident and was abruptly reminded of it only when my mother noticed he was tracking blood on her kitchen floor. Amused over his forgetfulness, he forked the missing toe out of his pocket, saying something like, «Well, I'll be damned.»

Loretta suffered a worse accident with the same harrow, and would have been mangled had it not been for the obedience of one horse in the four-horse team pulling the machine. Because my father was concerned about teenage Loretta driving four horses abreast, he always harnessed the big, powerful Dan in her team, the best trained workhorse on the farm. When out disking the last year's cornfield, Loretta managed somehow to fall off the seat and into the assembly. Her legs caught, she screamed, «Dan, whoa!» He did, bringing an instant halt to the team. Off a ways, Marius was working with another four-horse team. Hearing Loretta's distress call, he leapt from his harrow and raced to help her, to pull her legs out from the disc assembly. But he hadn't brought his own team to an orderly halt. The horses were confused; one or two had stopped, the others kept moving; the team was soon entangled in their traces and reins. Only after Marius and Loretta caught up with them did Loretta realize that her pant legs were torn and her legs bloody, and that she'd lost a good part of one heel. «That's when I started to cry,» she said.

Recalling the tire swing my father or perhaps Marius hung from the huge maple tree in the house yard, my sister Bethel said in a recent letter, «Our tire swing would probably look like an instrument of torture compared to swings sold by K-Mart and Target stores for children of this era.» Yes, the tire swing was terrifying. A single sisal rope hitched to a sturdy limb that was twenty-five to thirty feet above the ground; the seat, a car tire. When pushed to and fro, the arc of the swing was up to forty feet with one's body fifteen feet above the ground: the tire gripped under one's knees with legs going numb from lack of blood, arms holding on for dear life. Contests over summer hours among older siblings involved how close one could pump or be pushed above the horizontal line. And it was not exceptional for any one of us to be pushed higher than our nerves could endure. The family swing at my uncle Casch's farm down the road a ways was a gunnysack half-filled with sand and hung by a rope from a high tree limb. Grasping the sack between one's legs and holding onto the rope while being pushed to and fro to near horizontal, we suffered the thrill of spreading our make-believe fearlessness over the hostile land, like young Spartans tested for military mettle. To be called chicken or fraidy cat was the most traumatic scorn a farm boy had to bear. Grown-up men were entertained by our misery; the brave were bragged about, the meek were teased. And that's how survival of the fittest works: sissies must be culled while still children. It is said in Danish lore that boys too sissified to satisfy a lusty girl were castrated by the girls and trained as ponies to pull their milk-carts.

I recall at age five or six being taught by much older brother Marius that I must break my own future workhorses to the lead. One of a weanling colt pair was haltered, the rope from the halter snap tied to my right wrist. I was dragged all over the barnyard while my brother whooped, cheered me on, and laughed. I didn't break the colt and was lucky to have survived the lesson without my body being shattered. Those were the days when folks tossed little kids into deep water and yelled at them to learn to swim, when unwanted kittens and puppies were put in a sack with a hefty rock and tossed into the creek. Children exposed to this sort of event, who shortly before had been awed by the mystery of birth watching the family dog whelp, would fall asleep with an image in their heads of drowning in a birth-sack and awaken in the night with post-natal screaming, pawing at the darkness, as helpless as a turtle on its back. For many years, Loretta suffered nightmares from having been held by her ankles over the side of a boat by our Uncle Clem, pretending he was going to dunk her. She was three or four years old; my uncle was just having fun. Thereafter Loretta feared water to such an extent that she would never learn to swim.

Which brings to mind an event that at the time was amusing because all went well, and even today is unforgettable. Our father had hitched a team to a wagon to haul something, I don't recall what, to Hinton, which borders the Floyd River. Loretta was to go along, but because she had other things to do in town, she saddled a horse and rode beside the wagon. On coming to the bridge that passed over the Floyd, the water level, having risen over the night due to heavy rainfall upriver, was a good six inches deep over the bridge's road bed. Dad brought a halt to the team, paused for a moment, and said to Loretta, «Ride over the bridge to see if there's any holes in it.»

Loretta hesitated: «What if there are holes? What if the road falls in? I can't swim!»

Dad came right back at her: «Your horse can swim. Hang on to him.»

And at that, Loretta headed out over the bridge.

My greatest fear at the age of five or six was being kidnapped and chopped up. The igniting event for this illusory horror occurred one afternoon when I was walking along our country dirt road near the intersection where a left turn led to school. Down a ways, I saw a vehicle pull to the side of the road. Two men got out. They didn't look like farmers. From their car they withdrew some strange harness-like equipment and a stick with what appeared to be a saw blade at one end. I knew in a flash they were kidnappers with leather straps to tie me up and a saw to cut me into pieces. I scurried off the road and into a cornfield, down its rows of stalks, higher than my head. On rushing into to the house, yelling for someone to get the shotgun and describing what

I'd seen, my mother calmed me down with assurance that the men were telephone linesmen, the harnesses for climbing poles.

I may have emotionally assigned this incident of panic to being told about the kidnapping of the Charles Lindbergh boy. But the catalyst was more likely a closer-to-home event. When I was five, somewhere in the county, a man named Hickman kidnapped a young girl, age eight or nine, walking a country road to school, murdered her, cut her body into chunks and put them in a trunk. If he'd sexually assaulted her, and he probably did, it wouldn't have been reported in the news, for sex was not to be associated in the public mind with children.

Thereafter, my sisters avoided roads, and when they couldn't, they hid when an oncoming car came into view. Even in the harshest weather, they chose hiking to school over fields through mud or snow rather than taking the road. One late spring afternoon, when sisters Bethel, Fern, and Esther were returning from school by the overland route, as they came to the orchard area downslope from the house they spotted a strange man in the yard just standing there, looking around. Not sure if mother was home, they dared not approach the house with a child-murderer blocking the way to the door. They scampered up a fruit tree and hid among its branches until at last a car drove up, delivering our mother from a neighbor's.

The strange man was a hobo wandering the countryside looking for an odd job or a handout. Mother never failed to find something in the pantry for a hungry stranger, directing him to a place behind the house where he could sit and eat in the shade. Over the Depression years, rail-riding hoboes were a common sight at both Hinton and Leeds, for both were major railroad switching stations (At Britt, Iowa, the national hobo convention is still held each August at which a new king of hoboes is crowned). Many unskilled workers moved from town to town in search of jobs; some had adopted vagrancy as a way of life. Like the gypsies, hoboes as a class were not dangerous to children, but how could one tell when encountering one?

Whether walking a country road or climbing up a ladder it is usually along a route that danger is encountered. Along country roads, when visiting neighbors or herding cows, one can pause to gather flowers if one is a girl—bouquets of white daisies and purple clover

heads—one can daydream, watch clouds passing over, see a storm developing far off and imagine it's a tornado that might whip one's way. Yet country roads were dangerous, like jogging paths today. When about five or six I encountered a wolf. I was alone on the road, returning from the furthermost boundary of our farm, the intersection about a half-mile away where a left turn led to the school house. The wolf appeared out of nowhere. It jumped a fence up on the bank to my right and was halfway across the road when it spotted me, stopped cold, and angled its head my way. I froze in place. We stared at each other for a long moment. Then it trotted on. At the foot of the downsloping bank at my left, the wolf bounded over a fence and was soon lost to sight in a stand of waist-high corn. I walked on hurriedly to the farmhouse, told my mother and a couple of sisters in the kitchen what I'd seen. They laughed and teased, told me that it must surely have been a dog.

I remember the ridicule as vividly as the wolf. It was a wolf. And when reflecting on why I wasn't afraid, why the wolf didn't attack and eat me, still to this day I feel love for it. We were both by ourselves and out wandering. Because no one believed me, the wolf was mine alone, never to be shared; to others it was just a dog. Later I tried to understand why the wolf and I met at that crossing of our perpendicular paths. He had no home base, so wherever he went he wasn't lost. To be lost one needs a missing place. To be home is to be safe and sound, even when playing baseball and safely on base, when driven to the home plate and being called safe. To do anything like that, one needs others. When alone, one is never safe. But to be entirely one's own self, one needs no one, and no home base.

On crossing a road, look both ways. On climbing a ladder, never look down. Ladders on the farm were not leaned like house painters' ladders but straight up—the steel-runged ladder up the seventy-foot-high windmill, the wood-runged ladders to the hayloft. One's life could depend on a quarter-inch diameter bolt that may have rusted, or a pair of 8-penny nails in a strip of wood that may have split.

One fine afternoon, sisters Loretta and Bethel, when both were very young, decided to climb up the windmill. On getting half-way up, they may have panicked over getting down—an ascent easier on the nerves that a descent (just ask any cat, or a paratrooper), so they kept climbing up toward the platform on which one can stand when making repairs to the blades. A wind suddenly came up; the fan-blades began turning furiously. The girls laid down on the platform and called for help, their screams not heard over noise generated by the fan. By chance, Marius looked toward the windmill, no doubt concerned that when high winds come up the blades must be braked by a lever at the mill's base. He saw the girls. After braking the blades, he climbed up to them, and like a fireman, brought them down one at a time.

After the move to Sioux City, I was obsessed with a wish to overcome a fear of height, that emblem of cowardice, a negative merit badge. Recklessly, I climbed near vertical clay banks in quest of confidence. Comically, I proposed in junior high school that the human species had evolved from an inferior species of apes that kept falling out of trees, that human intelligence emerged only when it occurred to some really smart primal ancestor that the solution to survival was to stop climbing trees and stay on the ground. After this height-fearing, cowardly simian had influenced other cowardly tree-climbers to do the same, the entire race of ground-dwelling, height-fearing *Homo sapiens* gradually evolved, while all those silly tree-climbing anthropoids that didn't fear heights remained stunted on the evolutionary ladder as monkeys and apes. «And so,» I said, «humans matured genetically from those apes that feared heights; human intelligence emerged only when thinking became grounded, and human speech evolved as sublimated screams of terror recapitulated in the screams of human infants.»

Chapter 6

*Dirt farmers are as basic as
dirt, manure, beasts, and
when gotten right down to, sex*

On that Hinton farm we were dirt farmers. Dirt is a powerful signifier. The concept of civilization excludes dirt farmers and herders. The curse put on Adam and Eve's sons, Cain and Abel, was that one became a grain farmer, the other a sheep herder. A civilized farmer is a gentleman farmer, one who does not actually farm, never touches dirt, like corporate lawyers who won't take a criminal case, or physicians who won't work below the navel. Cultured and enlightened behavior is reserved for civil bodies, metropolitan people removed from the land, distanced from animals, not governed by natural laws. Farm produce is at the bottom of the food chain. The farmer stands on the bottom rung of the social ladder, just above animals and plants at the ladder's feet. John Steinbeck's *The Grapes of Wrath*, which reached a vast public in the 1940 film featuring Henry Fonda, brought the tradition of the scorned dirt farmer up to date in the urban mind. Peasant uprisings, enraged farm folk, armed with pitchforks and shovel-handles as weapons, have terrorized the nobility and the urban bourgeoisie from ancient times until today: ancient non-Romans to the north—dirt farmers, sheep and cattle herders, woodcutters—were barbarians, we are told in standard history books that generalize the rural masses no less than farmers do weeds and varmints.

Having wasted a lot of adult emotion claiming to be still a farmer, even as a scholar working his field, I've tried to understand why certain unwelcome behavioral patterns of my adulthood persist in recollections of farm boy experiences and still affect my behavior. I've appealed off and on to history and sociology, with some recompense gained on finding that the abrogation of farmers is elemental throughout civilization, which I find ironic, since the dawn of civilization is generally envisioned as the first instances when the human species took control of nutrition by supplementing food gathering and hunting in the wild with crop planting and animal husbandry.

The historical scope of this prejudice had a focus within range of my childhood experience that helped rationalize why heavenly pictures of farm life hanging behind my eyes look so unpleasant when seen out front. A farmer's insurrection, known in Iowa chronicles and the minds of very old people as the Farmers' Holiday movement magnified during my youth the urban belief that farmers by nature were vitiated and uncivilized. The movement followed on the Wall Street crash of 1929 that resulted in an inordinate number of bank failures and insurance company foreclosures. The gray blanket of misery from the East layered over Iowa farms, concurrent with the devastating droughts of 1931 and 1932, which were severest in northwest Iowa, at which time I was three and four. The two counties, Woodbury and Plymouth, that figured in my life, had three times as many mortgages called as any other county in the state when prices paid farmers for their produce dipped lower than the cost of production.

Over the 1932 summer, farmers pressed for legislation that would guarantee prices for their produce at least equal to the cost of production plus a family-sustaining profit. An event making morning headlines across the state erupted one night on the highway between Leeds and Sioux City. On August 8th, local farmers met to decide on a plan of action against purchasing agencies that were driving them into bankruptcy. The next day, the Sioux City Milk Producers Association was organized as a collective force. The roster of members included farmers from Iowa and those nearby in Nebraska and South Dakota, who regularly had their raw milk and cream trucked to Sioux City dairies. On the evening of August 11th, a mass of farmers—my father, Marius, and Loretta among them—blocked trains and trucks hauling milk into the city. Deploying logs to halt trains, straw bales to stop trucks, and armed with pitchforks for use on tires that didn't stop rolling, the irate strikers clambered aboard train cars and truck beds, uncapped twenty-gallon steel milk cans, and dumped thousands of gallons of milk onto the road—not emulating the Boston Tea Party, which was a kindred event, but following the age-old paradigmatic strategy of punitive abstinence as an agent of war against oppressive authority.

This rebellion had a long history behind it, recalling the early 1920s when European countries recovered from World War I and depended less on imports of agricultural products from America. When the post-war boom of 1920-21 favored agriculture, many farmers were encouraged to take large loans and buy additional acreage, breeding stock, and machinery. *Wallace's Farmer* was on the side of machinery manufacturers, leading farmers to believe that prosperity would be forever theirs if they invested in scientific farming. Banks in Iowa played a relatively small role in promoting farm mortgages. The big insurance companies, however, were awash with capital. They aggressively nudged farmers to increase their land holdings by mortgaging farmland they owned outright. «What is a farm without a mortgage?» was a sardonic pleasantry among farmers then.

Equitable Life and Bankers Life, plus a few smaller firms, had made Des Moines the insurance center of the Midwest. Farm machinery manufacturers advertised heavily to promote modernization of farming and led farmers to believe that without the latest equipment they couldn't compete and reap the profits of a booming economy. But as post-World War I foreign trade dropped off and prices declined across the country, farmers found themselves accused of over-producing during deflation. When the Wall Street stock market collapsed in 1929, many lost their savings when loans were called by the lending agencies. Over the next nine years, banks and insurance companies foreclosed on so many farms that by 1939 they collectively owned the equivalent of eight Iowa counties. Most of the confiscated farms were rented back to the farmers who'd lost them, so the farmer's pride in ownership was converted into humiliation as tenant farmer whose efforts to scratch out a living were monitored by insurance agents living in the city. By then, Iowa's farm population had dropped by five to ten percent—my own family's move to town would reduce the count by eight.[11]

Three years earlier, in 1929, dairy farmers had battled the state on a related issue. At the outset of the Depression, the state made an ill-timed demand on dairy farmers to have their cows tested for bovine tuberculosis. Although testing had been going on since 1919, it suddenly became not only compulsory but also so brutally enacted and on such a large scale that farmers felt both insulted and economically threatened. The state's investigation ignored most of the local veterinarians who politicians thought might be too friendly with farmers whose stock they regularly serviced. A special force of testers was hired from out of state. Cattle reacting to the test were to be destroyed, the farmer receiving compensation from the state only after the loss had been evaluated.

As the testing and destruction progressed county by county, many farmers claimed they were not receiving fair compensation. Some were convinced by quacks that the test results were not uniformly valid (Norman Baker, a Muscatine radio spokesman for a cancer cure that cured no one, was a daily provocateur). As entire herds were being decimated, the farmers around Muscatine and Tipton rebelled, driving off the state's veterinarians with shotguns. Although sympathetic—he, too, a farmer—Governor Dan Turner sent troops to the Southeastern counties. The testing continued under armed guard. In 1933, the Democrats took over the governor's office. They disbanded the state testing squad. The Cow War, as the imbroglio came to be called, ended when Iowa's dairy farmers were allowed to work with their local veterinarians. By 1940, bovine tuberculosis had been eradicated.

Milk was not an exportable product; refrigerated transport not yet available, so milk sales were not affected by the decline in produce sales to Europe that followed on Europe's economic recovery. But milk-producing farmers were in serious trouble by the early 1930s anyway. Big dairies that processed and retailed milk were also suffering from the financial collapse of 1929, and were struggling to remain solvent by paying as little as possible to the farmers. Robert's Dairy, the largest milk processor and distributor in northwest Iowa at the time, was not about to give in to farmers' demands for higher prices. Some farmers accused the dairies of enhancing their own revenue by overtesting and downgrading the milk they collected, leading a few dairymen to take deceptive action. It was not uncommon—even on our farm—to bang in the bottom of the milk cans we filled so the sediment would collect around the inside's bottom edges and miss the tester's collecting tube, which would most likely be aimed down the middle. Another common practice was to keep the filled cans upside down in the cooling tank until collection time, so when turned upright the sediment particles would be distributed throughout the milk long enough not to be detected.

Farmers at the time were being paid about one dollar per hundredweight of 3.5 percent butterfat raw milk, while the cost of production was as high as two dollars. To allow for a reasonable profit over and above costs, the farmers were demanding $2.17. When Robert's and the other big dairies refused to negotiate, thoughts of rebelling and withholding their produce from the market began smoldering in milk barns. By early August 1933, picket lines, manned by hundreds of farmers, began the blockade of trucks and trains loaded with milk from entering Sioux City.[12] On August 12th, an editorial in the Sioux City *Tribune* supported the farmers:

«The strike that has been engineered by farm leadership is the first expression of open rebellion against oppressive conditions. Other, and perhaps more drastic steps will follow unless relief comes soon. Events are hastening the farm belt toward a crisis of some sort. Agriculture is sinking, slowly but surely. Driven to desperation, it promises to go down fighting. The farmer's fighting spirit has come to the surface.»

A larger order of protest called the National Farmers' Holiday Association had been formed in May at a convention of some ten thousand farmers meeting in Des Moines at the instigation of the Iowa Farmers' Union kingfish, Milo Reno. Reno was a flamboyant old-time Populist organizer. The vice president of the Union, John Chalmers, was from hard-hit Boone County and just as bombastically assertive in promoting the Holiday movement. The word «holiday» was a pejorative slur against bankers, parroting their penchant to declare a bank holiday whenever they found themselves short on cash or verging on insolvency; on several occasions during the 1920s, the banks had induced farmers to waive their withdrawals for a specified time. But just taking a holiday was not action enough to satisfy the farmers' urgency to force prices upward.

The Milk War spread to the ranks of hog, beef, and grain producers. Local and state politicians were put in a quandary, for many depended on the farm vote to keep them in office. J. R. Roberts, president of Robert's Dairy Company, had told the Sioux City *Tribune* a few days earlier that he anticipated no trouble from the Holiday movement, that most of his company's milk producers were not in favor of the strike, and that, anyway, the dairy had a sufficient supply available for Sioux City. But milk could not be stored in those days before refrigeration, when ice blocks were the only coolants; dairies had to be restocked daily. On August 16th, 1932, the *Tribune* took a stand in favor of the farmers. In a front page editorial the paper warned dairies that the situation was indeed grave:

«It is a deep, damning shame, a blot upon the record of government, and a challenge to American intelligence, that the good, substantial farmers of Iowa, South Dakota, and Nebraska should be driven to their present straights. Made desperate by their losing battle for economic survival, the farmers have resorted to the extreme measure of striking in order to dramatize their plight before the eyes of the nation.

«The farmers are acting in good faith. Theirs is a righteous cause. They are to be commended for their self-restraint. They are not sporadic reds or professional malcontents. They live in the best farming country in the world and are not content to be denied subsistence and security for their investments without a struggle. They have an inherent right to fight for their homes and families.

«All signs indicate that this matter is moving to the point when state or even federal recognition may be necessary. But what sort of action will government take? Anything short of a general elevation of the price structure of farm commodities will not afford relief nor remove the cause of vexation. Economic justice and fair play cannot be denied much longer.»

During the wartime 1940s, Iowa's per capita income would be $930, about what it had been during the previous boom of 1919-20. But over 1932 and 1933, the per capita income was down to $252, considerably below the figures for the eastern states that had an easier time economically and were not disposed to care much about what was happening in the Midwest. An editorial in the Sioux City *Tribune* of August 11th, 1932, a few days after the Milk War began, pointed out one glaring example of eastern indifference to the farmers' plight. In keeping with the «dumb farmer» motif, the editorial was captioned, «Damn Dumb.» It recalled that when speaking in Spencer, Iowa in 1928 (my birth year, you will recall), the U.S. Vice President, Charlie Curtis, told a farmer who'd tossed a discomforting questions at him on the subject of the failed farm economy, «You're too damned dumb to understand.» Then, in 1932, on his way to the Olympic Games to represent Herbert Hoover during the presidential election campaign, Curtis paused in Las Vegas for a speech and again exposed his crudity when a verbal exchange occurred between him and a group of heckling farmers who compared their plight to that of thousands of war veterans who found themselves without jobs and impoverished:

Heckler: «Why don't you feed some of those ex-soldiers in Washington?»

Curtis, to the farmers: «I've fed more than you have, you dirty cowards! I'm not afraid of any of you.»

The Damn Dumb editorial continued:

«Evidently Curtis is conducting his 1932 campaign unchastened in mind or spirit by the events of the past three years. Such remarks, uttered by a supposedly enlightened man, reveal either one of two things—an infantile, childish mind, or a callous indifference to the mass of suffering humanity, or maybe both. Evidently Curtis agrees perfectly with P. T. Barnum's statement that there's a fool born every minute. We are tempted to say that, in our opinion, Curtis must have been born right on the minute, as he places the war veteran in the same category with the farmer. Can you imagine such an addle-headed mind as this Mr. Damn Dumb Curtis, if he is again put in the Vice President's chair, attempting to guide the machinery of our government during the next four years? Of course, we could probably forget our economic and financial ills in hilarious amusement at the antics of Dolly Gann and Curtis settling social problems, but it is hard to laugh on an empty stomach.»[13]

This connection between destitute dumb farmers and returning dog soldiers was not without history. The *Tribune*'s columnist wasn't aware that since at least ancient Roman times conscripted farmers made up the bulk of called-up armies. The phrase, «plowshares into swords» reflects those times when front-line soldiers were mostly farmers with the crudest of weapons and minimal armor that they, themselves, were required to fabricate They were the progenitors of «cannon fodder,» as line soldiers would still be called in WW II—expendable and replaceable, like child laborers and assembly-line workers. Even in ancient Roman times, recruits who survived slaughter and managed to get back home would usually find that senators had expropriated their farms, not figuring the owners would return.

Iowa's milk production could not be curtailed: cows had to be drained to the last drop twice a day or their bags would dry up and produce not a squirt until coming fresh after a winter's pregnancy and calving the next spring. So, as milking continued, milk was put to any use that would avoid spoliation. My parents were among those who held back. Milk from our cows was spun through the hand-turned cream separator up at the house; the skim milk was fed to pigs and chickens, the cream sold locally or consumed at home as whipped cream atop anything cake-like or fruity. We downed enough cholesterol to last a lifetime. The larger dairy farms delivered thousands of gallons of milk free of charge to hospitals, the orphanage, the old age home, and to the poor at the city's edge and in small towns.

Woodbury County's sheriff John Davenport handled the enflamed situation with caution and fairness. He was obliged to deputize about sixty men, but they were not armed. Few truckers would risk manslaughter by driving through a blockade, and fewer farmers would risk being charged with assault or murder. The strikers were effective, but when the full effect of the milk strike was felt in the city and nearby towns, with only ten percent of daily milk needs getting to back-door home deliveries and retail stores, Robert's and other large dairies counter-attacked by contracting for milk from Nebraska, Kansas, and South Dakota, iced and shipped up by train from Omaha. The expense of icing and stabilizing raw milk for shipment soon exceeded the increases demanded by the farmers. So the Milk War ended after three weeks with a capitulation from the dairies. In Sioux City, the wholesale price paid to farmers was raised from 2 to 3.6 cents a quart, while the retail price in creameries and door-to-door deliveries mounted from 8 to 9 cents. Omaha dairy interests fell in line with Sioux City's, agreeing to pay $2 a hundredweight for milk instead of $1.45, while Lincoln, Nebraska dealers raised the price forty cents to $1.80. These concessions were interpreted as plain-fact admission that the dairies hadn't been paying fair prices to the producers. The raises didn't do much more than energize the farmers' wrath against exploitation involving hogs and grain.

Encouraged by the success of the Milk War, a greater farmer's rebellion, incited by the National Farmers' Holiday Association, would soon bring the still-glowing embers into flames that spread to heat up the Midwest's hog, sheep, and beef-cattle producers. While dairying had been Iowa's first farm industry (forty years before this strike there were 165 cheese factories in the state, and by the turn of the century as many as a thousand creameries), few of the farms in Woodbury and Plymouth counties were specialized dairy farms after 1900. The importance of milk production to the diversified farmer was that, like eggs, it was produced daily to generate regular cash income, unlike most livestock, such as feeder hogs or cattle, or corn, oats, and flax, that could be marketed only once or twice a year.

Sioux City's Mayor William Hayes was quick to see that threats might soon turn to action worse than the short-lived Milk War. On the 22nd of August, he was quoted in the Sioux City *Journal* saying:

«For the past week, Sioux City has been the center of a movement that threatens to sweep the Middle West states like a prairie fire. In my opinion, an emergency of the first magnitude exists in this section, one in which I detect a potential threat of serious consequences to the entire nation. To minimize the seriousness would be a grave mistake. The suggestion has been made through the press that a conference of the governors of the affected states should be called. I believe that should be done, because the situation transcends local interests.»

Before anything useful came of Mayor Hayes' effort to find a way out of the dilemma, the first acts of violence had already occurred. On the 21st of August 1932, a mob of farmers halted a livestock train outside Sioux City and released the animals into the countryside. Sheriff Davenport was then in a pickle, knowing that the farmers' swing vote had already cost him re-election and now could prevent him from any sort of future in politics. He was a lame duck, while the victor, Sheriff-elect Ed Petty, one of Davenport's former deputies, was praying to the Lord God Almighty that by the time he took office the conflict would be over. Davenport was obliged by the code of his office and prodding by urban reactionaries to muster his deputies and arrest pickets who refused to abandon the blockades. On the 25th of August he was quoted in the *Tribune*, saying that, while he realized the farmers were receiving far too little for their produce, he would not tolerate violence. «I've been patient beyond measure,» he said, «but it is my duty as sheriff to see that all highways in Woodbury County are kept open, and I will do all in my power to keep them open.» The newspaper also reported at the time the farmers' typical response, that the sheriff was lucky not to be a candidate for re-election.

At the height of this rebellion, two thousand farmers took positions along the nine truck routes into Sioux City; staked out tents and set up kitchens. Armed with pitchforks, rotten eggs, 4th of July torpedoes and fire crackers, railroad ties, logs, hay bales, planks and threshing machine belts studded with tire-puncturing nails, they brought to a near halt the flow of livestock trucks. On August 17th, 1933, a swarm of fired-up farmers laid siege to the Sioux City stockyards and set about releasing animals from holding pens and off trucks that had evaded the barricades and hadn't yet unloaded. Deputies and city policemen managed to drive off the vandals before too much damage was done. The magnitude of this event made national news; the entire nation had become aware of the rebellion. On August 27th, even *The Literary Digest* covered news of the strike as an editorial headed «The Farmers Are Embattled Again,» followed by a quotation from the *Boston News Bureau*: «This time Sioux City is their Lexington, Massachusetts. They hope the metaphorical shots they are firing will be heard around the world.»

Other newspapers expressed caution. Sacramento's *Bee* concluded that, however well-intentioned the move might have been, it was extremely doubtful whether the strike would accomplish anything: «Too many farmers taking part could be persuaded to withdraw and sell their products if a tempting offer were made. It is hard to refuse money when the banker is clamoring for his interest and the sheriff is threatening eviction,» *The New York Journal of Commerce* said. And it continued:

«Such pathetically misdirected efforts at self-help show plainly that many farmers are incapable of realizing that they are infinitesimal units in a marketing organization that embraces a vast area of the entire world. The chief sufferer from a farmers' strike is usually the farmer himself. After a crop is made, the average farmer must sell in order to live, and sales at any price that covers the cost of getting commodities to market are better than destruction of the product or ignorant gambling on the chances of future improvement. The farmer must institute production strikes, not sales strikes, if he wants to improve his condition.»

Cooperating sheriffs and deputies soon arrived in Sioux City from all parts of the state to ride shotgun for those truckers bold enough to challenge the blockades. Not until September, however, did Iowa's governor Turner take remedial action: he convened the governors of Iowa, Minnesota, North Dakota, and South Dakota in Sioux City to confront their common problem (Nebraska, Ohio, Oklahoma, Wisconsin, and Wyoming sent representatives). Five thousand striking farmers and their urban sympathizers highlighted the opening day of the three-day conference by holding a peaceful protest march— «in the sprit of Gandhi,» they said. A good many influential people were called upon to address the conference and speak about the farmers' plight. After the affair ended, the governors compiled a report and forwarded it to Congress and President Hoover asking for a protective tariff for agricultural products, an expanded currency, an extension of the Reconstruction Finance Corporation, and a national moratorium on foreclosures of farmed properties. But not one of the governors was willing to do much of anything within his own state, if only because farmers across the states were themselves in conflict over the Holiday Association's action.

Farmers in Woodbury and Plymouth counties found the Governor's Conference report sadly lacking in anything that might be immediately helpful. Shortly after its conclusion, members of the Association voted to continue picketing around Sioux City until prices for their produce reached at least a break-even level. Mayor Hayes, Sheriff Davenport, and County Attorney Ralph Prichard took up the threat with governor Turner, proposing that he authorize the use of National Guard troops. But Turner was cautiously on the side of the farmers and feared an unpopular precedent. He would soon be coming up for re-election. Shooting farmers would cost him the farm vote, especially because the powerful Des Moines *Register*, sympathetic to farmers, would bury him under negative editorials and other Iowa newspapers would follow suit.

The rebellion would wind down by September 15th, when I was four, but foreclosures continued across the state and in farmlands throughout the country: over the nation's agricultural lands, 65,000 farm mortgages were foreclosed in 1931 alone. As elected officials, county sheriffs were stuck with enforcing foreclosures, thus raining down on their heads the wrath of farmers and hamlet dwellers who depended on farming (Robin Hood's battle against the Sheriff of Nottingham, was not just a tale in Iowa farmers' minds—like all myths, those of Robin Hood were based on realities). In late January of 1933, about twenty-five miles north of Sioux City at Le Mars (where ten years later, at the age of fourteen, I will work as a farmhand), a feature writer from *The Nation*, Charlotte Prescott, wrote a good story. Following a summary of the farmers' revolts, she, deployed an interview style for the matter of foreclosures:[13]

«Early in January 1933, at the farm town of Le Mars in northeastern Iowa, a mob of a thousand farmers seized the attorney for an insurance company, dangled a rope before his eyes, and threatened him with immediate lynching. They also held the judge of the district court in his chambers and defied the county sheriff to do anything about it. And they got what they wanted—the withdrawal of foreclosure proceedings against one farmer and the defeat of a deficiency judgment against another. It was the opening engagement between an organized rural population and established authority—social revolution in the cornfields of Iowa.

«This was startling news, but the incident at Le Mars was no sudden or isolated outburst. Dissatisfaction among farmers in the Middle West is profound and widespread. Over two years ago the agent for a farmers' loan company told me: Unless you get out into the country, you don't know what's happening there. The farmers aren't making even a bare living. And men don't see their families going hungry without doing something about it.

«They began doing something about it last summer. Their first gesture against doing things as they were was the 'cow war,' in which, with shotguns backing them, the farmers refused to have their cattle tested for tuberculosis. Then came the far more important Farmer's Holiday movement, an attempt to raise the price of farm products by keeping the products on the farm, by force if necessary. The attempt was unsuccessful. Prices they now get are even lower than last year's, when they were the lowest in history. Through delinquent tax sales, the foreclosure of farm and chattel mortgages, and deficiency judgments, the farmer is facing the loss not only of his farm but also of his seed grain, livestock, and machinery as well. His home, his tools, and his place of business are all threatened.

«A Farmers' Council of Defense has recently been organized, composed of ten leading farmers of Iowa and South Dakota. This council, which stems directly from the Holiday movement, heads a large organization of farmers and acts as a judiciary body to decide upon the grievances of the farmers. If it decides, for example, that the foreclosure of a certain farm mortgage is unjust, word is passed along to a thousand farmers and the foreclosure is halted.

Now starts the interview. The interviewee probably fictitious, but it doesn't matter.

«You want to talk to me?» The whiskered little old man wearily closed one eye, as if he had looked at the world too long, and gazed at me out of the other. «Yes,» I said, «if you could spare the time. I want you to tell me about the farmers' revolt.»

«We were standing in the lobby of the hotel, which has long been a landmark for the 5,000 inhabitants of Le Mars. The little old man sighed and seated himself in a worn leather armchair, while he pulled on a pair of overshoes, which zipped to the knees. Then he rose and adjusted a sealskin cap over his eyebrows. «I never have any time,» he said, «so you may as well come over to my office now.»

«We climbed a steep flight of wooden steps, and settled ourselves in his office. «I tell you,» he began, «the farmers' slide to ruin really started a long time ago, but it speeded up considerably soon after the war [1919-1920]. The farmer was urged to raise all he could and he got big prices for his crops. All sorts of companies sprang up. Potash companies, and packing houses, and oil companies. A salesman would say to a farmer, «You're getting 4 to 4½ percent on your government bonds. Well, our company pays 8 percent.» So farmers bought everything under the sun. All kinds of farm machinery, one, two, three, four automobiles, and all the land they could get their hands on at three or four hundred dollars an acre.»

«Things went along pretty well for a while, until the price of farm products went down and farmers began borrowing money on their farms. It was easy to borrow. The came the crash in Wall Street, and Eastern companies called back their money and started foreclosing the mortgages they held. Often the farmers had deficiency judgments rendered against them. When a farm is sold after a mortgage is foreclosed, if the amount it brings doesn't equal the amount of the mortgage—I told you that the land was borrowed when the land was sky high—the court issues a judgment to cover the difference and attaches the farmer's grain and livestock and machinery. What makes it worse is that the mortgage holder can send a receiver out to the farm right away to run it and collect the amount of the judgment, so the farmer is done out of the year of redemption after foreclosure that he's always been allowed before in Iowa. You don't have to be a radical to sympathize with the farmer. I've lived in this community fifty years and I know the people around here pretty well.»

After concluding this interview, the reporter questioned one of the county officers about the farmers having mobbed the courthouse. «Last week's battle,» he answered, «was mighty serious. According to the law here in Plymouth County when a mortgage is going to be foreclosed, the sheriff announces the sale of the land and the sale has to take place outside the north door of the courthouse.» He continued:

«Last Wednesday a sale had been advertised and crowds of farmers began to gather along about nine o'clock. When the sheriff and the lawyer for the insurance company came out on the north porch, the lawyer made his bid. The trouble with foreclosure sales nowadays is that the folks who hold the mortgages are usually the only ones who bid, and naturally they aren't going to bid very high.

«Well, this lawyer bid somewhere around $30,000 for 320 acres of land. Good land, you understand. That left about a $3,000 deficiency. Someone in the crowd yelled, «You'd better bid the whole amount of the mortgage!» The lawyer said, «I can't bid any more than I'm told to bid.» Then the farmers grabbed him and threw him down the steps. And they got him down on his back in the yard and told him again to bid the full amount of the mortgage and he said he couldn't. The sheriff tried to get over to him, but the sheriff was a slight fellow—anyway, what could he do against so many? Someone had cut a piece of rope from a swing in the courthouse yard and they threatened to put it around the lawyer's neck and hitch it to the back end of a car, and if he couldn't keep up with the car it would be just too bad.

«Finally they asked him if he would send a telegram to his company in New York. He said he would. So they dictated a telegram to him. I didn't see the wording, but it ended with «My neck is in danger.» Everyone felt sorry for the man who was losing his farm. We call him one of the good Johnsons. He's seventy years old and his folks broke the ground on his farm with a pair of oxen. At his age it would have gone pretty hard with him if he'd had a debt settled on him besides losing his farm. As it is, I suppose he'll rent his farm from the insurance company. Oh yes, Lawyer Lampson got word back from his company to bid the full amount of the mortgage.»

Following this affair in Le Mars, over five hundred farmers at Logan, Iowa, ganged up to prevent the eviction of a farmer because of a $700 deficiency judgment. In a southeastern Iowa county, a sheriff was driven off at the point of a rifle without being able to serve a single writ. At Dennison, Iowa, the sheriff of Crawford County attempted to sell the chattels at the farm of a much liked and respected family. He had on hand several deputies to keep order. The sale was proceeding quietly, with two cribs of corn already sold, when truckloads of farmers swept down on them, halting the sale. Some reports say that the sheriff was handcuffed and had his head dunked in a horse tank, and the foreclosure lawyer made to kneel on the ground and kiss the American flag while being told that it was un-American and unpatriotic to dispossess helpless farmers without giving them time to pay their debts. By this time, some of the farmers called themselves Minutemen, identifying with the colonial revolutionists of Massachusetts who railed against the oppressive tax-collecting British.

All this was happening during the few months before our Hinton farm was taken, before my father had to sell (privately and at auction) his horses, livestock, machinery, equipment, hay in the lofts, and feed in the granary. So it is not just scholarship that causes me to dwell on the subject of the farmers' rebellion, on the foreclosures and other degrading miseries that many farmers endured due to the collapse of eastern industries and financial institutions. In Iowa, where forty-two percent of the farmland was mortgaged and forty percent of state taxes on farmland delinquent, by 1933 about one farmer out of six had been foreclosed on, or had surrendered his land in the face of a sheriff's order to vacate. Large insurance companies—mostly those in Des Moines—then owned 3.5 million acres of the best agricultural soil in the world.[14]

In January 1933, *The Christian Century* published an essay on the foreclosure auctions—back then called Penny Auctions, at which farmers would collude at a deficiency sale and agree that, at risk to life and limb, no one would bid higher that one cent for a hog, two cents for a cow, three cents for a horse, and so on. Because the law forbids the mortgagor or its representatives to place bids, an entire farm could be outfitted with machinery and livestock for a dollar. After the penny sale, the horses, cows, chickens, and machinery would be handed back to the foreclosure victim. The sales were usually festive events, with farmwives setting up tables with coffee and baked goods to feed the participants. The *Christian Century* essayist, John Ellis wrote of one sale that turned to violence:

«Soft January sunlight fell on the farm buildings and the groups of men casually looking over the stock and farm machinery spread out for sale. Soft sunlight in January! In Iowa! This has been a mild winter, for which men say, «Thank God.» It is easier to keep warm with the light fuel picked up here and there—corn cobs and wood gathered in the groves.

«This sale was to clean Ab Willet of his farm implements, horses, hogs, and cows. Willet had been on this farm for five years, and for three years had not been able to pay the cash rent due on the pasture and hay land. Willet had farmed well and worked hard, but the times had been thumbs down on him.»

Ab Willet's cruel years were much worse than our cruel years. But for our farm, as for Ab's, that soft January sunlight wasn't so soft when summer came and reveled in parchedness. And what the sun didn't shrivel, swarms of invading grasshoppers ate. Without a hefty corn harvest to fill the silo with chopped stalks for winter cattle-fodder, and hardened ears to feed pigs, the beef and hog market collapsed; even chicken mash was too high-priced to support a moneymaking flock of broilers and fryers. The hog-to-corn ratio that Henry Wallace had calculated in 1920 as a guide to corn production couldn't be synchronized. It took twelve bushels of corn to bring one hundred pounds of live hogs to market weight. In 1930 there were about nine million hogs in Iowa; by 1934, when we lost our farm, the number had dropped to six million. What corn could be salvaged in the afflicted counties had to be held for seed.

Ellis' essay continues, saying that the mortgagor's attorney had advised that the mortgage on Ab Willet's horses, livestock, and machinery be foreclosed.

«A deputy sheriff was on hand to direct the auction. Willet's neighbors all came to the sale. They gathered in knots in the yard, walked around the farm buildings, talking about the depression, the low prices. Sam Wood, a man who'd been active in the Holiday movement of last summer [1932] gathered a group about him in the barnyard. He was a nervous man, his face twitching with emotion as he spoke. Men, this thing has got to stop! They have taxed the bread out of our mouths and the homes and land out from under our feet. Now, here today, do we propose to sit around and see them clean Ab of all he's got? If farmers don't get together and help themselves, they are a lot of jackasses, a bunch of yellow dogs deserving to be kicked.

«Ben Harris, a large man with a thin, shrill voice, was standing directly in front of the speaker. How're you gonna stop it? he asked. You can't go against the law. Two wrongs don't make a right. If we're going to have laws we can't go around busting them.»

«Wood's eyes burned with crusading fire. «You're right, Ben. Two wrongs don't make a right. But when has the farmer had any rights in the last ten years? You fellows—I know this crowd—and there ain't a man among you that ain't broke. You know it for a fact! You're all busted, whether you admit it or not.»

«Wood did know the crowd. Ora Hicks, standing a ways away in a faded worn-out coat and ragged overalls, a few years ago had been a prosperous renter keeping a boy and girl in college. Last spring he'd sold out and since then had been living in the village, getting county aid. John Heisel had put thirty thousand dollars into a farm in boom days, and last month had been forced to hand over the farm to the insurance company that held the mortgage. Henry Munn's father had left him a quarter section of unencumbered land. He bought another quarter to go with it, and, after years of struggle, lost both places and had a deficiency judgment against him for $5,000. He and his wife had put the best years of their lives into that farm. John Owen, also dressed in a shabby coat and baggy trousers, was standing beside Harris. Owen had thought he was smarter than his neighbors. He'd sold his land when prices were high, and salted away $20,000 in the bank. Last summer the bank failed, a total loss to the depositors.

«The farmers had come to the sale walking, or grouped in wagons. A good many of them still used their automobiles, but many had not been able to pay to renew their licenses.

«A truck came to stop in the farmyard bearing a score of men, among them two men in sweaters [in those days, hired hoodlums tended to wear sweaters]. The two men leaped to the ground lightly, their quick movements separating them from the slower moving farmers.»

[Note. This writer I'm quoting is an Easterner with the usual prejudices, such as that farmers move slowly, think slowly, drawl, wear baggy trousers, and so on. I'm aware of this defaulting, and am able to smile at his text now and then, recognizing that, being a big-city man, he is well meaning but rather naive. So I've transposed a few of his words, such as «git» to «get» and «goin'» to «going» and «seen 'em» to «seen them» and «them fellers» to «those fellows.» Anyone thinkin' these here farmers was hicks is a yeller-bellied jackass]. The text continues:

«Who are those fellows?» asked Heisel.

«John Owen's mouth parted in a wide grin beneath the sandy awning that shaded his upper lip. «I don't know all of them, but the two in sweaters are coal-miners, and they're boxers, too. I saw them in a fight at Fort Dodge last spring.»

«The sale was to start at one-thirty. Five minutes before that time, the auctioneer came out of the house followed by the lawyer. Sam Wood stood up on a corn planter and began to speak to the crowd. «Listen men, before this sale starts, there are something you'll want to get straight.»

«The attorney and the auctioneer stopped to listen. The attorney was a large man, standing half a head above the average man in the crowd. He wore a pearl gray hat and a light gray topcoat.

«Wood's voice was heard, shaking with emotion. «Men—I'm talking to you farmers now. I've got something to say before this sale starts. There will be just two bids offered on this stuff. A man chosen by Ab will make one. The second bid Ab will make. There the bidding will stop. No one will raise Ab's bid.»

«The deputy pushed through the crowd. «Get off that planter, Sam,» he ordered. «And keep your mouth shut. This sale will be conducted according to law.»

«There was an angry growl from the crowd at these words. «Bust him, Sam, if he touches you,» called a voice. «We'll stand by you.»

«One of the sweater-clad men had pushed between Wood and the deputy. The lawyer had been watching the incident, a bulldog expression on his face. He now spoke sharply. «Deputy, do your stuff. If Sam is here to interfere with this sale, arrest him.»

«The second man in a sweater pushed up to the lawyer, saying something or other. The lawyer retorted, «It's none of your business.»

«Oh, isn't it?»

«The sweatered-man's balled fist hit the lawyer smack in the middle of his face and he went to the ground, catching himself on his hands. When he struggled to his feet, blood was running down his face and his nose lay flat against one cheek.

«Sam Wood was still standing on the planter. The deputy was a determined man. He laid a hand on Wood to bring him down, but then wrath of the crowd erupted. The man grabbed the deputy and the lawyer and pushed them out the farmyard gate.

«The crowd of farmers, having realized that the two fighters were sent by the Farmers' Association to help them in case of trouble, forced the auctioneer to conduct the sale. As sole bidder and for a total of fifty dollars, Ab Willet ended up buying his own horses, stock, and machinery—a complete outfit to satisfy the mortgage and continue farming.»

This was Iowa in 1933—a part of it. The actions taken by the farmers were not right by all measures. There are at least two sides to every story. The mortgage holder on Willet's stock and machinery was a widow on state aid, whose taxes on the farm she'd rented to Willet were greater than the crop-sharing rental income she received from him. Faced with medical bills, she'd been obliged to take a mortgage on the land that Ab farmed as a sharecropper. By the time her lawyer had his nose back in shape, she was probably in the poor house.

The ugliest incident occurred on April 27th, 1933 at Le Mars. While on the judicial bench considering a court decision to allow a farm foreclosure, the district judge, Charles Bradley, was set upon by as many as a hundred farmers who pulled him down and dragged him outside the court house. As he was being roughly handled on the porch steps, one of the participants yelled, «Let's take him to the country and show him what a farm looks like.» The judge was tossed into a truck and driven a mile or so east of Le Mars. Somewhere on a country road, a rope was put around his neck, axle grease was smeared in his hair. His pants were taken down and he was threatened with indecencies, perhaps with castration. Grease and dirt were put in his pants that were then bunched up at his ankles. The tormented but principled judge refused to swear that he would no longer sign a foreclosure order; he would meet his fate rather than betray the laws of his court. He was allowed to pray before being sent to meet the Lord. Depending on which account one reads, cooler minds prevailed, or the judge's courage and his entreaty to the Almighty shamed the mob; the judge was released, or, as some say, he passed out while praying. In any event, the crowd scattered, leaving the judge to find his way home. «We shouldn't have done it,» one of the mob said later. «We should have gone after some of the lawyers.»[15]

After the Bradley abduction, Governor Herring declared martial law in Plymouth and six other counties where matters had become intolerable, and sent troops to run disperse mobs and supervise farm sales. The Des Moines *Register* had also had enough of such degrading hooliganism that had made national news and disgraced the State. «It is an outrage against the great multitude of law-abiding farmers,» an editorial read. «It cannot be condoned in any sense or in any degree.» Throughout the country, other papers expressed outrage. The Cleveland *Plain Dealer* called for an exploration of the economic maladjustment behind this social explosion. The Wichita *Beacon* commented, «That such an incident could obtain in a highly civilized community in a state having the lowest percentage of illiteracy in America is difficult of belief.» In the *Savannah News*, it was said, «One can not but wonder in how many other cities and counties there are dynamite bombs of a similar character that may explode unless the efforts at Washington put forward for relief quickly come into effect.» The New York *Journal of Commerce* wrote, «As a plan for raising farm prices by violence, it betrays a pathetic ignorance of the causes and the possible remedies for adequate prices.» The Hartford *Courant* made a reasonable assessment of the affair, while typically overgeneralizing both the extent of the violence and the personality of Iowa farmers:

«The farmers of Iowa are not anarchists by nature. On the contrary, in normal circumstances they are perhaps the most conservative, the most orthodox, and the most peaceable individuals in the nation. When they act as they have recently, the conclusion is unavoidable that they have been placed in a position so desperate as to nullify all their instincts and all their traditions. The fact is ominous, for it means that a situation has arisen that demands extraordinary consideration. The situation is not simply a problem in economics. It is also a problem in maintaining order.»[16]

Not much was gained from this poorly financed revolution that too many mean spirits let get out of hand. Hog and wheat prices paid to farmers bent steeply downward as slaughterhouses and mills ordered imports from out of state; urban vegetable and legume consumers reassigned their taste to tinned produce shipped in by railroad from all over the country; local banks and other creditors bore down hard on the strikers, punishing them by curtailing credit and calling delinquent loans. The spread between what wholesalers paid farmers and what consumers paid in stores widened dramatically. By the fall of 1933, the price of corn paid to farmers had made its way down from two dollars a bushel to ten cents, and hog prices, established in Chicago, had fallen to one dollar per head—two and a half cents per pound.

A summary of the cause behind the rebellion and its sad consequences had appeared in *The Nation* on September 7th, 1932. It included this statement by one of the dissident Iowa farmers who'd managed to run a gauntlet of rotten eggs to get some produce to town. He told reporters, «I own a farm near Boone. My share of the oats crop from twenty-four acres on this farm was $40. My tax on this same land was amounted to $44.16. Before prices took a jump, I could buy a 400-pound sow for 90 cents a hundredweight, or $3.60. At the same time I went to a meat market and priced a 20-pound smoked ham. It was $3.20. I told the sales clerk to go to hell. I'd buy a whole hog and cut off a ham.»[17]

The Milk War and the Farmer's Rebellion reinforced in city-dweller minds images of farmers constituting a violent class of coarse and unruly serfs. Near Cherokee, Iowa, several pickets had been wounded when fired on by deputies. A milk truck driver was killed en route from South Dakota to Sioux City, but it may have been the result of an accident. According to lore with a grain of truth to it, the truck driver was a young man who failed to halt when ordered to do so. «It was a freak shot,» an eyewitness recalled. «But the kid was just as dead anyway. Well, a bunch of picketers leaped up on the back of the truck to empty the milk cans. And what do you suppose they found in the cans—not milk but bootleg whiskey! The damned-fool kid, if he'd only stopped and told them he had whiskey, not milk, in those cans, they'd have let him through.»[18]

At Council Bluffs, a ways below Sioux City, some fifty picketers were jailed for unlawful assembly. Word of their plight spread rapidly and truckloads of farmers came from surrounding counties to storm the jailhouse. Deputy sheriffs, armed with sub-machine guns that few would have known how to operate, took stations all around the jail. The mayor sent for a unit of the National Guard. The sheriff boasted that he'd stop the rebellion if it took enlisting fifty thousand men to do it. «These farmers are hoodlums,» he said in a newspaper interview, «as much so as Chicago gangsters.» Carnage was avoided when a clear-headed farmer volunteered to put up his mortgage-free farm as bail for release of the men. The sheriff was more than happy to agree, grasping for any straw that would get him out of a dynamite keg ready to explode at any minute, considering the number of nervous fingers on unfamiliar triggers.

Heated battles, like dramatic wartime clashes, were attractive to the media. Eastern papers, literary and academic journals began doing more than just reporting facts. Reporters will be reporters, and media essayists must tell stories that keep a reader's eyes glued to the page. Thus much of the literature focused on the farmers' plight was rendered with humor and even sarcasm, at times exaggerating, at other times obfuscating the key economic issues.

An article in the *Literary Journal* of September 10th, 1932 opened with: «The Bread-and-Egg Expeditionary Force is digging in for a long siege:

Not 'till hell freezes over,' declare these striking farmers in the Mid-West, will they quit their fight to force up prices of farm products. Each day brings new and exciting developments as the farm holiday movement intensifies and spreads. It is one of the strangest phenomena of that breeder of anomalies, the depression.

A poll conducted in the autumn of 1933 by the Des Moines *Register*, found that 77.15 percent of the farmers had been opposed to the strikes, 14.28 percent had approved, and 8.57 percent were indifferent. The *Register* also reported that the rebellion had been confined to a few areas, the western edge of Iowa from Le Mars down through Sioux City to Council Bluffs, and parts of Minnesota and Wisconsin, and that the Association had only a few thousand dues-paying members (but the number of non-members, who were nonetheless part of the movement, may have numbered several thousand).

This poll accelerated a backlash against the Holiday movement. The *New Republic*'s essayist quoted the polltaker's results and concluded, «After reading a mass of these reports, and checking them against my own observations, I am convinced that they give a truthful picture of the farmer's state of mind. I wish that space permitted me to quote the replies of these farmers at length. For candor and common sense they certainly compare very well with an average number of statements on

the same themes by an equivalent number of average college graduates.»
(What a surprise to find that average dumb farmers can think and write
as well as average college graduates! The professor writing this essay
then tries to recover, while not erasing what he'd just said: «Many Iowa
farmers, of course, hold degrees).»

As I said, Loretta was with my father and Marius that night when
the first skirmishes between farmers and truck drivers happened, when
a train en route from Hinton to Sioux City was halted, the milk cars
opened, the cans emptied onto the roadbed. She was sixteen and sea-
soned to rough and tumble rural life but emotionally shaken on seeing
her father and other men she knew as kindly neighbors acting so coarse-
ly, worked up and violent. I was too young for direct experience of the
episode, but over the years my father told and retold the story to his
children—about armed sheriffs and deputies atop tractor-drawn hay
wagons, threatening to shoot but scared half to death they might, knowing that one deadly shot would be to their own demise. My father was,
after all, a Viking in my child-eyes, and a wagonload of vikinging farmers can bear down on hostile adversaries like a war-boat of rapacious,
bloodthirsty warriors of yore.

Chapter 7

No fairy godmother was paying
attention to Leeds, growing so quickly
from meiosis to adulthood

We left the Hinton farm before planting time in the early spring of 1935 when I was a few weeks short of seven, when the Depression was at its lowest and after the 1931-32 crop failures due to spring hail and summer grasshoppers, when Plymouth and Woodbury counties also experienced the worst of the Midwest droughts. The release of emergency corn supplies brought the farmer's price for a bushel to its lowest level. Our farm recovered because we had pigs fed on cheap corn, and we could have survived as a subsistence farm, raising our own foodstuffs and enough cash crops to pay the rent. It was not my father's ill fortune that would determine our fate, but our landlord's, a Leeds businessman, Martin Riediger. He owned a prosperous hardware business in Leeds but had plunged into a financial bog during the early thirties when farmers were unable to afford new tools, fencing wire, and other ferrous materials. About to lose his store to bank foreclosure, he was in desperate need of cash. A young local farmer, Walter Stusse, wanting to marry Riediger's daughter and take up farming on our spread, offered him a twenty-five-thousand-dollar incentive to have us evicted—an enormous amount, considering that our farm's net cash annual income at the time was about three hundred dollars.

Some years later, when my father revisited Sioux City, Martin Riediger was still apologizing for the deed that saved his business but had poisoned his conscience and aged him. From my present perspective, Riediger's guilt was wasted on me, and not one of my older sisters regrets being put off the farm, although they still speak of it at times with sorrow, as if expressing feelings grounded in reality.

Over the 1930s, America became primarily urban, its industries more technological. The invention of the gasoline engine had a drastic effect on farming. By the time I was born, there were about 250,000 vehicles in Iowa, more than half of them owned by farmers. This mobility lessened the farmer's isolation; automobile and truck speed increased the pace of farm life, allowing shorter farm-to-market cycles that reduced need for hay storage barns, corn cribs, and silos. Family farms were becoming businesses and scientific farming was underway, spurred by the World War I campaigns saying, «Food will win the war.» But those days had passed. We were now destined for town life, a house in town and city schools.

The advent of school busses and consolidated schools meant that farm-raised children were becoming better educated, while careers other than farming were holding carrots out in front of maturing noses that preferred to chase money at less risk and less labor. As families dispersed, the tendency for their grown children, especially the boys, was to seek employment in towns and cities rather than hire themselves out as farm laborers. Truck driving and auto repairing were the usual first trades for farm boys exiting farms. And farm girls were meeting marriageable non-farming boys in the urban schools— «How're you going to keep them down on the farm once they've seen Sioux City?» This dynamic was a one-way flow: farm-bred boys can become most anything—doctor, lawyer, merchant, professor—but a city boy meeting and marrying a farm girl cannot become a farmer, at least not the sort of farmer that physically works a farm. By the final year of high school, a farm boy has had ten or twelve years of on-the-job training. Farmers are born as farmers, not fashioned out of city folks.

It was difficult for my father to give up farming. His family was large and farming was what he knew best for providing support. Still, he took the eviction like a man, and was not a man disappointment could put down. And I suspect that my mother looked forward to the move to town, her agricultural labors reduced to a vegetable garden, and egg gathering to picking up a dozen at a grocery store to which she could walk. My parents had, of course, sold the milk-cows, cattle, sows, horses, mules, machinery, equipment and tools. My uncle Mark bought two weanling colts destined to be my team when I got old enough to handle them. I saw the matured pair five years later—majestically muscled, both sorrel with golden manes and tails and nearly matched white markings on their faces and feet—and a lump formed in my throat.

Constrained to become townsfolk, we moved to Leeds, a ways north of Sioux City. The town's population then was just short of one thousand, less than it had been in 1900. Prohibition had ended, and although whiskey could not be sold by the drink, beer could. My father bought a beer parlor at 3919 Floyd Avenue—the street named after Sergeant Floyd—which was a segment of Highway 75 running alongside the Floyd River and the railway that still bears half-mile-long trainloads of grain and livestock to Sioux City's mills and stockyards (during Prohibition, Highway 75 was the prime thoroughfare for black Cadillacs hauling bootleg liquor to Sioux City from Winnipeg).

Andy's Place, as my father's beer parlor was called before long, had the usual bar and a few tables, and, at the back, a dance floor with a nickel-slot jukebox. Hanky-panky was the only live entertainment. On any occasion when local politicians were bribed sufficiently to let up on anti-gambling laws, the dancing area transformed itself into a poker room. The entire place—which with lucidity I recall in my hypothalamus where the smell of talcum powder and newly mown hay endures—stunk of stale beer, decaying cigar smoke, gaseous spittoons, and oily sweeping compound. On using the single toilet, one could barely suppress the gagging reflex, the farm odors of hog manure and rotted horse urine having given way to the stench of men.

Saloons back then were cultural and social centers—low culture, to be sure, if measured against the urban gentlemen's club. Except in very small towns, such as Leeds, they were usually on the edge of town and always on the edge of the law, denounced by schoolteachers and condemned by clerics. A world all its own, with its own culture, rules, and morals, a saloon was much like a farm. My father's customers were animals being tended, lined up at the bar like hogs at a feed trough (It's not surprising that such drinking places came to be called watering holes, places where thirsty animals come to wallow and drink). It wasn't long before everyone in the town and countryside knew Andy's Place, and no one questioned my father's role as a supporter of the new Lutheran Church, or thought it incongruous that my sister Bethel, daughter of a public sinner, was the organist. The preacher and the saloonkeeper in any small town are the two most socialized men and usually the most liked—what woes beer didn't alleviate on Saturday night a dose of religion might cure on Sunday morning.

Perhaps my father may have been encouraged to open a beer joint by his brother John, whose saloon and pool hall in Correctionville managed to survive during those brutal years. He and my father were inseparable brothers, so as a child I knew more about him than any other of my relatives. In 1911, John had sailed back to Denmark to fetch the girl he had left behind, his beloved Maren, returning with her in early 1912. To avoid being drafted into the Danish army while there—a world war threatening—John spirited himself and Maren to England. There they booked on the Titanic, to sail in two weeks. But fate was with them. Anxious to get to Iowa, they seized a chance to sail without delay on a smaller ship charging less than the Titanic's fare.

Uncle John and Aunt Maren married, worked hard and saved money, but lost it all in the bank failure of 1932, their property impounded and sold for taxes due. (Their son Richard had died from pneumonia in 1931 at the age of fifteen. Times were so bad over the next few years that it took seven years for John to pay off the cost of Richard's funeral). Like my father, but earlier, John had settled on operating a saloon, and in time managed to buy an eleven-table pool hall with beer service next to Correctionville's sole movie theater. Before long he was known all over the county for his joviality, fairness, and peculiar business habits. Concerned that his customers with family responsibilities might get drunk and blow their weekly pay on Saturday nights, he would take the better part of their money and lock it up in a safe behind the bar, not allowing the customer to have it back until Monday night. Over the worst of the Depression years, he allowed dead-broke customers to commiserate in his friendly place where a farmer or trucker might come by saying he needed a worker for the day. John once came home at the usual late hour, and said, «I must have had seventy-five people in the pool hall today, and not one of them spent a nickel.»

Even when times got better, John's generosity continued to accrue fame. On an occasion when a train's carload of Negroes were sent to town to repair the tracks, they were required to live in a boxcar, and no one in town would allow them into their store or restaurant. John recognized their plight and invited them into his pool hall, where shortly before he'd set up an electric hot-dog machine. His white customers exited in disgust and went to a nearby bar. The blacks played pool, drank soda, and ate hot dogs; not one of them asked for alcohol, and unlike his regular customers, none of them swore or got into a fight. Those with a bit of money paid as they went; those with no money but a pay-day coming due signed IOUs. After a few days, John had a hall full of friends. Every black that owed him money paid up, and after they'd moved on, he received several postcards expressing thanks. One by one, his virtuous white customers came back and the drinking and cussing resumed. One returning customer remarked, «I'll bet they left owing you money.» Uncle John replied, «They all paid up, and that's more than I can say for a lot of white folks around here.»

So friendly to everyone and everything was Uncle John that he failed economically with his mini-farm on the side. Wanting to keep his hand in farming, he'd put together a few pigs and sheep. But rather than fatten them for the butcher, he talked to them, got acquainted with them, gave them names. He may have had the only pigs in Iowa to die of old age. And he had a weakness for buying everything that was for sale—houses, furniture, and cars. He even bought two abandoned railroad stations, the Illinois Central Depot and the Northwestern Depot. His son Harley took to answering the home telephone, «Hello. This is the Andersen's. We buy everything and sell nothing.»

I was not often around the other uncles on my father's side. Uncle Andrew, whom I can barely recall, farmed across the Missouri in South Dakota. He had a still under his barn in Vermillion. The operation of it landed him in jail every few months, helping the local sheriff fulfill his quota for peacekeeping arrests. John and my father would have to drive up to Vermillion to bail him out so he could get back to his farm by milking time. Local bootleggers were not severely punished in those days when sheriffs and judges were cautious not to dry up their own sources of booze, or lose an election over excessive morality, so fines were minimal and Andrew's still remained intact.

The uncles on my mother's side were those I knew best, because in my early teens I worked on one or the other's farm. But before those days of field labor, I had to get through my pre-adolescent years in Leeds, which wasn't much of a town; in my memory, just a main street with a few streets off it, lined with maple, oak, and box elder trees, and many grand houses left over from a brief period of affluence when Leeds was promoted as the industrial town, in contrast to Sioux City's regional fame as a booming metropolis, its economy fed by the stockyards and meat packing industries. Leeds was only 45 years old the year we moved there in 1935, having been platted in 1889 on 154 acres of treeless prairie with nothing to say it was a town other than a signpost—a child named before being born.

Leeds was annexed to Sioux City in 1890. Before that year had ended, the town had its own newspaper, the *Leeds Leader*, with a circulation of 1,000, advertised as an *Independent Republican Weekly*. In June of 1890, thousands of people from Sioux City took the free Sunday excursion train out to see the new manufacturing suburb for the first time. With three trunk lines of railway and the Floyd River for dumping waste products that spring floods would flush with the efficiency of a modern toilet, the Leeds Investment and Land Company promoted Leeds as the safe and profitable place to invest in real estate and establish manufacturing industries. The town's name was itself a crafty act of plugging—named after the manufacturing center of Leeds, England, and advertised as the future Pittsburgh of the West. Street names assigned by the developers were meant to prognosticate its profitable future: Carnegie Street, Pittsburgh Street, Altoona Street, Chester Street, Sheffield Street, Birmingham Street, Manchester Street, and Floyd Boulevard, which displaced the ancient Floyd River Road, a section of buffalo trail extending from Spirit Lake to the Missouri—from trail to avenue in one historical move. The heavy promotion was aimed at eastern industries and land speculators who responded with enormous amounts of capital and bank lines of credit, for large tracts could be bought cheaply, subdivided, and sold at high capital gains.

Within months, the second largest flourmill in Iowa was built on ten acres of the virgin plat. Named the Mystic Milling Company, it milled Robin Hood Flour from Dakota spring wheat. The Sioux City Engine and Iron Works relocated in Leeds in 1889 on twelve acres, constructing a building two-stories high, 400 feet long and 225 feet wide, and was soon manufacturing engines up to one thousand horse power and well-digging machinery that could drill as deep as 3,000 feet. The Daniel E.

Paris Stove Works relocated from New Hampshire and built a brick, stone, and steel complex that matched the Palais du Louvre in size: covering ten acres, its main building measured 75x700 feet with support buildings as large as 150x300 feet. Aside from manufacturing the famous Paris stoves, with such alluring names as The Paris Imperial, The Paris Cottage, and The Iron Crown, this factory also boasted the largest ballroom in the West—100x200 feet with a forty-foot ceiling; the grandest ball ever held in the territory, the Military Ball of 1893, took place there. This self-proclaimed «Finest Stove Factory in the World» lived up to its promotion as also the largest stove factory in the world; with its 400 windows, it was also the best lit. Other factories soon appeared, and after schools and churches were built, the residential community of Leeds quickly took shape along gridded, tree-planted streets.

But no fairy godmother was paying attention to Leeds' growth so quickly from meiosis to adulthood, skipping infancy altogether. Within three years, the town's decline was as steep as its whirling ascent. The finest stove factory in the world passed into receivership, its stock and machinery sold. Dynamic entrepreneurs with dollar-shaped eyeballs had miscalculated the cost of shipping raw materials from the East. And Mother Nature wasn't protecting Leeds either. In 1892, after six days of incessant rain over a large area of the northern Midwest, the Missouri River flooded to a record high and backed water up the Floyd, which was already at a flood stage. On May 18th, a six-foot high, and at places a half-mile wide, wall of water rushed down the Floyd Valley, destroying everything in its path, killing at least ten persons and sweeping 500 homes not caught by trees all the way to the Missouri. The next year the National Recession blanketed the big Eastern cities and sank many big banks where Leeds factory owners had secured deposits. Known as the «Panic of 1893,» the collapse of the eastern financial institutions hit the Midwest like the Floyd River's tidal wave, destroying wealth and halting industrial development. When the Columbia National Bank of Chicago, which had outstanding loans far in excess of deposits, failed and was unable to honor payroll checks, Leed's most attractive industry, the Engine and Ironworks Company, made a hasty retreat to resettle in Illinois, closer to the natural resources of coal and ore. Within a few years, all the major factories in Leeds were insolvent, out of business, abandoned, or in receivership.

Not everything could be blamed on the flood of 1892 and the National Recession of 1893. Pioneering is not a trade for the meek, and ordinary confidence can produce only ordinary results; the meek don't inherit the earth, as the Bible says, but tend get run off it. Yet, too many otherwise sensible businessmen had made the entrepreneur's usual mistake of believing their own propaganda. In the rush to profit, they'd invested beyond their means, and when the anticipated markets failed to materialize, they lacked reserves. Even before the flood, and when financial markets in the East were still strong, the Floyd Valley Flax Company had gone belly-up. The Rathburn Manufacturing Company lasted just two years, abandoning Leeds in 1892. The Sioux City Shoe Manufacturing Company plant in Leeds also shut down that year.

After 1893, the downslide continued. The Floyd Valley Mattress and Bedspring Works moved to metropolitan Sioux City where there was still a local market to offer subsistence sales. The Lyons Brothers Broom Works held out for five years, only to be ruined in 1900. Leeds Brick and Tile Works, which had manufactured one million superior bricks and tiles per month, was rebuilt after a fire in 1898 but entirely dismantled in 1914. The Morley Twine and Machinery Company moved to Sioux City in 1906 and then failed as the importation of cheap foreign hemp weakened its market; its empty buildings in Leeds were destroyed by fire in 1907. The Pioneer Stove Foundry suspended business in 1908. All told, between 1882 and 1915, Leeds was created and then devastated. Promoters who'd predicted that the industrial town would rise to the status of a metropolis and reduce Sioux City to a suburb had either grotesquely miscalculated or gotten away with a majestic scam. Most of the land speculators had made mammoth profits and sent the money east, while a few who'd excessively leveraged their ventures found themselves with worthless holdings. As a boomtown, Leeds boomed for less than four years and then fizzled out. The entire campaign to create an industrial city was a deflationary boondoggle from which the town would never recover.

After 1895, a few enterprising men ventured to start businesses in Leeds, but lucky charms were as scarce as hens' teeth. The most successful was the American Popcorn Company. In 1914, it became a viable industry, for its raw material was locally grown. Popcorn was a novelty then, even though in Sac County, Iowa, farmers had been planting and harvesting it since 1885, and long before, Indians had munched on fire-scorched corn. Cloid Smith (a precursor to Frank Purdue, the first to brand-name a chicken) foresaw a vast market for popcorn if it could be properly packaged and promoted with a magnetic name. Shelled corn had been selling in 150-pound bags or packed in cracker barrels if still on the cob—few stores would handle it in such bulky portions. And popcorn was still generic. Cloid Smith and his son Howard started their business in the basement of a house in Sioux City. They created the first brand name, Jolly Time, printed in bright green letters (from which the pea cannery got the appellation Jolly Green Giant). Their first popcorn packages were of cardboard, which failed because moisture passed through the box; the corn dried out completely and would not pop. After experimenting with glass jars, Cloid Smith handed the problem over to the American Can Company, which in 1924 developed an airtight metal can specifically for popcorn—the prototype for the modern beer and soft drink can. In short order, Jolly Time Popcorn became nationally recognized; the small plant in Leeds expanded gigantically to meet an onslaught of popcorn vendor carts and wagons, refreshment stands in movie theaters, and home poppers. Thirty-two percent of this nation's popcorn is still produced in Iowa.

The great Leeds oil boom was the town's last hurrah, ignited in 1914 when two workmen digging a well beside Floyd Avenue struck oil. The news spread fast; speculation was rampant; geologists were called in. On January 14th, in the midst of a freezing winter, the diggers worked their way down, excavating a large open well that produced 30 gallons in six hours. By that time, residents all around had begun to recall oil slicks they'd seen on still-water ponds. Leeds was sitting right on an oil field! The Levitt Investment Company from Sioux City was quick to buy land options and set a gang of men to digging and blasting for asphalt and oil. But as most everything went in Leeds, the boom didn't last, didn't even make it through the final two weeks of January. On the 24th, it was discovered that the vein of oil was coming from two 500-gallon leaking oil tanks owned by the Independent Oil Company on Floyd Avenue near the discovery pit. All those oil slicks on water, everyone had to admit, were from air pollution and run-off from weed-control oil sprayed along the railroad tracks.

But not all was folly and failure. The first automobile trunk was another of Leed's contributions to the world's economy. Two years before I was born, two brilliant inventors, Ernest Arndt from Nebraska and Robert Lier from South Dakota, moved to Leeds and established a factory. Arndt had developed and patented a steel trunk that would become twice its size when folded out, while Lier had patented a galvanized steel band attachment to affix luggage to the rear of the Model T Ford. They had met at a county fair—the usual place for inventors to demonstrate their ideas and attract a manufacturer. One or the other of the two men hit on the idea that their individual products could be combined as one: a steel foldout trunk attached to an automobile. The Kari-Keen Karrier—the first automobile trunk—would allow farmers to haul their own milk and cream cans to town in a car rather than a truck, make it possible for stores to offer small deliveries at cash-and-carry costs, and allow traveling salesmen to sell from the back of an automobile. After adapting the invention to fit any model of car and carry up to 400 pounds of weight, the Kari-Keen Manufacturing Company, advertising in the *Saturday Evening Post*, produced and sold some 450,000 trunks worldwide. The company engaged excellent marketers; even the popular comics Laurel and Hardy were brought to town after town to promote the Karrier.

The rear-end carrier forecast the pickup truck—a car that functioned as a truck. So Kari-Keen's swift success was also the cause of its demise. By the end of its third year of business, the Karrier's popularity had prompted every automobile manufacturer to build large trunks molded into the rear end of their cars. The demise of the cash cow Karrier also brought an end to Arndt and Lier's innovative achievements in speculative aircraft manufacturing.

Had I been born a few years earlier and moved to Leeds before 1930, I might have hiked out to Leeds Airport's Kari-Keen Test Field to watch one of the most advanced airplanes in the world take off, soar, and land. The Kari-Keen mono-wing coupe was the first airplane manufactured in Sioux City. At the Leeds airport—built and owned by Kari-Keen—the coupes were tested, promoted, and used to develop a flying school.[19] This side-by-side two-seater was shaped like a glider with a wingspan of 30 feet and an engine that could get the speed up to 100 miles per hour. Delicate, balanced, and not terribly clamorous, it was the first airplane in the country built with cantilevered wings requiring no struts or braces. By the time my family moved to Leeds, the Kari-Keen Aircraft Company had disappeared, its demise caused partly by the crash and death of a pilot flying in the 1930 Sioux Falls air show, but also because the entire country's economy was by then stalled in the pits—not many people could afford a private airplane. Only a few of the thirty to forty coupes produced during the four years of Kari-Keen's existence were still flying at the close of the 1930s.

Take-ups by large companies of ideas and products put into the market by small-scale entrepreneurs were typical of the way things went in this country—not structurally different from how the Wild Kingdom functions, with animals taking over the kills of other animals, hyenas and jackals moving in, then vultures, then ants arriving to glean, and microbes to clean up the residue. When a small, home-developed industry in small-town Waterloo, Iowa produced an engine known as «The Waterloo Boy» that rapidly found favor with farmers across the plains, the big John Deere Company of Moline, Illinois bought the company and moved its entire tractor manufacturing plant to Waterloo, becoming soon thereafter the state's largest employer of labor. In 1927, the Downee Products Company, a small manufacturer of infant clothing situated on Leed's Floyd Avenue, invented and manufactured—miraculously in time to provide me with their product—the first soft and absorbent Didies on the market (later to be called diapers). But firms that dominated the infant products market, such as Johnson's, the maker of baby powder that soothed babies' diaper-rashed bottom, soon expropriated their product, the Downee Didee. By the end of 1934, the Downee Products Company was on the skids; in 1936 it disappeared.

Most of Leed's small service businesses failed when the big company payrolls they depended on for customers were strewn to the wind. In 1893, Leeds had supported seven hotels and an array of barbershops, pharmacies, clothing stores, hardware stores, and sixteen saloons. By the time we moved there, the town has been reduced to one hotel, one physician, one lawyer, two barbershops, two beauty parlors, one hardware store, one general store, one gas station, one bakery and confection shop, three small dairies, several truckers, a few other one-man enterprises, and one bank, which was robbed the year I was born. The bandits put the bank's president, a customer, and a cashier into the vault, but the cashier was a very cool lady; as the hostages walked obediently into the vault, she tripped a lever on the door that neutered the lock and made the door operable from the inside. The robbers were expeditiously apprehended the next day, one in a Greenville barber's chair, the other as he stepped off a bus in Chicago.

In 1935, when my father opened Andy's beer joint, there were only two other bars in Leeds: Leeds Tavern and Ed's Tavern. My father's evening bartender, Dolphine Girard, called Shorty, was a daytime barber with his shop nearby, a man in need of two jobs to keep food on the table. The only industries offering employment to more than two or three workers were the venerable International Milling Company, the Fur and Tanning Company, a tool manufacturing plant, a lumberyard, a coal yard, the Jolly Time Popcorn factory, and the railroad yard where rail cars and schedules were sorted out before being headed into Sioux City. In 1937, a government-financed firehouse was built in Leeds, providing several bricklayers and carpenters with a few months of full-time employment. Floyd Avenue was by then a broken-down strip of road with weedy shoulders coated with creosote and with wriggling streetcar tracks down one side, packed with dirt, for during every heavy rain storm, clayey mud washed down from higher ground and coated the streets.

Leeds had been a localized concentration of the ingenuity in invention that characterized Iowans. Iowa had taken the earliest lead in aviation and was up front in the design of automobiles. William Morrison's electric car, which could seat twelve persons and still attain a speed of twenty miles per hour, was unveiled in Des Moines in 1890; it was the first triumphant horseless carriage. The first gasoline-fueled car built in Iowa was the Mason Car, featured in 1902; the Mason-Maytag Car's assembly plant was in Waterloo, Iowa. The car known among automobile buffs as the greatest ever built in America was the invention of Frederic and August Duesenberg of Grinnell, Iowa. The refilling lever-action fountain pen was invented by an Iowan, the Fort Mason home-mechanic Walter Sheaffer, after whom the Sheaffer pen was named. Fred Maytag was the first to equip the old hand-turning washing machines with motors: Maytag made Newton, Iowa the washing machine capital of America. Cold cream—a moisturizing cream blended with face powder—was invented by a young Iowan, Carl Weeks, and for a good many years his «Armand» facial cream made Des Moines a center for ladies' cosmetics. Sioux City engineer Telemachus Johnson is credited with inventing concrete pavement; 110,000 square yards of paving was laid in Sioux City in 1911, and at one time Sioux City had more paved streets than any other city in America. This invention, born of need-plus-ingenuity, came about after three successive floodings of the Floyd River had convinced city engineers that the asphalt-impregnated or creosoted cedar blocks that made wonderfully level and quiet streets tended to become dislodged and float off when flowing river water inundated the low-lying district. Following Sioux City's example, under the slogan «Pulling Iowa out of the mud,» the Iowa state legislature pushed for a comprehensive program of paved roads.

Iowans' proclivity for inventiveness also gave the world a few extraordinary cons. In the vicinity of Fort Dodge, Iowa lie some of the purest gypsum deposits in the nation. In 1858, two men, George Hull and H. B. Martin from Marshalltown, Iowa, managed to purchase a 7,000 pound block of very fine gypsum from a ledge near town, send it by railcar to Chicago, and have it carved with exceptional skill into a human figure about ten feet high and weighing 2,990 pounds. Under cover and avoiding detection, they trucked the giant to New York State, where they buried it on a farm near Cardiff. This relic of an ancient pre-civilization was discovered (ho, ho!) in 1869 and put in on display as a petrified ancient American. The hucksters had no problem getting P. T. Barnum interested, and Barnum had no problem getting a noted geologist to swear that it was «the most remarkable archeological discovery made in this country.» The famous American sculptor, Hiram Powers, admired by Thomas Jefferson and fresh from the Academy in Rome, proclaimed that, «no chisel could have carved such a perfect man.» This gypsum wonder of the world attracted over 50,000 amazed people, at fifty cents a look, until word spread that it was an ingenious fake.

I add this story, having happened so many years before the period this book covers, to point out that Iowans were not only, on the whole, expert farmers, imaginative inventors, but as well, ingenious hucksters. Years later, the giant, dubbed «Iowa's largest native son,» was purchased by Gardner Cowles, chairman of the board of the *Register* and the *Tribune* in Des Moines, and put on display at the Iowa State Fair. In 1948, it was moved to The Farmers Museum at Cooperstown, New York, where it can be seen today. The perpetrators were not prosecuted. In the Louisville *Courier-Journal*, an editorial read, «A hoax may become a valuable commodity if, in the end, we can all laugh, and particularly if the laugh is on us, and nobody has been hurt.»

That event happened many years before those bracketed by this book. I could have cited others more recent. But none more entertaining or remindful of Iowan ingenuity.

Chapter 8

An undulating sheet-metal slide
kept slick by boys sliding down with
waxed paper under their butts

T he move from the Hinton farm to Leeds caused an abrupt
change in how I fit into the world. My sense of personal geography was no longer of a whole. On the farm, everything within my scope belonged to my family: the land, buildings, animals, field
mice, gophers, jackrabbits, meadowlarks, barn swallows, butterflies,
bugs. I could wander over fields and along the creek and easily find my
way back to the house. In Leeds, nothing belonged to us but a house on
a plot of ground no bigger than our forsaken farm's chicken yard. On
the first day in town, I got lost one block from the house and was found
much further away by a search party of older sisters who refused to
accept that I was not lost at all, just looking the town over. Even at that
age, I couldn't tolerate being wrong and would go to the stake arguing
my case rather than back down. Later I will most likely attribute that
illutrious defect to my father's influence, but here I might as well confess that it was congenital.

My mother was happy to live in town, eager to enjoy the higher
standard of living that electrification allowed. Over the 1920s, a steady
drift of farm families moved into towns and cities. Historians of the
period refer to it as a women's movement—women wanting what city
women enjoyed: better schools for the children, close neighbors, elec-
trical appliances, and ease of socializing. The first things my mother
bought after settling in were a radio and an electric iron; then came a
vacuum sweeper, toaster, waffle iron, and washing machine. Had we still
lived on the farm when our county was finally electrified, it would have
been all those things plus an electric water pump and heater to service
an indoor bathroom, an electric brooder, cream separator, poultry water

91

warmer, and in time a feed grinder and milk cooler. By 1935, Iowa farmers on Rural Electrification lines made more use of home and farm appliances than the average number of farm cooperatives throughout the United States.[20] Although Dad's saloon was electrified, drinkers back then were accustomed to tepid beer from the tap and a rush of foam from an uncapped bottle—probably ten percent of all the beer served in the 1930s was streamy overflow wiped up with bar towels. I once displayed to my father a glass of beer I'd managed to draw that didn't have a bit of foam on it. His response quicly reversed my glory of achievement: «Beer without a head on it looks like piss,» he said, leaving me staring at the glass and reluctant to take a sip from it.

Conveniences and appliances enhanced the quality of our practical life but the family was suffering from fragmentation. Dad was no longer at home days or evenings, still in bed during breakfast, not around for lunch or dinner, but at his saloon until well after midnight, and sometimes coming home after too many short beers tossed down while jawing with his customers. A saloon being a social center, customers expected conversational bartenders. Marius had become a long-haul truck driver and was on the road to and from Chicago much of the time; when not trucking, he usually bedded in a rooming house in the nether part of Sioux City, not a place where deer and antelopes roamed but where wild women were at free range on the streets. Loretta was by then married, expecting a child, and had gone off to live with her truck-driver husband in a Sioux City house. Bethel commuted by streetcar to Central High School in Sioux City, and Fern by school bus to Woodrow Wilson Junior High, also in the city. Right before my eyes, the family was being dismembered.

E motion alone, whether felt at the time or as residue, is what makes one happy, not what people say or do to you. So by remembering few people outside my immediate family in Leeds, I also can't remember much happiness outside the house, and am mired at this moment in nebulous residual emotions not distinguished by the age of their first arousal. Yet I recall just about everything, and not a moment of unhappiness, from attending country school. During recess and at lunchtime the games my uncomplicated age group played imitated adult activities: little kids riding horseback on bigger kids, or playing barnyard chickens, clucking like brood hens, making nests in tall grass and protecting them against other kids pretending to be foxes or weasels. Games involving chase were most kids' favorites: blind man's buff, hide and seek. When snow was fresh on the ground we played Fox and Geese, getting pre-adolescent training in courtship by chasing down and tagging girls. When the snow was very deep, we dug roads and tunnels through it and built forts to defend against snowballs. When snowdrifts had hardened under their own weight, we carved out rooms in them, or sliced the snow into blocks with a long corn knife and crafted igloos as hideouts. One-room country schools did not have play equipment; they were schools, not playgrounds. Our teacher neither instigated nor supervised games out of doors. On occasion, when snow or rain kept us inside, and when ordered to by the teacher, forcing boys to hold girls' hands, we shoved the desks aside and played Ring Around the Rosy, and London Bridge is falling down, falling down, my / fair / lady.

Play activities are easier to remember than school work, but even in the schoolhouse life was enjoyable—learning to tell time and to count and recognize numbers and words from phonics cards the teacher held up. I remember the standard nursery rhyme stories but must have known most of them before entering school. I could read simple texts before kindergarten, and storybooks I couldn't read I would make up from the pictures. At some pre-school Christmas or other while on the farm, I'd been given a copy of Piper's *The Little Engine That Could*, which remains indelibly with me. I also owned Potter's *Peter Rabbit*—Peter, who burrowed under a fence to get at Mr. McGregor's cabbage patch, lost his coat and shoes to the farmer's scarecrow and almost ended up as rabbit pie. I still think that his siblings Flopsy, Mopsy, and Cottontail were my sisters, because surely in the midst of them I was the rabbit always getting into trouble. Bannerman's *Little Black Sambo* remains unforgettable—Sambo, in his purple pants and red shoes, under a green umbrella, outwitting the fierce tigers, causing them to churn themselves into butter as they raced around the tree in which he was safely out of reach. I don't recall if I encountered the boring and sanitary daily life of city-dwellers Dick and Jane until attending school in Leeds: «See Dick. See Jane. See Spot. See Spot run.» It was a test of oral skill and restraint to whisper to a desk-mate, «See Spot pee,» without giggling. More inter-esting were stories such as Jack and Jill going up the hill, because, someone told me—I don't remember when—that they went up the hill not just to fetch water, but I wouldn't have puzzled over that until I was nine or ten. Milne's *Winnie the Pooh* stories still haunt my psyche: stuffed animals that come to life without having to imagine them. And I haven't forgotten Toad, Ratty, Otter, and Badger and the chorus of field mice singing carols in Graham's *Wind in the Willows*. I remember *The Story of Ferdinand*—the bull that preferred smelling flowers to fighting picadors. At some point after moving to Leeds, I recall getting sensually aroused when recalling Burnett's *The Secret Garden*, and somewhere along the line, maybe by the age of nine and before moving to Sioux City, I read Barrie's *Peter and Wendy*—Peter Pan, who never wanted to grow up. I fell in love with pubescent Wendy, whom Peter had taught to fly and who never seemed to get out of her white flannel nightgown. By age ten or eleven, my infatuation with tractable Wendy had to compete with Flash Gordon's amply developed girlfriend Gale, whose skin-tight space suit was optically traceable to render her naked, aiding in the development of my competence to see through women's clothing—a capacity Superman had with his x-ray vision, but lacking a dirty mind, hadn't put to its fundamentally biological use. Such is what I can dredge from memory; not classrooms or teachers in Leeds but all sorts of things that make me feel at this moment vaguely sinful.

It may have been hard for me to figure out what to do, how to behave, when living not in my own but in an other people's world. For my sisters, town life was adventure and relief from chores outside the house. City schooling was better than the rural school, offering more options and enhanced socializing within one's own age group. But not enough time had elapsed to gain self-assurance before the indoor bathroom and faucet water had lost their charm. We faced then an excessive need to adjust and redefine our intimate world, which would change so often—the farm, four different houses in Leeds, four more coming up in Sioux City. Perhaps these discontinuities and social upheavals fashioned my own inability to settle down in one place or to live in a proper house. Still today, so many years later, so many addresses behind me—calendars and address books trashed. I move laterally and in any direction, like my birth-sign, Cancer the crab. And I avoid houses as if, also like a crab, I were carrying a protective shell on my back. When I undertook these opening paragraphs a few months ago, I lived in

Arizona, having returned from five years in Paris, and now live like a imperial pigeon in an industrial loft in Boston's Leather District, right between South Station and Chinatown, reluctant to memorize my telephone number for fear I will move again and waste the brain cells needed to record it.

Hawthorne School was at 44th and Central, the only school for the Leed's population, serving kindergarten to the sixth grade. The school had a long history, relatively speaking. Before 1890, the undeveloped area had had a one-room country school, the Krummann School. When the town was platted, and after a few families had built houses and moved in, the country school was torn down and classes were moved to Floyd Avenue, held there temporarily in an abandoned building that had been a saloon and dance hall.

The new school, built in 1891, was a fine brick structure of eight large classrooms, with one teacher, who was also the principal, and five assistants, all women and by rule unmarried. Over that decade, a Parent Teachers Association was formed; speakers were brought in to offer parents such topics as care of children's teeth, precaution in handling raw milk, safety in the home, and instructions on the three basic food groups (promoted by beguiled dietitians to foster midwest agriculture). The population of Leeds declined over the next three decades, but when school busing moved deeper into the rural areas, one-room schools were abandoned in favor of consolidated schools like Hawthorne. The building was enlarged in two stages, in 1913 and 1917. In 1934, when I was enrolled at age seven, classes at all levels were still overcrowded. Principal Charlotte Osborne and thirteen teachers coped with over 400 pupils, aged five to twelve. A high school wasn't built until 1939, too late for my older sisters.

The first rented dwelling we occupied was an average-sized clapboard house across the street from the school. Just Esther, aged nine at the time, and I attended the school, which, by Iowa law, had to teach reading, writing, grammar, spelling, arithmetic, and geography. Not until after the sixth grade did United States history, physiology, and principles of American government become required, along with recommendations for special studies of the effects of stimulants, narcotics, and poisons, physical education, and elements of vocal music. How I adjusted to this town school, I can't remember. Deep in my mind now is the thought that Esther was teased over her home-made clothes, pretty as her print and lace-edged dresses were, and over the sandwiches she brought for school lunch: home-baked bread, hand-cut in thick slices, and layered with such country delicacies as head cheese or bacon lard or heavily salted roast goose grease drippings that thicken when cool and spread like butter. Town kids ate city-type sandwiches: peanut butter and jelly, minced ham, bologna, and processed Velveeta cheese layered between slices of Wonder Bread, and preferred chocolate to natural milk. My mother soon converted to lunches that would help the girls fit in, and was careful to mix white margarine with dissolved color tabs to make it appear yellow like butter. Back then it was illegal to sell colored margarine that might be sold by unscrupulous merchants as the genuine thing.[21]

Probably because on the farm we were tightly packed and sociable from birth—early to walk, talk, and work—we were mentally advanced over most of the town kids. Bethel, Fern, and Esther were hard-working students of the type our country school produced. Esther, the youngest of the three sisters, was obliged to skip grades to keep herself in line with others at the same learning level. (nicknamed «Andy,» she graduated from Sioux City's Central High School in 1941 while still fifteen).[22] Fern commuted to Woodrow Wilson Junior High in a rather shabby section of Sioux City. There she found herself stirred in with several hundred pupils and different teachers for each subject. Distressed by the lack of environmental and social coherence that typified her farm life and the country school, she shunned classmates and organized her days and evenings around schoolwork, becoming introspective and introverted. Marius had stopped at the sixth and Loretta after the eighth grade in country school. In 1902 the Iowa General Assembly had made school attendance compulsory between the ages of seven and sixteen, but the law was largely overlooked in rural areas. Farm youngsters older than fourteen were needed at home to work in the fields and help with chores.

Bethel was the first to go beyond country school. A precocious learner, she'd completed the eighth grade at the age of twelve and taken Plymouth County's top honors for grades. To continue, she'd had to attend school in Hinton—a small junior-senior school four miles from our farm, but no busses, not even horse-drawn, served our part of the county's farmland. Some students came to the Hinton School on horses or ponies. Bethel chose to room in town and work after school as a companion to our landlord's aged mother. By then she'd mastered the piano, and at fifteen, when we moved to Leeds, had become the organist at the Calvary Lutheran Church—established and built that year under the leadership of Reverend Kettler and Pastor Waldemar Hinck, with the participation of businessmen, including my father and the hardware store proprietor, Martin Riediger, who'd put us off our farm and received forgiveness. In Hinton, Bethel accumulated money by doing household jobs when time permitted, and ironing the pastor's white shirts. With cash income to spend, her wardrobe was soon independent of home-sewn print dresses that, though pretty enough with ruffles, pleats, and lace, were not appropriate for a girl coming into womanhood under scrutiny by sophisticated city girls reading fashion magazines. By the time the entire family moved to Leeds, she went directly to Sioux City's Central High—by then wearing store-bought dresses, her shapely legs clad no longer in long white cotton stockings with an elastic band at the thigh but in rayon silk stockings, her feet in stylish high heels.

Bethel stands out in my memories. Over the years in Leeds when I was seven to nine she was fifteen to seventeen, a medley of piety and sensuality so different from my other sisters that at times I suspected she'd been adopted. Were she not my sister, I could have loved her differently than the others, and perhaps I did. She was the only sister that aroused me as a teenager and the first female I'd seen almost entirely disrobed, by chance having passed by her bedroom door when I was eleven and spied her standing before her dressing table mirror, brushing her hair. The sight of her perfect body fixed an ideal beauty for me, and I've cherished her for that virginal experience. At the age of sixteen, in her last year at Sioux City's high school, she was dating, by seventeen going steady; at eighteen she married her handsome young man, the Marine who fell in battle on Guam. Later, also when eighteen, sister Fern married a soldier who distinguished himself heroically in the conquest of Nazi Germany and would retire a colonel. Both she and Bethel were pregnant when their fresh husbands went off to war, which was how men going off to war staked their claim and the left-behind women pledged their fidelity. It wouldn't do for a soldier to return after four years to find himself the father of a two-year-old. Those weddings of promise jiggled the statistics for divorce in this country within the first five years of marriage. Prior to the attack on Pearl Harbor in 1941, only seven percent of marriages in Iowa ended in divorce; by 1946, when most of the G.I.s returned, seventeen percent were destined to fail.

Over the first year in Leeds, we lived directly across from the school playground where, during summer weeks, an activities director checked out basket and volleyballs for the older kids and plain rubber bouncing balls and tossing rings for the younger ones. Swimming lessons were offered at the town pool up the hill at Carlin Park. My apostate nature obliged me to swim only under water, a skill I would perfect over the next few years while remaining hardly able to swim on the surface (Somewhere in the world is a woman now in her fifties whose near-drowned six-year-old body I brought up from the deep when surface-swimming, would-be heroes couldn't get down to the depth she had sunk).

Across the street from the last of the four houses we occupied, at the corner of Harrison and 41st, was Leeds Park, which was laid out in 1911 at the confluence of 41st with Central and Harrison Avenues. The park was a nice grassy place with huge lilac and bridal-wreath clumps that shielded secret acts and offered a bedding-down place for hoboes. There was enough ground area for basketball and volleyball games and for men to toss horseshoes. Benches were clustered here and there where neighbors could congregate in the open air. The park was outfitted with the usual chain and wood-seat swings, a pair of long teeter-totters, and a steep, undulating sheet-metal slide that was kept frighteningly slick by boys sliding down with waxed paper under their butts (bread loaf wrappers were waxed back in that pre-plastic era and handily recycled as butt-sliders). Leeds Park was a good place for little children to burn off baby fat getting terrified on high swings while being taught courage by their fathers, and where older children could break arms and legs falling out of trees and off the iron-pipe monkey bars. Throughout the summers, free movies were shown weekly after dark on an outdoor screen, while vendors hawking ice cream, cotton candy, popcorn, frozen Snickers and Milky Way bars pocketed kids' allowances and lawn-mowing earnings a nickel at a time. Today the park is a rather disconsolate space—a few deranged trees pruned by ice storms, wind, and decay, the shrubbery cut down to deny teenage sex and frustrate muggers and rapists in need of places to set ambush. The current playground equipment is made of glaringly colorful plastic that violates the landscape. Families can picnic in a small pavilion of sorts, but kids hang out nowadays at an amusement center nearby, pitting their bravery and emerging skills against extra-terrestrials and asteroids.

Some pleasant things must have happened in Leeds over the long, damp, cold winters that weren't, in themselves, miserable. We were used to harsh weather and were dressed for it—fleece-lined oilskin coats, flannel-lined sealskin caps, wool mittens that itch when the hands sweat, buckled rubber boots over woolen socks. Snowsuits had recently been invented, so young girls had more to wear than plaid woolen skirts over thick stockings with tight elastic tops and flannel bloomers secured with elastic bands at the upper thigh. Leeds was a large-family town, so there were plenty of opportunities to find playmates. I must have had at least one or two. I remember having built a tree house, and swiping green apples and cherries dozens of times from trees close to an alley. Fruit stealing was as common a juvenile crime back then as smoking dry leaves rolled in a piece of newspaper. Some years before our time in Leeds, an irate man had shot six boys out of an apple tree, wounding a couple of them with shotgun pellets. At his trial, he pleaded innocent, insisting that he was unaware the boys were in the tree and that he'd aimed at a rabbit on the ground. With no greater accuracy, perhaps, I hunted birds with a slingshot at the edge of town, but mostly aimed at insulators atop telephone poles, which older boys shot with rifles. With a wire mesh food strainer I caught tadpoles in eddies along the Floyd River banks that I would take home in a jar, add to the family fish bowl, wait for them to turn into frogs, and then dump them back into the river along its weedy banks. Probably not one of those frogs would remember having been raised as a foster child in a coral castle set in pearl pebbles. Every shape of bird nest could be found among the plant growth on the riverbank, and in the denseness of low branches and tall weeds were giant webs of the garden spider and sometimes a hermit's house to avoid—a pile of brush with a tarpaulin or tarpaper roof. Along the weedy berms of the rail bed running beside the river, butterflies, attracted for some reason by fumes rising from the oily gravel, were as plentiful as flies—yellow and white sulfurs, swallowtails, buckeyes, blue-skippers, and monarchs mostly.

Yet I don't recall a single friend at my side during after-school hours or on my outings. Maybe I didn't have any. Maybe I was taken as a dumb farm boy and not sociable. Maybe I wasn't sociable. Leeds wasn't all that urban: quite a few retired farmers had moved into town, leaving their land to be worked by grown children, and farm families came to shop in Leeds, to social clubs, dances, church, beer parlors, and pool halls. I've tried to recall more about what Leeds was to my child years, but all that came to mind were fragments, like the litter of a dream one can't reassemble, a jigsaw puzzle with only a few frayed pieces to work with. Leeds was not a hometown, not like the final stage of expansion from one's cradle. Still, I could color those pre-adolescent years with mythical blessedness and tell a few charming tales, but I would have to make them up, and to do that would be to deny the terror in favor of soft inner illusions that would fail to confront reality at the time. I could say that Leeds wasn't a serious town, and perhaps I was too serious a child. Many people protested the cost of building a high school, considering it would raise their taxes, and passed off the pedagogical need by saying kids older than fourteen could travel to a Sioux City school. Town festivities included a baby beauty contest, a smiling contest for girls, pie-eating contests, and one of the most famous boys was a nine-year-old, «the dandelion champion,» who dug 4,974 pounds of dandelions to win a contest that grossed 17,000 pounds of the weed I admired like any other flower. Digging dandelions was not respectable farm work.

Lilacs and zinnias, my favorite flowers—and moss roses. Robin's eggs as blue as a pale sky, and miniature sparrow eggs fifteen to the nest and the size of fat jellybeans. Gray squirrels in the churchyard across the street, and box elder bugs, and bats at night darting, squeaking, and scaring the life out of my sisters who wore bandannas skin-tight to keep them out of their hair. We rooted for Wendell Willkie in the late 1935 presidential election year, even though all we knew about him was that his local campaign office gave out little cardboard boxes with his portrait on them; when one pulled a resin-coated string from inside through a tiny hole in the box, rasping sounds formed the squeaky words «We want Willkie.» (Franklin Roosevelt won again that year). Joe Louis knocked out somebody in the first minute of the first round about the time the Ringling Brothers Circus was in town and I'd seen a gorilla and a freak show, and been taken to see the elephants bathe in the Big Sioux River and the midget auto races at Riverside Park. And that was about the time when my mother went to work at the Cudahy Company meat-packing house in Sioux City, commuting by streetcar, and quit after a week because, although she could deal with the blood and guts, she couldn't take the foul language of her co-workers. While standing where the walk to our Harrison Avenue house had been, I looked at the spot where, on trying out sister Esther's bicycle without her permission, I caught a wheel in a rut at the edge of the walk before I'd gone ten feet, fell over sideways and broke a forearm. I must have screamed like a stuck pig, for Marius rushed out of the house in nothing but his underwear to pick me up. My arm was set in plaster at St. Joseph's Hospital in Sioux City, where I raged against the ether mask and knocked the ether can out of the anesthetist's hand, spilling its contents about and all but putting the surgeon to sleep, as the kindly, forgiving anesthetist later told me.

These fragments don't make a complete picture. I can't get the four years we lived in Leeds into any sensible sort of order. I recall an old rusty scooter, and can see myself pushing it along the few paved sidewalks in town. Envisioning the small ice-skating rink on Floyd Avenue next to the fancy Illinois Central Depot, a long block from our house, I see myself skating as best I could with a single buckle-on left-footed skate, as if it were a scooter. To warm up on zero-weather days, the older boys at that rink would build a big bonfire and share the heat with anyone who was suffering. The depot offered a toilet for anyone too far from home—not that the stationmaster was fond of kids, but he needed a solution to boys peeing most anywhere, like dogs that leave yellow stains in the snow. That station was so beloved by townsfolk that today it stands rebuilt as a historic memorial.

Every passing train was a spectacular event—the enormous engines with whistles that could shatter one's eardrums. Those that stopped at the station for car-switching blew steam clouds more furious and heated than dragons or Old Faithful—of that, I'm sure, though I'd never seen a dragon or the famous geyser except in geography-book pictures. The steam smelled oily and metallic; when standing close to an engine in icy cold weather and taking deep breaths, one could warm one's face and lungs like Turks in a steam bath. At night, when the town was asleep, the clankety-clank rolling of heavy freight trains would shake the ground and rattle every loose object in our house.

Leeds had a baseball team, the Red Socks (emulating the misspelled but famous Boston Red Sox), made up of young men who worked days and practiced in the evenings for boisterous competition with teams from neighboring towns. The players paid for their uniforms and equipment by compiling the town's telephone book and selling ads to be placed in it. And there were a few other sports for people to enjoy. Ignoring the Depression, the Petersen brothers, sheet metal fabricators, took a financial gamble in 1932 and built a nine-hole sand-green golf course at the southeast edge of Leeds, with a clubhouse big enough to hold their metal shop in the basement. Sand-greens were packed mason's sand, regularly oiled to keep from blowing, and smoothed with a strip of carpet at the end of a stick. The green fee was a quarter. A found golf ball could fetch a nickel, the price of a candy bar, a pack of Black Jack Gum, a bottle of Royal Crown Cola, or a try with the drugstore's steam shovel's claw in a glass case for grabbing a whistle or toy truck; failing, one was left with a dose of jelly beans. On a good day of beating the weeds and shrubbery all around the course, a kid could make a quarter, buy a bag of marbles, and still put away a dime in the town's bank, where, at the height of my affluence, I had forty-five cents on deposit. This golf course continued in use until 1942 when few men were around to play. By then most of the older boys were in military service and many men had vacated Leeds for employment in the war industry. The Petersens rolled up the sod that year and sold it to the Sioux City Airbase to be placed around the newly built barracks, leaving the fairways to become farmland again.[23]

By the age of nine I was hooked on adventure stories promoted by late afternoon radio serials, especially Jack Armstrong, the All-American Boy, whose strength and virtue was attributed to eating Wheaties; and also an admirer of the straight-talking, straight-shooting Tom Mix, featured by Ralston's shredded wheat cereal. The gender of children was vigorously defined by most everything one heard and did—for me, muscles and guns; for my sisters, a Shirley Temple doll with hair one could brush.

An older cousin, Violetta Bollmeyer, who still resides on a Hinton farm next to the one that was ours, told me that, as a kid on the farm and in Leeds, I was devilishly clever and prone to trouble. I cannot imagine this was true, yet am willing to admit that throughout my life I've tended to be provocative and an adept prevaricator, as if nourished by conflict like Popeye by spinach. As a child I was a target for others to test their mettle against—and that has never changed, other than from the physical to the intellectual. Books I've written tend to be confrontational. Back then, in Leeds, as it would be in Sioux City, I vacillated between fearing and fearlessness, cowardice and courage, and I recall that fearlessness was my greatest fear. Even this book, while being written, is a cause of apprehension that at times keep me awake all night, so much of its laying bare my life in ways that others sanitize. Too early in life, I think, I developed a romantic temperament: emotional, sensitive, adventurous, eager for novelty, erotic and rather disorderly, and knowing at all times that, even if I tried, I could not be typical.

To and from school, or when wandering about Leeds on weekends looking for something to do—or, as my mother would say, some kind of trouble to get into—I was often confronted by hostile boys—always a group, never a single risk-taking boy. I remember two traumatic fistfights: right now, in front of my eyes, I see the face of one boy about to throw a punch at me—short, stocky, pudgy, and freckle-faced, backed by a half-dozen others who'd put him up to it. Then I see that boy's body doubled over and hear him moaning and gasping for breath. Respectful that he wore glasses, I'd hit him full force in the stomach before he could hit me in the face, then turned and walked away as if unafraid, while every muscle of my body trembled in fear the gang would muster enough grit to beat the life out of me. The molesters did chase me home, keeping themselves at a safe distance. When I came into the house through the back door to the kitchen, they gathered outside and jeered like milksops in any mob, bolstered by their number and the closed door between us—and one or two of my older sisters teased me for being chicken, not knowing I had felled my opponent with a single blow and strategically retreated so I could one day fight again.

For a while after that I was left untested, but later on, during winter, when sledding by myself on Carlin Park Hill, the only hill in Leeds, still crowned by a water tank, a dozen boys ganged up to punish me, if not for that dubious victory over vice, for whatever was on their brutish minds at that moment. I was nine and had a Red Runner racing sled with paraffined blades, a Christmas gift from my parents. To escape what would have been a thrashing, I didn't hesitate to slam my sled down hard and speed toward the bottom of the hill, not thinking until halfway down—the curs a ways behind yapping for my demise, like bull-dogs chasing a fleet deer—about what would happen when the downs-lope ran out. To my right was the top edge of a retaining wall built to allow flat excavation for the town's swimming pool. Between the wall and the pool was a chain-link fence. I thought that if I shot off the top of the wall I could clear the fence a few feet beyond it and land in the pool, which was deeply filled then not with water but with snow. I swerved and took flight off the wall okay, but made a near-fatal pilot error. Unmindful that the fence was not much lower than the wall, my magic-carpet-sled didn't clear the fence but crashed into it. I crushed a shoulder, the collarbone shattered, and my right arm broke near the elbow. The lusty pursuers, out of sympathy for a fallen combatant or maybe just in awe of my aerobatics, stood silently and watched as I hauled my sled homeward, one arm dangling awkwardly.

At times I've thought that my youth had too much violence, per-haps because so much of it was in the context of saloons and dance halls, both sites of drunkenness and bawdy behavior. I will never know whether the lingering sense that my pubescent years in Leeds were violent had to do with having come off a rural platform on which severity was essential to survival. On the farm my childhood had been more nettles and bull thistles than flowers—not that I'd missed out on affection. With so many children under her wing, my mother was strict yet gentle and routinely loving; but I can't recall if she ever touched me after the diaper-changing age, or when getting me into and out of cloth-ing. My father was gentle and funny, usually in good humor, gentle-hearted, and proud of his children, but unpredictably fierce at times. My big brother Marius was a huge man—six-foot four, about two hundred and sixty pounds—temperate by one set of instincts and cruel by the workings of another. In our culture, men beat their animals more than they trained them; brothers were entitled to reprimand sisters while obligated to protect them from despoilment by others. Marius was

Loretta's buddy and co-worker but tough on the younger girls, slapping them around with impunity. When at the age of nine Bethel had a severe headache and begged off milking, rather than console and protect her, Marius accused her of lying; to test her excuse, he smacked her throbbing head with an open hand.

Shortly before our move to Leeds, my father killed two of our three dogs because they'd behaved badly in the barn yard one night—the third dog, our terrier, got run over by the mailman's car when both were running in the same deep snow rut and our dog stopped to look back. Snow banks had made the road narrow, almost impassable; the snow was white, our terrier was white; the mailman didn't see him.

My memory of my father's violent deed differs from that of Loretta's. I recall an afternoon when our two mixed-blood German shepherds—defenders of our livestock from coyotes and stray dogs—harassed milk cows with full udders. Enraged, my father chased them down and bashed in their heads with a hammer. Loretta says I remember it wrongly, that the dogs had raised hell with the horses during the night, driving them into barbed wire fences, and that the next morning our father took the dogs to the woods, killed them with a shotgun, and buried them there. (Maybe in my subconscious reworking of the event, focused on milk cows, I made it into my father killing someone who'd molested my mother). And my father almost killed our service boar with a club when, out in the pig-lot, the boar attacked my sister Esther (maybe I dreamed that he did!). My father heartlessly whipped a team of run-away horses after they'd shied in the field and raced back to the barn. On entering it, still hauling a manure spreader wider than the door, the team snapped the leather traces and the spreader caved in at the front. (I was atop the bed of that spreader when the horses spooked. Maybe I caused the runaway!)

As for those two farm dogs, I had no love for them. They were an occasional cause of apprehension and sadness. Sometimes at night they would howl mournfully at the moon. Having been told a dog's nighttime howling meant someone nearby was about to die, we children laid awake wondering who it was, imagining what death for humans was like, having seen so many dead animals. At my very young age, I couldn't distinguish between myth and reality, between jokes and truths. Stories of werewolves and howling dogs could keep any kid from sleeping and make him afraid of his own shadow when walking in moonlight. Even in the city, whether true or not true that one broke one's mother's back by stepping on a sidewalk crack, I looked down as I walked.

Farm men were not sadistically but functionally and stupidly cruel. Horses were whipped for most any misstep or misdeed. Marius brutalized the mule team, Jack and Jenny, and kept them in such a nervous state that no one but he dared enter their stall. Milk cows were beaten in their milking stations for swishing a manure-laden tail into the milker's face. My uncle Henry on my mother's side of my pedigree ruined one of his best dairy cows that had kicked and knocked the pail out from between his knees while he was milking her. Furious, he grabbed a hayfork and poked her behind her hind legs, daring her to kick again. The sharp tines punctured her kicking leg; within a few days she was racked with a bacterial infection and could no longer be milked. Barn cats were kicked out from under one's feet—always getting in the way, especially the half-dozen at milking time that wove in and out between one's legs and shrieked when stepped on; the only way to settle them down was to fill their big metal dish with milk from the first bucket drawn.

When I was five or perhaps six, my father punished me for a crime I didn't commit. I'd been out in the tool shed for a while playing adult with adult tools. Later, back in the house, my father burst through the door in a rage, blood filling his face, having just gone to the shed to get his wood-boring brace, not finding it there. Figuring I'd mislaid it, he grabbed me by an upper arm, hustled me outdoors, and with a kick to my butt aimed me in the direction of the tool shed. On the way, while I stumbled along not understanding what I was being punished for, he kicked me a couple more times, and when we arrived at the shed, he told me to look for the brace until I found it. He left me there, but no brace was to be found. I snuck back to the house after awhile by a circuitous route through the wood lot, hoping for my mother's protection. Marius was in the house when I reached it. He asked what I was so distraught over, and my mother said, «Dad punished him for mislaying his brace out in the tool shed.» Then she said to me, «Did you find it?» My brother said, «How could he have found it? I'm using it out at the cob-house and it's still there.»

Young children have the gift of amnesia. One of the Golden Rules handed down to sanction civilization is to forgive and forget, but when five or six, a child can only forget, not yet knowing how to forgive; that capacity awaits a later stage of development. After moving to California, I spent a more time with my father than I had as a young child. I was not the easiest son to raise. He was more forgiving of me than I'd been of him. When at the age of sixteen out there, while living at home for a while, I cut the fenders off his 1938 Chevy sedan, painted the carcass fire engine red, and punctured the muffler so the motor would roar like a racecar. Few fathers would have tolerated that foolishness while also thinking of it as amusing. He loved driving that hot car, saying, «When drivers up ahead see me coming, they think I'm a fire engine and get out of my way.» On occasions when in that fire-engine red Chevy, my father hauled me and my side-men to play a dance job somewhere in town, usually in Oakland or Vallejo—the bass fiddle lashed to the top of the car, the drums on back seat laps—it didn't occur to me, because I wouldn't know it until years later, that on the Hinton farm when I was a toddler, he'd painted a stake-wagon lipstick red, and with it hitched to his rubber-wheeled tractor, would haul the Hinton Farm Girls baseball team to nearby towns. On entering a town, he would parade the girls up and down Main Street before they undertook devastating yet another luckless team with Loretta pitching. So he must have been reliving a memorable precedent.

Throughout my life, my father has been with me. I still hear his advice, and an image of him smiling and laughing appears out in front of my eyes. He loved his family, enjoyed family outings at Sioux City's Riverside picnic grounds, family boating and fishing on the Big Sioux, board and card games at home. I've told so many stories about him, his memorable absent-mindedness always taken with humor. He was in many ways a remarkable man, and under conditions that would have broken a lesser man, he shared with my mother the task of raising ten children. Regardless of what calamities we could recite, not one of us would have wished for a different father. While he wasn't a role model for everything, he was for many things. He instilled confidence, and in manageable ways could be empathetic. When tears came to my sister's eyes because he was about to slaughter a non-productive milk cow they'd come to love, he led the cow to a neighbor's farm and traded her for a victim for whom they had no feelings. As a man who farmed well he had to judge animals according to their usefulness. Even when he killed those two dogs, he was obliged to do it. Once a farm dog goes bad, when the wolf in him surfaces through the domestic membrane and threatens livestock, it must be destroyed. At age fourteen, I, too, killed two dogs, and with a shotgun. They were marauders, sheep killers. I was not acting violently, not with cruelty, just being a good shepherd.

My father was a natural protector, like my uncle John. He managed by his own wits to keep his family well housed in the best part of town. Not even in the worst years would we suffer the terror of poverty, or attend less than the best public schools. He ran his beer parlor with humor and efficiency; his clientele admired him. He looked after his customers, making sure they didn't get so drunk as to pass out, cutting off their beer orders when he felt they'd had all they could handle. He wouldn't allow any regular poker-playing customer to lose a week's pay needed to support his family or buy seed for planting or feed for live-stock. If an out-of-town card shark came to his place, threatening to win big and take his winnings out of town, my father would get into the game, nick a few high cards; then, in a sudden rage leap up and accuse the shark of cheating. A couple of my father's burly friends would pin the shark's arms behind his chair. Sure enough, after inspecting the cards and finding the nicks, the shark would be judged hands-down guilty, his chips and his money taken. My father would keep any expro-priated cash not needed for redistribution among the losers after benev-olently poking five dollars into the shark's pocket before he was carried across Floyd Avenue and tossed onto the first freight train that passed by—hopefully, as my father would say, onto a flat-car hitched behind a carload of hogs that hadn't had a bath since they were born. I once asked my father if that was fair, considering that the shark hadn't been the one nicking the cards. He replied, «All's fair in love and poker.»

On one occasion in Leeds when I was eight or nine, I had to fall asleep thinking my father had killed one of my uncles—which one I didn't know because it would have been either Uncle Hans or Uncle Chris, identical twins. They were my mother's brothers, sojourners on disability pensions who'd had to accept their lot. American-born Germans, they'd fought in France against Imperial Germany in World War I and were gassed in a trench battle. As a consequence, both were tubercular, drank heavily, and were always broke. Doomed to a short life, they were drifters with neither hope nor ambition, although on occasion they would drive to Chicago, load their car trunk with Lake Michigan fish and ice blocks, then race back to Sioux City, getting there before the ice had melted in time to peddle their catch at a busy street corner and then stock up on booze. On occasion, they came to Leeds in need of a place to hole up for a while.

My mother couldn't handle her twin brothers when they'd been drinking. My father did his best to keep them restrained. One night very late I recall an awful fight that erupted on the front porch. The noise woke me. One of the twins had showed up in the middle of the night, slobberingly drunk. My father had arrived home from his saloon at that moment and refused to let him into the house. I still hear my father's fury, his sundering shouts and curses. From a window, and in the spooky streetlight, I saw him drag a man's body across the street to Leeds Park where he dunked the man's head over and over into the birdbath, towed him off into deeper darkness, and returned to the house alone. When he came up the stairs to the bedroom floor, I asked him who was the man. He mumbled, «One of those god-dammed twins. Get back into bed.»

I laid awake for awhile in the light of an electric candle, thinking he'd killed that uncle—was told the next morning that he'd left him comatose to sleep it off on a bench. Those uncles were ghosts in my mind. Having no fixed location in the world, just appearing and disappearing, with one looking exactly like the other, they lacked physical reality.

Chapter 9

Toilet odors were
aphrodisiac in those days

After three years in purgatorial Leeds, each year in a different house, we moved to Sioux City. My father had sold the Leeds beer parlor and bought a larger one in Sioux City at the lower end of Fourth Street, a nefarious part of town where down-and-outers, boozers, and prostitutes roamed, and where today, fifty-five years later, the same saloon at 1008 Fourth Street shares a dingy block with Francis Canteen, an adult book, lingerie, and video shop; across the street is an exotic-dancer bar.

When visiting Sioux City in 1997, I stopped by to check out what had been Andy's Place. The street-front window had been redesigned but on the inside was the same bar, and at the rear of the dance floor stood a set of drums where small combos still play on Saturday nights. The walls are still painted in a creamy tan enamel, the stamped tin ceiling is still up, the booths along a sidewall were removed to make room for a pool table, and a ladies toilet had been added next to the old one. Back in my father's days of ownership, the one toilet serving both sexes was furnished with a condom and comb dispenser and decorated with girlie calendars and ads for hemorrhoid ointments and Lucky Strike cigarettes. Women using it under its single naked bulb risked confronting their names and essential body parts inscribed on the walls—traces of lewd secrets, bragging claw marks of territorial beasts; poems in couplets, quatrains, and free-verse—a class of literature without literary status, akin to poetry in dungeons. Toilet odors were aphrodisiac back when sex really was dirty. Upstairs, above the saloon and accessed from a separate street door was a parlor with a cushioned davenport, armchairs, and three or four bedrooms with iron-post beds and washstands, where my father served up women and verboten whiskey to

111

show appreciation for his best customers and neutralize the potency of alcohol-control agents. My father had a girlfriend Leona who resided up there and was in charge of the goings-on. Anyone who's seen a few Hollywood Westerns is familiar with the upstairs rooms and entertainment girls that work their charms not just in movies. And every one of those saloons had a Leona.

I will pause here to say a few more words about my father, to whose strong character and natural morality I have tried to hold up.

His moral values were not church-sanctioned but fitted to the sort of life that survives by wits; a natural trait of the natural farmer, upon whose basic industry civilization was built. It was his staunchness and indifference to risk that passed to me, not genetically but by osmosis, and perhaps as well, his refusal to accept hard luck as hard luck. «One doesn't cry over spilled milk»— but that was my mother's usual advice. My father's advice over my early years can be encapsulated in one phrase: «You won't know how to do it unless to try,» to which I might add a couple other points of advice that may seen ubiquitous but still ring in my mind as philosophical wisdom. On an occasion when helping him with some carpentry, I complained that his crosscut saw didn't saw straight. His response was quick: «Saws don't cut crooked. Arms do. Don't ever blame a tool. If it doesn't do what it's supposed to, you're using the wrong tool. If you're pushing too hard, you're not letting the tool do the work.» Plato could have said that to Timaeus.

«Don't ever back down,» he counseled me. «Only a fool admits he's made a mistake. Just figure a way to get around it.»

Often I've mused over an event in Sioux City when, in the basement of his saloon, he built a twelve-foot rowboat for the family to enjoy at the lake. I'd advised him on a couple of occasions, when invited down to see his progress, that the boat would be stuck forever in the basement because the only way out was a narrow back door to a narrower set of steps leading up to the alley. Not one to worry about any problem in advance of solution, he worked on the boat off and on until it was ready for the water. One Sunday morning, he shook me awake at dawn and asked that I come to the saloon after breakfast, saying he needed help hauling the boat to Brown's Lake. When we arrived at the saloon, to my amazement I saw that he'd already taken a sledgehammer to the basement's thick brick wall and knocked out enough of it to make way for the boat to pass through.

We maneuvered that boat out through the jagged hole that an errant bomb might have caused, hoisted it up to the alley, lifted it atop the car, and lashed it down with ropes. Halfway to the lake, it started to rain—a Midwest, mid-summer downpour out of a sky so black that cars were driving with headlights. In semi-darkness, we arrived at a place where private farmland had to be crossed, where a farmer would want a fifty-cent toll paid before he'd open the gate. By then the road was so muddy that my father had driven the last quarter-mile in low gear, and, as we would soon find out, the boat was accumulating inches of water in its belly. After tolerating a few horn-honks, the disbelieving toll-keeping farmer came out of his house wearing mud-boots, a slicker, and a piece of oilcloth over his head. He was cussingly angry with anyone being so dumb as to think he could drive the next two hundred yards to the lakeside without getting stuck. My father would hear none of that—dumb farmers are used to doing dumb things. He handed over the fifty cents and demanded entry. The dumbfounded dumb farmer opened the gate.

We didn't get to the boat-launching site where the lake shore was shallow, but only to the closest point of the lake's steep edge before the car sunk so deeply in mud that its running boards were flat on the ground. My father cut the car's useless engine and sat silently at the wheel for a few moments, as if awaiting orders, then pushed open his door saying, «Well, let's get it in the lake.» By the time I managed to open my door against the sticky clay mud, by then oozing over the running board, he had loosened the tie-ropes on his side. Neither of us were wearing boots, just street shoes; mine were sucked off my feet a foot underground, and I had to dig down for them with my hands and bring them up out of the muck, only to toss them onto the car's floorboards. By then my father was wallowing up to his knees, trying to pivot the boat so the bow would be aimed towards the lake, just a few feet from the car's side, where the bank sloped steeply downward about fifteen feet. He called out to me to come around to where he was holding up the stern; having pivoted it, the boat was perpendicular to the car. When I came around to him, he said, «Let's just push it off and it'll slide right into the lake.» That's what we did. We pushed the stern up, the boat slid off the car and down the bank. Weighted by its bellyful of rainwater, it plunged straight into deep water, stopping when the boat was half-sunk, the bow embedded. Through deep muck we came to the edge of the bank, my father's shoes and socks buried forever, our clothing coated with mud, and looked downslope at the disconsolate boat. He turned his face to mine, his big Danish smile melting my soul, and said, «Well, son, we got the damn thing in the water, didn't we!»

It took the dumb farmer's tractor and a two-dollar bill to get us back on the road to home and a garden-hose bath and car wash. That's the way my father was: impulsive, hardheaded, and compensatory. He was only five foot six inches tall, while his father and four brothers were all over six feet. Of his three sons, I stand as the shortest, exactly six feet; my brothers were six-two and six-four. He once told me that, as a youth in Denmark, he was the shortest boy in the neighborhood, and couldn't hope to survive a wrestling bout or fistfight with boys his age or older. His only defense was to act fierce, never back down, and hope to outwit an assailant because he knew he couldn't outfight him.

In 1942, Andy's Place and some eighty other saloons were in operation within Sioux City and the adjacent South Sioux City and Dakota City, with such appropriate names as The Bowery, Cornhusker Tavern, Dipsy Doo, Farmer's Tap, The Jitterbug, War Eagle's Cafe, and Dew Drop In, which, in earlier years, was Dutch Boynton's speakeasy. The city's population was divided during the 1930s on the issue of saloons, liquor stores, and dance halls, but ever since Sioux City's population was greater than one of each sex, as in the Garden of Eden, it has been a sinful town. When the first electric lights were turned on in Sioux City, one-fourth of the thirty-six light bulbs were in saloons.

This well defined Lower Fourth Street strip, now just two blocks long and cut off from the rest of Fourth Street during a recent phase of urban renewal, was to Sioux City what Storyville was to New Orleans—not really a red-light district but an underbelly zone known for hock shops, bath houses, used furniture stores, beer joints with accommodating bar maids, and a few street and short-stay hotel whores. I might mention that Storyville was shut down in 1917—too close to the port of New Orleans (all ports have a red-light district nearby). The government ruled that no prostitution would be allowed within five miles of a military base (at that time, fifty percent of the sailors were venereally diseased). Louis Armstrong, by the way, earned his daily fare over his first years as a trumpeter delivering coal to Storyville brothels.

Today the lower Fourth Street strip is preserved as historic property, the buildings looking much as they did back then—less grimy now, as coal-burning days have passed. The city's current alternative newspaper—the sort of smoldering rag that respectable people do not read, appropriately called *The 4th Street Revue*—is published just a couple of doors from the address of my father's former saloon. The Revue's publisher Cindy Waitt's «quote of the month» for her first volume was Albert Einstein saying, «Great spirits have always met violent opposition from mediocre minds.» So Einstein reigned on lower Fourth Street while in Las Vegas a huge sign at the Bellagio Casino announced that coming soon would be Van Gogh, Monet, Renoir, and Cézanne, with special guests Pablo Picasso and Henri Matisse, thanks to the New York Guggenheim Museum's expansive folly. What goes up, it is said, must come down.

In earlier years, the so-called «red joints» area of Sioux City was Pearl Street, the first commercial street, said to have been named after a much appreciated black cook on the Missouri River packet boat Omaha (but it could have been called that because at that time Sioux City was often referred to as «the Pearl of the West»). When the street was extended north as a residential street, the new portion became respectable Grandview Avenue.

As usual, red-light districts tend to become ghettos and come under fire for lawless depravity and demands for relocation as a city develops. In the late nineteenth century, Sioux City's most notorious center for fleshy vice, gambling, and assorted crime had been the Soudan district, also known then as the Soudan Colony. «Where will they go?» asked the Sioux City *Journal*, when the police announced that the colony could not stay where it was because the new elevated railway connecting the downtown with the developing Morningside suburb would be lowered to street level where it passed by Third Street, where passengers would need protection from the zone.

«Where to? If the city proposes to protect this goose that lays the golden egg, then the city should provide the colony with a suitable location situated on the riverfront and isolated from all respectable people. A high board fence could surround the ground, and thus being a compact, limited area, could be easily kept under police control. If it is public policy to foster and encourage the Soudan, move it anywhere you please except into localities inhabited by the virtuous poor. The rich will protect themselves.»

The Soudan Colony was indeed the golden goose. Not exceptional was belief among Sioux City's enlightened businessmen that doing away with saloons and prostitution would hurt business in general. Fewer traveling businessmen would lay over a day or two to enjoy activities they wouldn't dare indulge in their hometown. Fewer farmers and small towners would visit the city on Saturdays. Businesses would stop booking Sioux City for conventions and trade fairs, both of which flow with the undercurrent of an anticipated orgy. Even the ancient Romans knew that the construction of a public coliseum and a brothel was the quickest was to settle hostilities in newly conquered territory and to keep occupation troops from getting homesick.[24]

O ver the latter part of the nineteenth century, Des Moines boasted the largest distillery in the world, and Sioux City wasn't far behind in capacity to produce quality beer—Heidel-Brau, Western Brew, and Ace. The entire state of Iowa profited from alcohol taxation. Even though public sentiment was largely anti-liquor, politicians and businessmen had only to look downriver to see how many Missouri and Mississippi river towns were reaping huge gains from the liquor traffic while keeping down property taxes.

The Iowa constitution had been amended in June 1882 to forbid the sale of alcohol other than ale, beer, and wine, but lawyers engaged by the liquor industry soon found enough defects in the way it was written to cancel enforcement. In June of 1862, a statutory law closed all of Iowa's drinking places, except for those in Sioux City, where politicians and businessmen thumbed their noses at the legislature and continued to license drinking establishments in open violation of state law. Deploying a neat twist, the illegal operation of a speakeasy, or hole in the wall, could be made to appear legal (the term «hole in the wall» referred to speakeasy proprietors' practice of cutting a hole through the wall between adjacent establishments, so when tipped off about a raid, the liquor could be handed through and not found on the targeted premises. By time the police arrived, the joint would be serving soda pop at a prayer meeting). Once each month, each hole-in-the-wall proprietor would be arrested on some charge of disturbing the peace, such as using foul and profane language, and in court be expected to plead guilty and pay a one-hundred-dollar fine. If the proprietor refused to comply and confess, he would be charged with liquor-law violations and his joint shut down. Such scenarios of mutually agreed upon blackmail and benevolent police coercion were commonplace in the Sioux City area even during my early youth in the mid-thirties when the Depression was a flat line on the country's oscilloscope.

At the Iowa Democratic convention held in 1884, under the slogan «liberty of individual conduct,» the platform had repeal of Prohibition as the primary goal of the party. The wording read, «Use every means to blot that foul stigma from the face of Iowa» (an editorial in the *Des Moines Leader*, commenting on the Democratic candidate for governor, suggested that he might be right on prohibition but probably should stand for something else as well). In 1894, the state legislature passed an ingenious law preserving the spirit of prohibition while providing revenue in lieu of increased taxes by allowing alcohol sales. The law sanctioned only one saloon for each 1,000 units of a town's population if over 5,000, and continued to permit tavern owners to confess annually to breaking the law, pay a fine, and be exempt from arrest until the time came for the next year's confession. This so-called Mulct Law came under fire perennially from temperance groups, including a visit by hatchet-wielding Carry Nation in June 1903. The law was automatically repealed on January 1st, 1916 when statewide prohibition was again established.

Although voting itself legally dry three years before the Volstead Act of National Prohibition had taken effect, Sioux City hadn't gone dry at all but had made a jump-start on bootlegging. Iowa, Nebraska, and the Dakotas were wetter during Prohibition than they'd been before receiving orders to dry up. During Prohibition, bootlegging, gang wars, racketeering, and enfeebled law enforcement produced greater social ills, traffic deaths, assaults and murders than public drinking. Sioux City was among the most notorious of the midwestern cities for alcohol-related violence and crime, and had been for half a century.

After the repeal of Prohibition and legalization of 3.2 beer, all

117

across the state pressure was on to prevent dancing where beer was sold. Uncle John in nearby Correctionville partitioned off a part of his pool hall to make a dance floor. John's son, my teenage cousin Harley, had bought a junk car but hadn't enough money to buy a license for it. Driving about town anyway, he was arrested for not having plates and fined two hundred dollars—an enormous amount; even if he'd had a job; it would have taken six months to earn that much money. The exorbitant fine was a commonly deployed act of extortion on the part of Correctionville's mayor and police chief, who let it be known to Uncle John that if he didn't stop holding dances at his pool hall he would either have to pay the fine, which of course he couldn't, or see his son go to jail. John had no choice but to close down the dance hall.

B ack in the 1880s, when a confession and a hundred-dollar bill could keep a speakeasy operating in Sioux City under the blind eyes of the local government, nettling opposition came only from clergymen. A national «crime of the decade» took place in Sioux City in August 1886 when the pastor of the First Methodist Episcopal Church, the Reverend George Haddock, was gunned down near the public livery stable at Third and Water Streets. He had instigated a movement to apply «citizen's arrests» in order to bring liquor violators to trial without the benefit of less-than-charged confessions. For this, the pastor was threatened, insulted, and subjected to indignities; even some of his fellow clergymen had tried to quell his pontificating rage; male parishioners were hard enough to keep in church without threats to the city's economy antagonizing them. A saloonkeepers' association was formed to quash the preacher's prosecutions and punish witnesses willing to testify for the state. At a meeting on August 2nd, 1886, the entire cash-on-hand treasury of the association was put up as a bounty and offered to two German musclemen if they would waylay the preacher and give him the sort of whipping he wouldn't soon forget. As it turned out, the thugs took it on themselves to shoot the pastor rather than punch him into pulp.

The assassination of Reverend Haddock attracted the attention of the entire nation. Trial correspondents came from Chicago and as far as New York City. On March 23rd, 1887, the state court convened. The German goons were tried separately; one for murder, the other tried later for complicity. After a twenty-one-day trial of the shooter, and twenty hours of jury deliberation, eleven of the twelve jurists voted for acquittal. No truth had come out during the trial for the jurists to work with. Every witness was or had been engaged in the liquor business; even the witnesses for the state prosecutors were implicated in the conspiracy. The case was dismissed. In the fall of 1887, the accomplice was brought to trial for manslaughter, found guilty, and sentenced to four years in prison, but was immediately pardoned by the governor. The shooter came up for re-trial in December before a spiritless prosecutor. After a few moments of deliberation, the jury returned a verdict—not guilty.

Reverend Haddock was a true martyr. His struggle for a lost cause remains on the minds of some in Sioux City, even a century later. Still anchored in the pavement at the corner of Fourth and Water Streets is a marker, saying «Haddock Died Here,» followed by:

«Oh Haddock! We catch up the banner that fell

All stained by thy rich martyr blood;

And we vow that each drop to a torrent

That shall sweep off the curse with its flood.»[25]

In 1932, when I was four, Iowa's Democrats risked their state and local elections on the promise of beer for Iowans, winning a majority in the state legislature and seats on a good many town councils. Having faced up to social reality, they lived up to their promise of delivering this opiate for the masses. In April 1933, the state legislature legalized the sale of 3.2% beer. Although Iowa would still suffer droughts and grasshopper invasions, no parched Iowan mouth need shrivel up from then on for lack of beer. In Sioux City, which included Leeds, 218 beer permits were issued over the first few weeks, and more bottled beer was consumed over the first month than over the rest of the year. City and townsfolk guzzled what most of them had never tasted before. Heads spun like eddies and whirlpools in the flow of a flash flood that soon settled down to a steady foamy stream. By 1934, at the age of six, I'd already been sipping beer for two years—my father's home brew—so I don't recall the Beer Law as anything special.

Just a month after the state legislature legalized beer sales, the *Collegian Reporter* of Sioux City's Morningside College published a survey of student reaction. Twenty-five collegians responded: seven girls, eighteen boys. In general, there was scornful insistence that student drinking was strictly a personal matter. Even before legalization, fifty-five percent of the Sioux City college students drank beer on occasion and ten percent were hooked on it. The seven girls among the testifiers declared in a chorus that beer was not intoxicating, while five of the boys maintained that it was, one saying that one didn't need to drink a whole case of it to start weaving daisy chains, swinging chairs, or making violent love to ugly waitresses. One boy said, «The saloon is here and always has been.» Deploying the best of the Anti-Saloon League metaphors, some of the boys feared the girls would regress to Bacchanalian revelers, while other boys affirmed that the girls had a right to drink if they wanted to: «Let the sweet young things quaff deeply of the evil cup.»

It was bad enough that girls were drinking beer, even worse that in 1934 Muriel Hanford (the «Peacock Girl») opened a night club in Sioux City, The Peacock Inn. The club was situated over the thirties in the Jackson Hotel. Hanford's stage career began at the age of three as an angel in *Uncle Tom's Cabin* (as for her role as an angel, she said years later that she would like to be remembered as anything but that). During World War I, Hanford had already gained fame as the featured Peacock Girl in the Ziegfield Follies in New York City. She traveled the RKO vaudeville circuit, married a Sioux City millionaire, from whom she was promptly divorced, played bit parts in Hollywood films, and during part of the WW I years, drove an ambulance in London. Before opening her club in Sioux City, she established one in Arnolds Park, Iowa. She died at the age of seventy-five in 1965, still performing until seventy in a restaurant she owned in Fort Lauderdale, Florida.

When my father established his Sioux City saloon, liquor by the drink was outlawed. An effort by some legislators to overturn the restriction and allow cities with a population greater than 10,000 to decide for themselves as to that issue was defeated in 1939. So saloon proprietors had to keep two businesses going under one roof—beer over the counter and whiskey under it. Federal and state alcohol agents, deputy sheriffs, and local policemen then had the benefit of a second income from bribery, blackmail, and sundry payoffs to supplement their depressed paychecks for upholding a law most every lawman regularly broke.

In April 1941, when I was thirteen and could draw a beer with a good head on it, the Iowa legislature passed seven more beer bills. One outlawed dancing in establishments that served beer, while the other allowed a proprietor to promote dancing if the dance floor area was at least 1000 sq. ft. and on the same floor as the bar, thus preventing the smallest watering holes from siphoning off dancing-prone drinkers from larger pools of iniquity. Another of the laws, aimed to reduce hanky-panky under tables or on booth cushions, ruled that partitions between booths could be no higher than forty-four inches. Each establishment was required to have a full-time uniformed policeman or sheriff's deputy on hand at all times—so payoffs were conveniently legalized. The final law reaffirmed that liquor could be sold by no agency other than a state store.

Proponents of state sales soon conceded that the liquor commission allowed its stores to sell with reckless abandon, even a case of liquor every other day to the same man. «Of course they are selling to men who run beer joints,» said Representative Greene from Dennison. «That's why some of those places are dispensing hard liquor. The liquor commission is to blame for half our troubles.» As New York's mayor LaGuardia was saying at this time about his own city, «It would take 250,000 policemen to police the speakeasies, and another 250,000 policemen to police the policemen.» A legislator from Spencer, Iowa, agreed that the situation was deplorable. «But don't cuss the legislature for not passing laws,» he shouted to the chamber. «And don't cuss the police officers for not enforcing the laws. They wouldn't hold their jobs if they did. The responsibility is squarely up to the people of Iowa. They will not stand for officers, mayors, and sheriffs dictating their lives. What we need in Iowa is a campaign of Christian education.»

But it would take more than that to dry up the towns and counties of Iowa. The Church is the only institution that offers forgiveness of sins rather than jail time. Sinning is created and nourished by efforts to forbid it. Had all those saying they were without sin cast a stone anyway, Sioux City would have been buried under a pile of rocks.

During Prohibition, Canada was a major source of quality whiskey. On dark nights, Highway 75 north of Sioux City, passing through Hinton and Leeds, was blackened even darker by black Cadillacs with hollowed-out trunks loaded with alcohol coming from Winnipeg. Times then were economically favorable in the Midwest. A fortune could be made running Canadian whiskey down though Minneapolis and St. Paul to Sioux City, Omaha, and St. Louis. A secondary industry, riskier but lucrative, was hijacking, and a third was the management of local stills; yet a fourth was exploitation by mayors, sheriffs, and police officers. Paid off to turn their eyes and act discreetly, their rewards indirectly helped local economies: illicit profits were spread around in obeisance to the trickle-down principle of capitalist economics. A massive amount of fresh outside capital beefed up Sioux City's economy, by then one of the favorite retreats for bootleggers and mobsters when under the heat in Chicago, while St. Paul to the north was a benevolent hideout for the higher echelon of gangsters and mob leaders needing a vacation from their nerve-racking occupations. Dubbed Little Chicago, Sioux City even had a residence hotel called the Chicago House, located at the corner of 4th Street and Jones, just a couple blocks from where my father opened his saloon. Its basement served as a notorious poker room over the years when gambling was rampant in the city.

Some say that Jews operated the big-time gambling rooms. Indeed many of them were Jewish-owned. Around 5,000 Jews lived in Sioux City then (eight percent of the in-town population). As the saying went among them, their survival options were to change their noses and names, open a hockshop, jewelry or clothing store, or become a gambler. Many were immigrants who'd been seduced by land speculators into coming over from Europe in the 1890s to settle in North Dakota, but they arrived too late to buy or homestead the best farmland; Germans and Austrians, with deep-seated anti-Semitism, had settled there a decade earlier. Disillusioned, having found no Promised Land, most of the Jewish families resettled in towns.

I don't know what the ethnic situation was in the 1930s as to poker or dice games. Professional card players of most any nationality moved up and down the Missouri, and local sharks circulated among small towns in Iowa, Nebraska, and the Dakotas. A big winner couldn't stay for long in any one place, usually not more than a couple of days; if not waylaid and robbed, he would run out of people who'd risk playing against him. My father didn't come along as a card shark until about 1939 when we were in Sioux City. Poker was neither played nor even mentioned at our family home; it was a business, not something one simply played at. He taught me cribbage, pinocle, and how to play poker professionally, but I didn't make use of the lessons until my years in the Army when earnings from cards were a dependable source of income, supplementing off-base gigs in the murky outskirts of some Alabama or Georgia town—Anniston, Phoenix City, Columbus. On discharge from the army at Fort Benning, I bought a new suit and a new Chevrolet, paying with cash earned mostly at cards, so I could return to California in style. And I credit my father's card skills for my entrance into academic life. In 1945, a year after the move to California, he had enough earnings to buy a large student rooming house just one block from Sather Gate at the University of California, Berkeley (on that site the University Art Museum now stands). Over the few months I lived at home there, I became acquainted with university life, mostly by pretending I was a student and crashing sorority dances. A few years later, I would enroll.

Poker playing is artful and predatory when played at stakes high enough to keep the brain still oxygenated when one's belly is sucked in and stuck there. Poker is not a game of card tricks but of probabilities, facial expressions, eye contact, quick glances, hesitations, well-timed nervous twitches, and big raises with blue chips tossed in the pot as casually as if feeding hogs from the corn wagon when you've detected that your only opponent left with cards in his hand is holding his breath and turning purple. That's why the super professionals can play with only three cards in their hand. A wince at the wrong moment can cost you a pot, and scratching your crotch while contemplating your next bid can lead to a long night's sleep in a trash can. Even at a table of farmers risking their seed-corn money, a timorous shark will have starved to death by morning. Bottom feeders are not poker players but day laborers shoveling dirt at subsistence pay. In a game of four or five equally skilled players, the thinking man with his hands and his guts on the table will come out ahead enough nights a week to make good money.

Men who claim to know how to cheat at poker and brag about their prowess are, as a rule, liars. A skilled card player does not cheat but plays at a higher level than his losing opponents without letting on how skillful he is. My father taught me that when playing against skilled players, most of the men at the table not only know how to cheat but can detect right off if you are cheating. It wouldn't make sense to risk one's life nicking cards or bottom-shuffling when at least one man at the table will catch you out of the corner of his eye where he's put his eye-ball in focus, or feel the nicks, and no player who values his good-looking facial features, as I did, would try using a palm mirror when dealing, or substitute an altered deck when thinking no one is looking. Expert poker players are always looking. It's not like one sees in the movies when the winning hand is four aces or a straight flush—both are as rare as hen's teeth and three-dollar bills. When getting up to go take a leak, one had better walk away from the table with hands open and at one's side, and if a girlfriend is standing admiringly over one's shoulder, she had better not move about the table to look over another player's shoulder, like a Mata Hari carrying out espionage.

Ten years before I was taught to play poker, my teenage tenor sax-playing cousin Harley—Uncle John's son, you recall—was putting groceries on the family table and buying dance tickets, gasoline, and booze from his poker earnings. He'd been taught by the roving shark, Lee Strickland, who preyed on farmers in small rural towns and survived by losing enough times to make trusting people think he was not skillful but simply born under a lucky star. Harley was a risk-taker, but soon enough had found out that a winner loses friends in direct ratio to winning pots. When church leaders admonished the Sioux City police to crack down on gambling, Harley was more mollified by the reform than financially unsettled; by then he was getting paid enough playing dance jobs to make up the loss of poker earnings feeding his lifestyle, though sometimes when on the road, even at age eighteen, he would supplement the band's meager earnings with a few hours of gambling in towns where he wasn't known, didn't need friends, and wasn't about to hang around for post-game festivities in a dark parking lot.

Davie Berman, Sioux City's most famous card gambler, who went on to become one of this country's most infamous bank robbers, East Coast mobster, and hotel and casino owner in Las Vegas, having taken over the Flamingo after Bugsy Siegel was shot, was already a notoriously successful poker player in Sioux City at the age of fifteen. His time was a generation before mine, but his name still lingered in 1940s local lore. His daughter Susan Berman, an accomplished journalist, novelist, and one-time essayist for *New York* magazine and *Cosmopolitan*, came back to Sioux City in 1980 to excavate the history of her father, who'd died in 1957 when she was twelve.[26] All she'd known of him was what he'd been to her over his final years, that in Las Vegas he taught her what to do if kidnapped, built the first shul in town so she could go to Sunday School, hung her portrait over the Flamingo Hotel registration desk, drilled her in arithmetic in the counting room of the casino, took her to floor-show openings, and invited Liberace to play at one of her birthday parties.

Davie Berman was a scrappy Jewish boy of impoverished parents in a North Dakota one-room schoolhouse serving a desolate plow-resisting landscape known to the German farmers surrounding it as the Judendburgers, or Jewish Hills, on which immigrants lived not in romantic, picturesque poverty but in hungry, dirty, shameful poverty. Davie's regular occupation then, other than making high grades in school, was fighting with other North Dakota farm boys who were German and prone to using the word «kike» when referring to a Jew. After his family's sod hut, on an acreage of rocky hillside prairie disdained even by the sheep his father tended, had burned to the ground in 1912, Davie's parents, with children in tow, moved to Sioux City in mid-winter. They were given sanctuary by a rabbi until Davie's father got a job as a cream buyer for the Sioux City Bakery and could afford to rent a small house—at 620 Myrtle Street, just a short walk from the Orthodox synagogue Beth Abraham.

Age nine then, Davie, his two brothers and his sister came up against the usual prejudices. Their run-down clothing and peasant-like living conditions even embarrassed a good many of the city's established Jewish families, as mercilessly bigoted as goyim. Davie was raised on indifference as a means of survival—meaning just doing whatever one has to in order to survive. He went to work as a newsboy to help feed the family, hawking Sioux City newspapers, the *Tribune* and the *Journal*, paying a penny for each copy and selling it for two cents. He tried to succeed at every way a boy can make money—fishing the Sioux River for carp and bringing home sackfuls to be made into gefilte fish, carrying ladies' luggage at the train depot for fifteen cents a bag, operating a refreshment stand at fairs. He tried to land a regular job in any sort of store. But in those days, Jewish boys often weren't hired. At the age of fourteen after five years of struggle—doing well at school yet

125

knowing how few roads were open to him—he confided to his sister Lillian, «I'll make it as a Jew.»

As a newspaper vendor, Davie knew the town. Boyish, endearing, and personable, he also knew many people. Boys hawking newspapers and distributing handbills at the time recall that he was always looking for an angle. It's said that when a Yiddish-speaking boy came on line, the gentile news vendors would teach him how to hawk his papers by yelling, «Read all about it,» but actually, because he didn't understand English, they'd tell him the words were «Son of a bitch» or «Read about the bastards.» When Davie became the leader of the Jewish newsboys, he put an end to that practice. He'd become a protector for all the Jewish kids in town. His daughter says in her memoirs:

> «Once Davie and some other newsboys were in a drugstore drinking sodas. A strapping Iowa farm boy wandered in drunk with a friend. He said in a loud voice, «For a penny, I'll kill a Jew,» glaring at the smaller, obviously Jewish boys. Davie went to the cash register and asked for change for a nickel. Then he plopped a penny down on a counter in front of the boy twice his size and said, «I'm a Jew, take me on.»
>
> «They scrapped on the floor, kicking, biting, and pounding their fists into each other. Soon another farm boy joined in and then the other three newsboys entered the fracas. The two farm boys seemed about to kill their weaker rivals. Suddenly Davie attacked the farm boy furiously and there was blood all over. Davie Berman had a knife. The farm boys ran out; Davie's friends looked at him with awe. He put the knife away and said, 'You've got to use what you have to get by.' He had learned to live on the defensive.»[27]

This story may not be true in every detail. Susan Berman was as much novelist as biographer. At worst it is an example of inverse prejudice, for such stories, though happening in the city, tended to put a farm boy into the cast of characters as the rowdy and ripe-for-a-fight villain. It just couldn't have been a city boy who would have behaved that way toward Davie and his friends. One didn't usually find farm boys in a Sioux City soda fountain, even though by then the soda fountain was a popular place for all ages and types. It was common back then for city-folk to use such expressions as, «Now this big farmer son-of-a-bitch came through the door...» or, «Those burly farm boys, who were used to wrestling bulls and greased pigs, came bustin' in, and....» The standard Western movie promoted this myth of rural men as turbulent and rowdy, all muscle and no brains—brawls in town breaking out when ranch hands ride into town, whooping and hollering, shooting off guns in the air, soon to get roaring drunk and break up the saloon, smashing bottles, mirrors, and chairs over each other's heads, and hauling squealing, leg-thrashing bar-girls over their big broad shoulders to upstairs bedrooms—all that accomplished before having taken a Saturday night bath in a brothel.

Harassing Jews in Sioux City was not a farm boy amusement but a game played by urban urchins and hoodlums. About the time of Davie Berman's fight, a 1903 Sioux City *Tribune* headline proclaimed «Immorality Is Rife, Yet Sioux City Children Are Growing Better.» An optimistic probation officer had announced that, among other efforts, much work was being done to ferret out obscene notes in schools, and that among other recent notable offenses by high school teenagers were only six for persecuting Jews. The remaining 305 misdemeanor arrests were: one for reading dime novels, five for obscene writing, eight for being found in a pool hall, fourteen for drinking liquor, twenty-six for fighting, thirty-six for being in the penny arcade, fifty for immorality, 104 for committing larceny, and 121 for disturbing the peace. An additional 139 girls and 311 boys were simply taken off the street.[28]

By the time of my own transit from Hinton farm boy to small-town Leeds to big-time Sioux City in 1938, the statistics hadn't much changed. As for Davie Berman, by then he'd had robbed several banks, spent a few years in Sing Sing, had a run-in with Al Capone, and could boast an FBI file on him with more pages than my writing might fill in a lifetime. The class poem he wrote at the age of sixteen in the Central High School yearbook remained in Sioux City as a fossil print of a past era. The poem is titled, When 17 Year-Olds Are Has Beens:

Gathered in a spacious chamber
After many years of war,
Fully ten score Castle «has beens»
Were together as of yore.
They were all alumni members,

127

The Dirtfarmer's Son

Called from north, south, west and east,
To attend the anniversary
Of the High Alumni feast.
Everyone was known and famous,
Some gained victory on the field;
Memorial services were held
For those who there were killed.
Former belles are now old women,
Women fat, lean, short, and fair;
While the boys, now grown to manhood,
Some short, or fat, and minus hair.

Chapter 10

*I underwent a metamorphosis
that would pull me out of a
post-farm monochromatic lull*

The move to Sioux City obliged me to negotiate a final transition from farm to small-town to city life. My parents had leased a hefty white wood-frame house at 2216 Douglas Street on the respectable North Side, a block from Grandview Park—the very park where enterprising Davie Berman, when about my age then, rented pillows for people wanting to sleep in the open air on steamy hot August nights, and stood guard while his roomers urinated behind bushes. The park is still famous for its spectacular rose garden and band shell dedicated in 1935, with years of weekly concerts by the American Legion's Monahan Post band. Grandview Park is also the place where a host of people can recall themselves making out on automobile rear seats—a non-patrolled lover's lane where adolescent boys of my generation retrieved spent condoms tossed alongside its curvy moonlit roads. Yes, dating couples in parked cars did the same things they do today.

I entered the fifth grade in Hunt Elementary School on 20th and Jackson and there underwent the metamorphosis that would pull me out of the post-farm monochromatic lull in Leeds and send me down a multi-colored track towards adulthood. I was still a deeply tanned and sun-blond farm boy in overalls and work shoes, bluntly set down in the snobby North Side where people of my lowly class were labeled dumb farmers. But the fresh start I'd made in Leeds, when less equipped at the age of seven to adjust rather than conform, had now become another fresh start in Sioux City at age ten. Physicality was a supporting factor. I'd grown tall for my age—five foot seven, weighing about 150 pounds—was well-built, lean and sinewy, very strong as farm boys tend to be, and was Nordic, an estimable kindred even in a predominantly German and English city.[29]

I don't know and can't say for sure if the prevailing urban attitude towards farmers as half-baked and crude had been augmented in negativity by the farmer's Holiday movement and the violence with which it came to a close five years before we moved to Sioux City. Most urban adults remembered the event. It had brought some hardship to pregnant mothers and children in need of protein—at least that's what the dairies had to say about it, and had made news for journalists and a lively issue for politicians who believed an attack on farmers would give them a bigger share of the urban vote. While the newspapers hadn't turned against the agrarians, no reporter passed up a chance to embellish every act of violence perpetrated by the striking farmers.

In any case, it wouldn't have taken the Milk War or the Farmer's Rebellion to instill in urban people's minds that farmers were cultural and moral hicks, whether Kentucky hillbillies, Arkansas pig-farmers, Kansas wheat-growers, or Iowa corn-pickers, and by nature mentally blunted and violent, like natural beasts. The historian of the American frontier Frederick Jackson Turner, speaking before the American Historical Association in Chicago, said, «A frontier society should hardly be expected to show an intelligent appreciation of the more complex interests of a developed society.» By frontier society, he meant a society of agrarians still rooted in the soil.[30]

Dirty jokes that passed between men and older boys most often involved the dumb farmer and the farmer's daughter. Stories about the sexual exploits of traveling salesmen were built without fail on seductions of dim-witted farm girls, or dumb things done by farmers. A typical joke featured a young farmer whose town barber dispensed condoms (called «rubbers» back then) as barbers typically did, for barber shops were sinful places where one caught up with unpublishable gossip, heard dirty stories, and exchanged pornography—a barber with a good supply of jokes and racy magazines had steady customers. On concluding the haircut, the barber slipped a pack of rubbers into the hayseed's hand, saying, «Wear one of these on your pecker and you won't get diseased.» Compliantly, the farmer put one on as soon as he got back to the farm. And he wore it day and night, rolling it off only when he had to piss or when making out with girls in cornfields or at dances in town. Sure enough, he didn't get diseased.

Farm boys and men were equally caricatured in popular raillery. Even podium jokes by politicians to open speeches often debased farm folk instead of the speaker's wife, back when devaluing one's wife displayed power over her and strengthened bonds among men in groups. I recall a Nebraskan explaining why Iowa State's football team didn't have female cheerleaders. The reason: «Because ya can't stop 'em from grazin' the playing field durin' half-time.» Stories deprecating farmers may be as old as agriculture when put in contrast to urban centers. The 14th-century Italian writer of bawdy tales, Giovanni Boccaccio, tells of a farm-raised bride who returned to her father in tears from her honeymoon, having found that her groom's penis was smaller than her donkey's. Hundreds of other examples out of history can be cited, including, from our era, the country hick Li'l Abner as the leading newspaper comic strip of the 1920s through the forties. Sadie Hawkins in that strip was the husband-lusting, over-the-hill country nymph with an eye on Li'l Abner. Few city people could understand that Sadie Hawkins Day festivities, such as those staged annually by Sioux City's Morningside College—when single men and women dressed up as country hicks with artificially freckled girls chasing country bumpkin boys—were as insulting to the moral sensibilities of farmers as black-face shows to nonwhites. Red Skelton's popular radio character, Clem Kadiddlehopper, a dreary dirt farmer, clumsy in gait and speech, also epitomized the dumb farmer and entertained the entire country's radio and television audiences over the fifties. As late as 1972, the puppeteer Jim Henson, for his *Musicians of Bremen* television special, created a puppet named Lard Pork, a fat, beady-eyed degenerate chicken farmer.

The most popular radio show of the 1940s was ventriloquist Edgar Bergen and his smart dummy Charlie McCarthy. City boy Charlie was well-dressed, squeaky clean and well-groomed, but Bergen's second dummy, Mortimer Snerd, a real dummy, was a farm boy, a dumb farmer with unkempt hair, freckles, and the buck teeth of a gopher or jackass. So widely known was Mortimer Snerd that, in 1946, when President Harry Truman fired Secretary of Commerce Henry Wallace (the Iowa farm scientist who'd previously been Secretary of Agriculture), Edgar Bergen and the dumb farm boy Mortimer Snerd were deployed by *The Chicago Tribune* to ridicule Truman's action. Truman had fired Wallace over a speech he'd given in Madison Square Garden, a speech that had been approved by Truman but soured the president's closest colleagues, who were calling for Wallace's head. Truman's «stupidity» is displayed by dumb farmer Snerd:

> Bergen: *Mortimer, how can you be so stupid?*
>
> Snerd: *Umph, what was the question?*
>
> Bergen: *Why did you fire the man who made the speech after you said you'd liked it?*
>
> Snerd: *Did I fire him? I thought someone fired me!*
>
> Bergen: *Mortimer, you're hopeless.*
>
> Snerd: *What was the question?*
>
> Bergen: *That wasn't a question. It was a statement. You're hopeless.*

What I hadn't realized up until the move to Sioux City was that, though still socially awkward and plain in culture, I was intelligent, not just smart, and as mentally tough as physical. Over the fifth and sixth grades at Hunt School, I was a quick learner and dependable performer when called upon to speak up in class, shy when confronting certain conditions but inversely confident facing up to others; not yet argumentative and brash, just self-assured and self-disciplined. But it wouldn't take long for me to realize that intelligence can be a congenital defect—averages tend to erode extremes. To offset being teased, I lived up to the farm-boy image, took command of the playground and gained respect by reforming bullies and settling even fair fights that occasionally broke out. Impressed by my peacekeeping capabilities, the principal appointed me Captain of the Boy Patrol with a squad of ten boys to heed my commands. We patrol boys wore a cross-band with a big silver badge over a slick, white, knee-length coat; we kept order in hallways and on the playground, turned the stop signs at right angles at street intersections during coming-to-school and going-home hours. I was the one boy the principal could call upon during stormy weather to escort a pupil home who'd taken ill at school—a knight-protector.

And surely, although unknown to the principal, I was the only ten-year-old sixth-grade boy who took a girl on a date. Her name was Lorraine, a sturdy girl with curvy legs; red-haired, lightly freckled, an only child whose pre-school sensuality hadn't phased into sexual latency after age six but had skipped it entirely. Though anything but a tomboy, Lorraine could throw a softball overhand and insisted on competing in pentathlon with the boys. I may have used her as a supplementary backup threat to my well being, saying, «Don't mess with me or I'll sic my girlfriend on you.» If I didn't, I could have.

Lorraine's mother was a divorcé, and in those days when I could already imagine things without witnessing, a divorced woman who wore short skirts, spike heels, and lavish cosmetics, as she did, was an aphrodisiac just to look at—not a woman smartly dressed and made up as if asking for it but one who was getting it. A single mature woman dwelling in an apartment, unless she was a widowed old lady or wore spinster clothing if young, was plain as day a moral sinner, her income suspect and her sex life obviously outside marriage. Just being aware of this—fascinated erotically by Lorraine's mother—meant that I was slipping past childhood.

Lorraine, proud of her emanating breasts, was the only girl in school, she assured me, who wore a brassiere, not to hold up much of anything but to pad the petite rosebuds that put eye-catching points in the front of her blouse. On occasional Saturday afternoons, with her wearing one of her virginal print dresses with a Peter Pan collar and lacy cuffs and hem, we went to the movies and sometimes to the roller-rink where we skated as a pair, my right hand behind her waist, my other hand holding hers in front of us. Bashfulness, rather than any sense of morality, kept me restrained when occasionally after school we were alone at her mother's apartment and she would slip into her mother's silky robe and oriental slippers, put on bright red lipstick, and act grown up, sprawled languorously on the couch like a harem odalisque, sipping not the customary hot chocolate of pubescent courtship but a Dr. Pepper through a pink straw. There was nothing we said to each other at those times that wasn't absurd and silly, and to my recollection no classmate or teacher was exempt from our stinging judgment of their looks, deportment, and manners, born, as we were, into a world of idiots with grotesque faces. Lorraine's propinquity in my life, her upper crust temperament, precocious aptitude, and worldly wit surely helped to negotiate my transition from farm boy to city slicker. By the end of the sixth grade, I knew how to date a girl and cope with lust by monitoring my fickle shyness. In the fifth-grade class photograph taken with our horsy-faced teacher, third from the left in the front row, I'm dressed not in overalls, as five of the nineteen boys are, but in the trousers and vest of a three-piece suit—too hot that day to wear the jacket—and am the only one wearing a necktie. Third in from the left in the second row, one will find my sweet Lorraine.

«You're too smart for your own good,» my mother often said. For a bright kid, certain problematical vectors rush out far ahead of one's stage of comprehension only to turn back and tug one any which way. One risks getting ahead of oneself. «You're too young to understand,» one is told when one asks certain questions. But you hadn't asked because you wanted to understand, not knowing what understanding means, and maybe you weren't even asking because you wanted to know, but only to imbibe the mystery—not hungry but curious. «When you get a little older, you will...»—will what? «You're too young for that kind of thing,» and «Aren't you ever going to grow up?» and «Act your age!» and «Don't you think she is rather a bit too old for you?»

One's psychology develops in the context of denials and contrasts, to be this and not that, while it is less important that you become one or the other than that you don't become what you're not obliged to. So if I was singled out by teachers and fellow pupils in that final year of elementary school, it was simply because I was so noticeable. Being a country boy, I couldn't grow into being a city boy, considering I was already seven when I got to Leeds and ten when I moved to Sioux City. Without experience in city living from the first critical years, I had to do most everything by figuring out how to do it, rather than by social conditioning. I had to fashion my farm boy stuff into a city boy, with all the qualitative aspects of a vigorous hybrid. So when with Lorraine, I was not a ten-year-old ordinary boy but a self-created individual, and there wasn't a damn thing I was too young to do.

Chapter 11

Ye gods and little gold fishes,
what Iowa has done for those
dirty Danish farmers

In Sioux City's elementary schools, as across the state, nationality was at the brim of one's self-consciousness. While today pupils are categorized as white or black or Asian, in the all-white section of Sioux City we were distinguished by the bloodline of our fathers: German, Swedish, English. I don't recall anyone calling him- or herself an American; that designation didn't come about until mid-World War II. Polish derivatives suffered from the tradition of Pollack jokes. And Jewish children were not classified by national blood but by just being Jewish, with a bloodline but no nationality. Many Iowans had their foreign-sounding names changed or anglicized. Heinrichs, such as my father, became Henrys. So common was this practice during the wartime forties, with people wanting to mask their German and Italian names that jokes about name-changes passed around, such as the one about a man named Richard Shit, who appeared before a judge to get a new name.

«Well, with a name like that, I can understand why you wish to change it,» said the benevolent judge. «What would you like to change your name to?»

«John Shit,» responded the man.

I repressed the German half of me. That was easy to do in the 1940s, considering the United States had entered the war in 1941. Germany was our enemy and German the hated language. I was grateful for my Danish surname. Yet, still today, when I think of myself as Danish, a dark Germanic cloud passes over my mind and I think of my mother as being denied.

My maternal grandmother, German to the core, was living with us for a spell during my early teens in Sioux City. A drinking man, her husband, Christopher Steinhagen, had downed a bottle of bad whiskey; half-blinded and in agony, he shot himself. My childhood memory recorded that he'd hung himself from a barn rafter, but that may have been one of my uncles. In any case, I wasn't the only one to think that my grandmother had driven him to the end of the rope. She alternated unwelcome stays among her three daughters. My father had bitter arguments over cards with her, and also over Hitler, whom she called the Kaiser. She insisted that everything negative said about him in the newspapers was wartime propaganda. White-haired and near toothless, she had all the physical aspects of a village witch interred in a wrinkled old skin. On occasion, she would tell of her gift for laying on hands. When she laughed, even over the frailest joke, she cackled; when not gay, she was serene, relaxed, and as silent as a snake. She enjoyed being around children but sometimes put us in conflict with mother's advice, insisting we not brush our teeth because, she said, the plaque protected the tooth enamel from decay. Her incidental wisdom allowed her to take such imprudent liberties. My mother tolerated her, yet, although not betraying it openly, she secretly hated her. This grandmother—the only grandparent I knew and for whom I retain some affection—passed away in 1955, dropped dead on the living room floor at the age of ninety-six, shortly before an entire generation growing old had died around her.

Danes were not entirely exempt from racial prejudice, so I had to add that bias to the dumb farmer syndrome affecting me. Most adults in Sioux City were city-bred Republicans. Many older folks may have harbored resentment for the role Danish farmers had played in unseating Iowa's Republican governor, William Loyd Harding, who was born and raised in Sioux City. That election happened twenty years before I appeared on the set. Harding had verbally attacked Danes, saying they were insular, socially non-integrative, unpatriotic, and dirty. He was referring to Danish-American farmers.

The story behind this conflict was an important aspect of American history. Only in the 1950s, when living in the San Francisco Bay Area, did I come to realize how it might have affected my upbringing. The loyalty oath debacle of the McCarthy era has now dissipated with the aging or death of individuals within that generation. A few of the directly affected survivors remember that outbreak of suspicion and flagrant accusations of people as un-American. But that phase of moral discomfort wasn't the first time this odious malady affected my history. A few years after my parents married in 1912, a statewide ruckus arose over the patriotism of foreign-born Iowans. Many who trumpeted themselves as genuine Americans from colonial stock blamed newly arrived foreign elements for the non-success of the first Liberty Bond drive in 1917. Ill-advised, if not just short on common sense, Governor Harding, a resolute Republican superpatriot, gave in, perhaps gleefully, to the pressure that lobbyists for the Americanization of aliens were putting on the re-election agendas of Washington politicians.[31]

Faithful to his party and inspired by fiery speeches of Teddy Roosevelt, who was stumping the country to reclaim popularity, Harding organized a program to Americanize Iowa's entire population and reinforce his state's commitment to winning the World War in Europe. In May 1918, the year of the Red Scare, when my brother Marius turned six and sister Loretta approached two, Harding issued a proclamation: English must be the only medium of instruction in schools and public speeches; all conversation in public places, on trains and over the telephone, must be in the English language; those who could not speak or understand English were ordered to worship not in churches but in their homes. Harding was aping a national propaganda agenda promoted by the powerful Ohioan Wayne Wheeler. In Washington, Wheeler had set up office, and from there led a lobby that hitched Americanization of the foreign-born onto the fast-moving train of public sentiment toward prohibition. Henry Ford had taken up the same issue in 1914, figuring an assembly line of like components in serial order needed a new type of work force equivalent to military ranks and order: all workers sober, physically fit, and speaking the same language.

Harding's acrimony against the foreign-born, especially Germans and Italians who maintained love and respect for their motherland or fatherland, was fairly widespread across the United States. Almost any incident could set off an explosion of emotion against immigrant Germans. In 1918, at Morningside College in Sioux City (founded by German Methodists), the college president, Alfred Craig, decided to forbid women students to march in a downtown Sioux City parade. He was promptly derided as «Kaiser Craig» and hung in effigy from the college's flagpole. On the chapel's altar, students placed a sign: «Down with autocracy;» another sign reading «*Alles ist Verboten*» (Everything is Forbidden). On April 29th that year, students broke into the college's Conservatory Chapel, took all the German hymnals to the athletic field, tore them up and burned them. And with but one dissenting vote, the student body adopted a resolution asking the College Board to prohibit the use of German in Methodist Episcopal services.[32] The following month, the war fever prevailed in Dakota City where a German lodge was dynamited.

Two months after his proclamation, Harding delivered a July 4th Independence Day speech in which he singled out not Germans but Danes as the chief offenders. He cited Danish settlements in Iowa's Shelby and Audubon counties as examples of what he was trying to protect America from. «Young people of these communities,» he said, «were not getting an American upbringing. When they get through school they are full-grown 100 percent Dane.» As if politically suicidal, he made an even more appalling mistake. He asked his audience to just think for a moment of a man brought from «the filth of Denmark» and placed on a farm for which he paid perhaps three dollars an acre: «Ye gods and little gold fishes, what Iowa has done for him he never can repay.»

That «filth of Denmark» phrase dredged up the old ritornello picturing farmers as dirty. The Des Moines *Register* responded quickly to Harding's speech, condemning it as a know-nothing campaign, an ill-considered diatribe against people of foreign birth. The *Register*'s biting editorial reminded readers that Denmark was a wholesome dairying nation and a model for cleanliness. Nothing is dirty or rotten in Denmark. (Even this year, 1998, when I'm writing this chapter, the Berlin-based *Transparency International*, which rated 85 nations for corruption, cited Denmark as the least corrupt, followed by Finland and Sweden, with the United States as 17th, Russia 79th, and Cameroon the 85th. «What's rotten isn't in Denmark,» was a subhead in the September 23rd, 1998 issue of the Sioux City *Journal*, along with a reminder that on the same date in 1806, the Lewis and Clark expedition returned to St. Louis from the Pacific Northwest.

As for Danish patriotism during World War I, the Des Moines *Register* reported a few days after Harding's blunder that, of 163 men recently drawn from Audubon County for military service, 99 were of Danish extraction against 64 of all other parentage. That grotesque ethnic slur also collapsed a critical post under Harding's political platform, soon to be toppled. Throughout the state, Danes were painfully irritated. Many of Harding's supporters of every nationality distanced themselves from his office. Though relatively few in number, Danes commanded respect for their expert farming and picture-perfect farms. In the 1916 election, Harding had received 55% of the vote from predominantly Danish precincts. Two years later, at re-election time, the vote was less than 7%.

Iowa's Woodbury county, which embraced Sioux City, and adjacent Plymouth county, in which our picture-perfect farm had its place, had fewer Danes than nearby Shelby County and the town of Elk Horn, known as Little Denmark, the largest and most famous ethnic settlement in the state where Danish was the community language and hardly any English was spoken. Elk Horn is the site of the Danish Immigration Museum; my father's name is among those inscribed on the walls. Other counties, too, had Little Denmarks: Kimballton in Audubon County, Ringsted in Emmet County, and Fredsville in Grundy County. The 1915 census indexed about 19,000 Danish-born residents in Iowa, congregated tightly perhaps because their native country is so small and the agrarian population restrained by available acres.[33]

Ignorant of Denmark's history, Harding hadn't realized he was recapitulating the plight Danes had suffered with great land losses in the nineteenth century. At the Congress of Vienna, Denmark was forced to give Norway to Sweden, and in 1864, after the invasion by Prussian and Austrian troops, made to forfeit the duchies of Shleswig and Holstein. With that loss, Denmark had relinquished a third of its territory and much of its pride. Prussian officials forecast Governor Harding's proclamation forbidding the Danish language in schools, churches, courts, and public assemblies. To Germanize the Danish people, who were in the majority, Danish folk dress, stage plays, and music were outlawed. (My Danish grandfather, Mads Vesti Andersen, was fifteen, and my grandmother, Marie Johansen, was nine in 1864 when Germans put Denmark to the rack). Nonetheless, Harding's proclamation couldn't be ignored as the wave of jingoistic war sentiment was stripping the country of racial tolerance. Not wanting to appear unpatriotic, residents of

Danish towns went all out to display loyalty to America. Several young men enlisted during the first weeks of the war. Their departure in April 1917 occasioned celebrations among the Danes in Elk Horn and Kimballton, with American flags waving and the *Star Spangled Banner* repeatedly sung. That year, Elk Horn's citizens voted to build a new public high school devoted exclusively to the English language.

A few foreign-tongue farmers, especially Germans but some Danes too, found their barns splashed with yellow paint, and many others received anonymous hate mail. Protests continued to be bellowed from farmlands and towns across the state, especially by the Norwegians, Swedes, and Dutch; the Germans and Austrians were not in a position to complain. The governor's proclamation had cut much deeper than nationalities and languages to expose raw nerves and enervate muscle power that Harding hadn't anticipated. Not all the old-stock Iowans were impressed with Harding's politicizing of nationalities. He'd mistaken his governor's seat for a seat of personal might. In Iowa back then, real power was not with politicians but with the formidable Gardner Cowles, owner since 1903 of the Des Moines *Register*, with whom Harding had recklessly feuded on a personal level. Most local newspapers took their editorial contents from the *Register*, the dominant voice of Progressive Republicanism in the state, and few politicians dared veer from the prevailing demeanor of the press.

The *Register*'s editorials elicited many letters duly published as public opinion. Some writers connected Harding to the hated Kaiser. One letter hit the target that public sentiment had pasted on Harding's chest: an outraged small-towner, Peder Sorensen Vig, having rejected a name change to Peter Sorenson, said it would never occur to him that the use of Danish language, in public or private, was contrary to the Oath of Allegiance. «Patriotism and loyalty,» he wrote, «are not matters of the lip but of the heart, otherwise, according to Harding's logic, a parrot might be patriotic and a stammerer dying for his country on a battlefield would be a filthy slacker. The governor knows there are many Danes in Iowa, that they speak Danish and are not ashamed of it. And why should they be? It's no fault of theirs that they were born in Denmark. A person may be born Danish and still be a good American citizen, and a dog may be born in America and still be a dog. Language in itself is neither loyal nor disloyal. It's the use of language that counts.»[34]

This same year the state legislature passed the most stringent criminal syndicalist law in the nation, providing a twenty-year jail sentence for the conviction of any person who by word of mouth or in writing advocated sabotage or violence against the government or any industry when attempting to accomplish industrial or political reform. No major test of this law came until 1938, when I was ten: a senator named William Sentner was charged with inciting violence during the so-called Maytag strike that year, but his conviction was overturned by a higher court. By then, Harding's extreme antics were ridiculed in the national press, especially after news reached Eastern papers that five German-American farmwives had been arrested for talking German over their party line.[35]

I don't know how my father reacted towards the proclamation. He must have been gravely provoked. I recall an older sister, probably Loretta, saying that he didn't wish to be taken as unpatriotic, that where he was born should not matter, considering that every original non-Indian American was a foreigner from somewhere or another. He must have gained a fair mastery of English by the time he encountered my mother, for she spoke English and German but not Danish. His English was thick and from the back of the throat, like the Danish tongue, but not tinged with noticeable accent, and my mother's smooth English wouldn't betray that she also spoke German. The proclamation must have put my father on caution, however, for he made no effort to teach his children Danish, nor did our mother want us to speak German. In fact, she never spoke of her childhood, partly because she was German but also because she'd had a crude and miserable upbringing; not until leaving home with my father at her side could she wear other than overalls and plow shoes. I know nothing more than fragments about her past.

Chapter 12

*I became aware of the female
essence, that among women were
not just secrets but a secret life*

At age eleven in a family house full of furniture and people on Douglas Street by Grandview Park, I felt like a solitary boy embedded within a bundle of girls, a single Jack in a playing-card pack of age-numbered Queens—five sisters, ages eighteen, sixteen, eight, six, and three. The sixteen-year-old attended Central High School; so most of her social life happened out of my range. Eight-year-old Alice was still in elementary school. She was the only short one, very pretty with silvery blond hair and light blue eyes, pale as an angel but her lips and cheeks were full and naturally pink, and she still had her baby teeth. I'd put out the word throughout the Hunt School zone that she wasn't ever to be teased or mistreated. Little brother Harold was just seven, too young to relate to. The youngest of us shared beds, and the entire family made use of a single bathroom. So there was hardly a good night's sleep or moment of silence in that house. But I don't recall perilous outbreaks of fighting that might have threatened total war. Our mother was a strict and impartial referee, and arguments were put to bed before our bedtime.

I have often thought that I was defined within a context of sisters. This awareness probably dated from this year when the two still-at-home sisters, Fern and Esther, were blooming as adult-like girls and dating young men. Their manners and objects of allurement, which maturing girls deploy to enact their rituals of display and seduction—lingerie, hair brushes, perm-irons, perfume vials, face-powder compacts, lipstick tubes—set them apart from my juvenile world ornamented with fighter plane models, arrow heads, starfish, and crinoid fossils from limestone quarries—not entirely innocuous or innocent accoutrements. The girls

143

spent most of their home hours fussing with themselves. They had their own bedroom sets and mirror-topped vanities painted personal colors, and curtains they'd made for their windows—a normal transition from being single girls to married women. They had their pulp-novels, locked diaries, and fashion magazines, while I had my adventure books, scrapbooks, and notebooks in which I'd begun writing essays directed towards altering the world, for I would be a man of action, not to be molded by life but to define it. I had begun to think of these sisters as I imagined how boys they dated experienced them. Just by sniffing their bedroom air, contemplating objects on their dressing tables, sneaking a peek at their underwear in drawers, I became aware of the female essence, and that among women were not just secrets but a secret life, that my own secrets had no place with those sisters and no place in the house, the house being a girl's natural environment, her congenital territory, wherein she learns the truths about women's lives she has not yet lived. A boy must get out of the house, away from mother and sisters to find manliness or else stultify as a sissy. Boys and men belong in barns and garages. There were times in Sioux City when I wished that I dwelled in a hermit's cave where I could be alone with myself. I'd dug a cave in a vacant lot behind and out of sight of the house, but on flat ground with a wood-plank and sod-covered roof, so it was more like a grave than an abode, though I don't recall any notion of entombing myself. Just sinking into the earth was at times far enough removed from house and family.

In mid-September of 1940, school started at North Junior High where, on entering seventh grade, I was again at the bottom rung. And the move up the three-year ladder was to be made without my companion Lorraine. She didn't show up at school that September so I had to assume that during the summer her mother had moved away from Sioux City.

Except for summer months at one or the other of my uncles' farms, I'd been off the farm for six years. It had taken five of those years to adjust my manners to city life. At least in retrospect it would appear that it did. Most likely I repressed the first junior high year, now remembering next to nothing about it, only about activities outside of school—always work, never anything like the Cub or Boy Scouts. I made As on every test in school and had such an incredible memory that my homework assignments were completed over the homeroom hour, so for a couple of after-school hours three days a week, I did odd jobs, such as delivering a distributor's supplies to shoe repair shops and selling magazines door-to-door—*Redbook*, *Cosmopolitan*, *Ladies Home Journal*—which gave me plenty of practice talking to adult women. This left little time for myself, with the new winter darkness coming on an hour or two after getting out of school. During the school months, on every Sunday morning, I helped my father clean up the Saturday night mess in his saloon, pocketing coins I found under booths, suspecting at times that he seeded the floor with enough nickels and dimes to keep me enthusiastically employed, like one chums for fish.

My absence from the neighborhood lessened occasions for making friends, but I preferred loneliness to wasting time with others. I didn't need the presence of companions, or to be known intimately, and that hasn't changed, even though over the rest if my life I enjoyed many friendships. But as a child, anyone who got too close to me felt like an intruder; any implication of dependence was distasteful, suggesting that I couldn't stand alone. I remember only two boys my age in the neighborhood, but I spent hardly any time with either of them. Across the street lived one with the strangest name, Efram Everett Wallace, Jr., a tall gangly kid with excessive arm and leg lengths, whose father was a banana import agent and whose mother was British and very proper. Efram was mercilessly teased at school, not just for his name, which was cause enough, but over the knickers his mother obliged him to wear, knickers having gone out of fashion by the end of the 1930s except in Chicago where mobsters still wore them. Because he was my close neighbor, or maybe because I felt sorry for him, I intervened on the playground and along the sidewalk on the way to and from school to protect him from taunting boys.

I stopped by Efram Everett's house one afternoon to take up this matter with his mother. She was gracious and willing to hear me out as I told her of the tribulations her son was suffering. «Well, what should Efram wear?» she asked at last. «What I wear,» I think I said. «Denim or corduroy trousers, and he should not be called Junior and not Efram Everett but Effy.» So the following Monday, Effy showed up at school in brand new denim trousers and white tennis shoes, looking somewhat like a regular boy. But he remained an insufferable sissy so we had nothing in common. Nor had I anything in common with the other boy my age across the street and his passion for ugly snapping turtles he trapped along Perry Creek and kept in his backyard in a board-fenced mud puddle.

W hen school let out in early June 1942, I needed a paying job for the summer. My father had one lined up for me: selling two- to six-day-old chicks at Jack Boothe's chicken store on upper 4th Street near the Heidel-Brau brewery. The job lasted less than half the four-week baby chick season. I was doing admirably as a salesman. Customers liked me. I always gave them a few more chicks than they were paying for, knowing that a few would die before feathering out. Most of each day I was alone in the place while Boothe spent hours on end carousing in beer parlors nearby, including my father's down at the other end of the street. He was an indifferent man, with no feelings for animal life. He would pluck baby chicks with diarrhea, a fatal self-poisoning condition symptomized by half-closed eyes and disinterest in eating, out of the flat wire trays. He'd cradle their necks between the first two fingers of his hand, with his thumbnail sever their neck vertebrae and in the same motion toss them into a trash barrel. He was an inept mercy-killer, so when he was away, I'd reach down in the can to finish off chicks that were still suffering.

One afternoon when Boothe happened to be at the store, a lady came in with her heart set on purchasing three-day-old Buff Orphington chicks. I told her we were woefully out of them and suggested another variety. «But they're my favorites,» she wailed. «I adore their color.» Boothe overheard the dialogue. He came out of the back room in a huff and said to me sharply, «What do you mean we are out of Buff Orphingtons?» He guided the lady to a rack of yellow-ochre colored chicks. I stepped up and said to his face more forcefully than a sensible boy should have, «Those are Rhode Island Reds!» Boothe snapped back, saying to the lady: «This kid doesn't know a damn thing about chickens.» Slick salesman as he was, he sold the lady the bogus chicks. After boxing them up and taking them out to her car, he bawled me out for having almost lost a sale.

«But in a couple of weeks,» I retorted too firmly, «when their yellow fuzz is gone, those chicks will come out with red feathers.» I was fired on the spot. I went to tell my father what had happened, why I was thrown out. I thought he would be proud of me, would acknowledge my chivalrous integrity. But he did not seem proud of me. He was amused, saying with a smile at my sacrifice of a job for honesty, «The only difference between those chickens is their color. They all taste the same.»

I had long ago forgotten about this incident, had chalked it up as just another bad rap—boyhood innocence against adult jadedness when money is involved. But in the spring of 1961, twenty years after that baby chicken debacle, when coming to the end of my graduate studies in art history at Columbia University, it so happened that Frank Loyd, owner of the prominent Marlborough Gallery in London, was laying plans to open a branch gallery in New York City. He was looking for a director. One of the major New York artists he had secured under contract was Robert Motherwell, with whom I had an acquaintance. Motherwell proposed me for the position. Painter Mark Rothko and sculptor David Smith, both of whom I'd met in the mid-1950s, would also be in his stable, so Marlborough promised to be the top gallery for avant-garde art in New York. That I was still a student didn't figure in this case, because unlike graduate students who come directly from being undergraduates, I was older and had plenty of background behind me. Professor Rudolf Wittkower, the Department Head at Columbia and one of Loyd's advisors, was also backing me. He and Motherwell met with Loyd. Shortly thereafter, I received a call from Loyd asking that I come to see him. I did. His office was in a spacious gallery about ready to open on 57th Street off Madison Avenue.

Loyd put me through an interrogation to test my knowledge of art from various periods, to hear how I would go about selling whatever he showed me in photographs. I was doing fine with one item after another. Loyd seemed impressed. That is, until he handed me a photo of a Rembrandt painting, saying, «How would you go about selling this Rembrandt?» I looked it over, and was about to respond when suddenly I felt something wrong. I kept looking hard at the photo while Loyd prodded me for a response. Finally I said, «I don't believe this picture is by Rembrandt.»

«Of course it's a Rembrandt.»

«I'm sorry, Mr. Loyd, I don't think it's by Rembrandt.»

«Then who is it by?»

«I think it's by Jan Lievens.»

Loyd kept his eyes fixed on me, then said, «All right. Now tell me how you would sell it as a Rembrandt?»

«I wouldn't.»

And Loyd said, «Then you are not interested in selling pictures.»

That ended the interview. On departing, knowing I had let down Motherwell and Wittkower, had wasted their support, not knowing how I would explain to them what had happened, knowing I couldn't tell them much of anything because they were partial to Marlborough Gallery, though not part of what I had just experienced, the vision of chicken-dealer Boothe came into my mind, displacing Loyd. I saw Boothe laying into me for not selling that lady a hundred Rhode Island Reds as Buff Orphingtons, firing me for being honest, and now Loyd tossing me out because I would refuse to sell a Lievens as a Rembrandt. That small act of honesty cost me a chance at a lucrative post-graduate career starting from the top. And I could not tell a soul about it. David McKee, now the owner of a New York gallery on Madison Avenue, was given the directorship. He too had been grilled with photographs, but it's unlikely he could have told the difference between a Rembrandt and a Lievens, not having undergone the same training I'd had under the Dutch expert, Horst Gerson, and perhaps not the same eye for Old Masters. When I spoke of the incident with McKee a few years later, after he had opened his gallery, and when Frank Loyd and Marlborough Gallery were on trial for defrauding the Mark Rothko estate, he did not recall being interrogated on that item.

Chapter 13

She'd been my brother's girlfriend before taking up with my father

When I came to my father's saloon the Sunday morning after being fired by Boothe, he was washing up beer glasses and relieved that I'd arrived to sweep the floor, clean cigar-butt ashtrays and Bull Durham-sprayed spittoons, so he could go upstairs and sleep off the lateness of his Saturday night. I was semi-conscious of the fact that he was sleeping up there with Leona. He was fifty-five then. Leona was in her late thirties. She'd been my brother Marius' girlfriend before taking up with my father.

While we lived in Leeds, Marius roomed in the Pearl Street zone of downtown Sioux City. There he met a woman in a bar named Eileen Hicks, a dark-haired, shapely divorcée; they married about the time the remnants of our family moved to Sioux City, but were divorced shortly thereafter. Marius then took up with Leona, having met her at my father's saloon. On occasions, Marius was my father's evening bouncer. Whenever a problem arose in the bar or upstairs Marius would straighten things out. His gigantic presence was all it took to get the kinks out of any man who'd gotten plastered and out of line. If the man wouldn't settle down, Marius would just pick him up, carry him down the street a ways, and dump him in front of another saloon.

When Eileen, a better-looking woman, came back into Marius' life, he sloughed off Leona. My father took Leona's side, and soon took her in entirely. A fistfight over Leona broke out at some point between Marius and my father. Marius is no longer living, so I can't get to the details, and my older sisters have repressed the incident or had no clearer picture of it at the time than I did. While I recall only that my father had an arm in a sling for a few weeks, my sisters recall his bloodied and bruised face, and that in the struggle his arm had been broken.

Life had not dealt Leona a playable hand. Starkly white-skinned, fleshy, and sagging, she probably hadn't had a day in the sun since childhood, but she was good-looking and sexy, crude in manners and speech but warm at heart and loyal to my father. I knew nothing of her background other than that she'd managed to keep herself afloat as barmaid, having found as a teenager how to win approval in alternative ways. She'd had to sacrifice too much of her life to life, had been married and had a boy my age in a boarding school who was feeble-minded, and also a daughter living with a former husband. Maybe I substituted for the failed boy at times, and maybe in my mind Leona at least partially stood in for my mother, who wasn't much help to me; with so many children among whom to distribute affection, meals, clothes washing, birthday and Christmas gifts, and determined to treat them equally, she didn't treat any one of us very special. Her font of affection was always full but she didn't waste it on decorative displays once a child could stand on his own two feet.

Leona was my father's day-to-day partner, filling out for him what a wife with a house full of children could no longer provide. She lived upstairs and kept the girls and the customers in line to make sure there were no girls getting hurt or doing side-line whoring, for they would fight like polecats over special customers. They didn't get paid except what my father gave them, but got tips that Leona made them share all around. And they had to stay decent and clean-looking and give the men a good time dancing to the gramophone in the parlor, playing strip poker, or just horsing around with them. Leona kept track of the girls' personal boyfriends so there wouldn't be any beatings over jealousies or men going upstairs at all hours of the night. Air Force servicemen from Sioux City's military airbase were not allowed in the place because my father didn't want military police coming to make inspections.

Later in life, I connected my mother's general state of depression, and the migraine headaches that put her to bed for days, with knowing she'd been reduced to being a brood-hen, a reliable stable mate but not a man's daily companion. On the farm they'd shared every aspect of life, back when their days of post-marriage dating and dancing were not yet over. But my mother would have no share of the saloon in either Leeds or Sioux City. I don't recall her ever going to either place. Her contact with my father was limited to his slipping into bed at two or three in the morning, and to occasional Sunday visits to relatives or family picnics and swims at Brown's Lake or Riverside Park on the Big Sioux River. In his times of delight and gentleness, he was as lively and fun a father as any child could wish for.

When the saloon was sold in 1943, no business would keep my father and Leona together. In spite of their closeness, and determined to be a good man, my father's priority was to keep his family intact. After he'd gone out to California with Leona following, he split from her, maybe for the sake of the family, or maybe his libido was on the wane and Leona too was wearing down. Whatever brought about the rupture, Leona would soon escape from memory and fall in love with an adoring Italian deep sea fisherman from Martinez in the upper Bay Area near Vallejo, marry him, and settle down in a tiny house in the Rollingwood section of Richmond, just a stone's throw from where my parents and the younger children would live as a family again. From the day my mother arrived out there in 1944, her farm-type partnership with my father was renewed. Again equals, as they had been when daily life didn't segregate domesticity from income-producing labor, they lived together in close harmony, sharing pleasure in radio programs— Bob Hope, Fibber McGee and Molly, Edgar Bergen, Major Bowe's Amateur Hour—and the birth of grandchildren.

Every boy growing up should have a Leona in his early life, like Jesus had Mary Magdalene. Leona-types are mysterious, like sibylline women put on this earth to be thought about and puzzled over. She offered a wisdom of mortality that a mother can't give, for a growing boy needs to grow away from his mother, like offshoots of trailing vines that either root a good distance from the mother or suffocate under her foliage. Leona was the only mature woman available to talk to when I was too young to confront myself personally, to fathom my need to know more about life than what barroom chores, catechism, and ordinary schooling was teaching me. After the brief fling with Marius, Leona had no one over the Sioux City years but my father, and I was the only one of his children, other than Marius, who came to the saloon. Often on Sunday afternoons, after I'd finished my saloon-cleaning chores, she would descend from the upstairs, draw two short beers for us, sit with me at the bar drinking, and ask how my life was going, how things were at school, causing this essentially shy boy to blush when, with her pale wide-apart eyes looking straight at me, she'd ask how I was making out with girls.

Leona always looked like she'd just gotten out of bed. She would brush her hair flat and put on lipstick but still look puffy-eyed and slumberous. On most occasions when I saw her on Sundays, she hadn't gotten out of her knobby pink chenille robe. She'd settle on a bar stool like a perched bird with splayed elbows supporting a short-necked head, fumble in a little beaded drawstring bag and extract a crumpled pack of cigarettes, pull out a wrinkled smoke, stroke it smooth and stick it between her red lips, then light up with a wood match scratched expertly on the bar stool's underside, like poker players do under tables while keeping their eyes on the game. That vision of her is etched on my brain.

«You have a girlfriend yet?» She would always ask me that. And on one occasion when she did, when again I hesitated, she said, «Don't tell me because I don't want to know. I'm tired of being a girl. I want be a man for a while. And if I were one, I'd stay away from women. That's what I'm telling you. That's what I'd do.»

On some of those winter Sunday afternoons, she'd take me to a movie, always a cowboy film: Tex Ritter, Tom Mix, Buck Jones, Gene Autry, with Loony-Toon comedy shorts and RKO Pathé news of the war. Leona would dress to go out as if going on a proper date, her face made up with white powder and rouge, her hair shiny. She'd squeeze herself into her usual wool dress that made her torso look sort of like it was suffocating, and then layer on her balding mink coat with furry collar that I suspect was mostly dyed squirrel hair. In her unsnapped black galoshes, almost as high as her knees, her large black hat at a rakish angle and her white face puffed out like goose flesh, she would march me down Fourth Street, her cosmetics perfuming the gray sorrowful air as we walked without saying much of anything. I wasn't around over summers, so it would always be a winter day when we took in a movie; by time it let out, the sun would be low in the sky, the sidewalk slushy and gritty where icy paving had been sprinkled with crushed cinders. Hardly anyone would be walking the downtown streets at that hour on a Sunday. An empty streetcar might clamber by and make spine-tingling squeals as its iron wheels turned onto Jackson Street. A few cars might pass, going clankety-clank with tire chains, probably coming back to town from the country over icy mud roads.

The Orpheum was a big gaudy theater left over from Sioux City's glorious past. The plaster decorations all over the inside that had been gold-leafed were painted a rusty yellow and the red velvet walls, whenever the lights came on between features, were browned, streaked, and waffled by rainwater leaks and patches where the ancient cloth had been removed and the old plaster painted but the color not matched. The big stage was still wreathed in plaster roses and scrolls like a picture frame, with little cherubs and horse heads and other shapes that could hardly be made out when everything blended in the same color range. The red velvet curtain had been drawn shut years ago when highly cultured people moved west. In front of it, where conductors of orchestras once stood on a little platform and soloists were spotlighted and actors bowed to a full house, hung the biggest movie screen in Woodbury County.

At the candy counter Leona would buy some «lunch», she called it. Two large bags of double-buttered popcorn, two boxes of Dum-Dums and a giant cherry coke with two straws, was the usual fare. Then we'd climb cat-eyed to the top row of the balcony where there wouldn't be anybody to tell us to shut up. Up there the seats smelled oily and creaked like old leather saddles. We'd divide up our lunch, using seats on each side of us for side-tables, and would hardly get into our popcorn bags before some wicked masked men had held up a stage or shot a few ranch hands while rustling their cattle. When I reflect on those movie sessions, sitting in near-vacant darkness with Leona smelling like a damp flower garden, I feel erotic. Whether true or not, I want to believe that the double features she usually selected were of a cowboy film followed by a blue movie featuring show girls with plenty of dressing room undressing scenes—and that she understood why I kept my jacket draped over my lap.

I've tried off and on to recover the full context of a date with Leona, and am able to reconstruct one that is perhaps no less accurate than if I had experienced it last week. After the cowboy film was over, the war news came on. General McArthur was meeting on a battleship with an admiral after the Marines had landed on some Pacific island to kill Japs, but I couldn't follow the story because Leona was getting herself reorganized and saying over and over it was urgent she had to go to the bathroom. She got up and folded her coat and brushed popcorn off her lap and off the seat, then all at once sat down again and said she'd wait until the second feature started so as not to miss the beginning of it. While President Roosevelt was saying something about London being bombed by the Nazis, Leona asked me which cowboy I liked best, Buck Jones, Tom Mix, or Tex Ritter. She didn't wait for me to answer, but said that Buck Jones was the nicest looking and gentlest but Tom Mix was more manly and Tex Ritter was...

«No! No-oo! Will you look at that!» She interrupted herself. «Right...in..the...water!»

On the screen a fighter plane had been shot down and was burning as it crashed into the English Channel. I couldn't make out over Leona's disjointed voice if it was a good guy's or a bad guy's airplane. She went on telling about how it was that the good cowboy always shaves and dresses up smartly but never gets married, even though in every movie there's a beautiful girl who falls madly in love with him and would marry him if he would just settle down and buy a ranch or something.

«Kid, have you ever wondered why the good guys always ride off at the end of the movie?»

«Probably it's because they have to make another story,» I said. «That's why they never get killed or even hurt in a fistfight or shoot-out. They couldn't show up in the next movie married or with a black eye or dead.»

«Yeah, you're right on that score. You can't keep a good man down to one story. That's what I always said. The bad ones hang around, the good ones get away. Hey, Kid—»

«Yeah?»

For a moment she held up talking as she stared at a news clip about an earthquake in Guatemala. Then she asked, «D'ya know why good guys like Tom Mix and Buck Jones ride stallions?»

«Maybe.»

«Well, you know what a stallion is, don't you?»

«Course I do.»

But Leona told me anyway, in words that shouldn't be spoken but whispered, because she was thinking, not listening: «It's a male horse that hasn't been castrated.»

«Cripes! I know that Leona. I'm a farm boy, remember?»

«You know why?» Leona asked again.

«Why what?»

«Well, think for a minute.» Then she leaned close and whispered in my ear even though there wasn't a soul but us left on the balcony. «Stallions are loners and you can't keep 'em around other horses because their sexual urges are so strong—that's why male animals have to be castrated. You can't have stallions and boars and bulls runnin' around loose. That's why human people get married. Did'ya know that?»

«Know what?»

«Like I just said...», her voice now a loud whisper. She leaned away and looked back at me like I was ignorant. «It's to keep the men from runnin' around loose. You can't just castrate 'em or there wouldn't be any kids. Get it?» Then she relaxed back in her seat.

The Loony Toon was now playing but Leona had gotten herself lost in thought again. Before the cartoon was even over, she went down to the ladies' room. That gave me a chance to stretch my arms and legs and get resettled before she got back. The second feature had already started. Leona was again cloudy with cologne and she'd bought chewing gum. She offered me a piece, wanted to know what was playing. I told her «Back-stage Life»—about a small-town girl who'd gone to Hollywood to be a singer and dancer but was down on her luck and had just got herself stuck in a burlesque road show in a Can-Can line.

«That's a good place to start,» Leona said, and crackled her chewing gum a couple of times before evicting a husky wheezing laugh. «Gotta start someplace.»

But as the story went along and because of the girl's good looks and long curvy shape, she got picked to replace a strip-tease queen who'd run out on the show. The girl was a long way off from wanting to be a stripper, so in the boss' office, when the flashily dressed boss handed her a bird of paradise fan and told her she'd been picked to replace the queen and that she was to do a strip right there in front of him so he could look her over and give her some pointers, the girl refused and got herself slapped around and threatened with a whip that the boss lashed against a chair a couple of times to show her what it'd feel like. Then she started to strip—cringing and sobbing and hating every minute of it—and just when she was almost naked the good guy busted into the room and grabbed the boss by the neck and snatched the whip out of his hand to save the girl—Leona at that exact minute said, «Let's not stay for this one! This is not the kind of movie a boy your age wants to see.»

Leona gathered up her coat in one jerky sweep and without taking another look at the screen grabbed my hand and marched to the stairs with me following like a colt just broken to halter. In the lobby I shook loose and ducked into the toilet. On re-emerging, Leona was outside under the marquee gazing at posters of coming attractions. In the slanted afternoon light, her pale face looked like a soap carving, and down from it her whole body hung like a big dangling lump of fur. As I came up to her, she murmured, «Maybe we'll go to another movie-show next week.» We walked to the corner. Deciding I'd best go home, I said goodbye, turned back and headed up Jackson, the brittle air searing and howling through the streets, yellow light from swaying streetlights bouncing off snow-covered cars. I figured I'd grab a streetcar if one came along, but the town appeared so vacant that more likely I'd be most of the way home before that happened.

Chapter 14

*My pale blue eyes got
seared by the harsh sun and
invaded by hay dust*

Often when I had a school day off, I would ride along with my truck driver brother, Marius, because it was the only way I could see much of the world beyond streetcar lines. His truck loaded with crates of bottled beer, the kegs and barrels in an insulated compartment with ice blocks, he would make deliveries to saloons in a half dozen towns. While I unloaded the crates and loaded on empties, he would drink with the customers or shoot pool. Only when it came to the barrels would he lift a finger. Kegs I could lift, but not full barrels.

Other than those day trips I hadn't traveled anywhere. But I'd read *Around the World in Eighty Days*, *A Tale of Two Cities*, *The Golden Fleece and the Heroes Who Lived Before Achilles*, Robert Browning and Robert Frost poems, Jack London's *The Call of the Wild* and *White Fang*, Poe's *Raven*, Melville's *Moby Dick*, stories by Kipling, *Huckleberry Finn*, *The Arabian Nights*, *War and Peace*, a hundred *National Geographics*, most *Life* magazines, *Reader's Digests*, *Field and Streams*, and every comic and Big-Little book from Flash Gordon to Buck Rogers to Orphan Annie. I'd read just about every book and magazine worth reading in the school library and half the *Encyclopedia Britannica*. I'd read every billboard and Burma Shave sign that passed by a car or truck window in which I was riding, every label on every box and bottle in every toilet I'd ever sat in, even the Sears and Roebuck and Montgomery Ward catalogs, page by page, in the outhouses on our farm and when visiting uncles. But for all that reading and knowing, I'd never gone anywhere much beyond Sioux City except in a beer truck.

I had turned thirteen but looked a bit older and had no trouble saying I was sixteen, which got me a job on Saturdays and alternate Sundays as a stable boy at an equine club where Sioux City's gentry boarded horses, rode at hunt, and jumped fences in an outdoor arena wearing equestrian attire. The club, Sunset Stables, was a couple miles out of town on Stone Park Road. By then I had a bicycle for getting around, a bright red Schwinn with white-walled tubular tires, and a battery-powered horn and headlight, a timely gift from my father. When snow and ice on the road kept me without wheels, I flagged down friendly cars for a lift.

The horses at Sunset Stable were not the sort to which I was accustomed, not big brawny harness horses but slender, long-legged sleek hunters and jumpers with refined heads and attitudes. My experience in riding had been sparse and confined to plodding along bareback atop work horses and an occasional hell-bent-for-leather race atop a Shetland pony my cousins on my mother's side, Eldo and Everett Bollmeyer, owned, a creature put on this earth to run flat out, halt stiff-legged and toss kids onto the ground, breaking their bones. My cousins won a lot of races with their pony at the county fair—both cousins still living, still farming, and able to walk. That pony had bitten into enough human shoulders and thighs to be re-classified as a carnivore.

I worked at Sunset Stables as many weekend hours as I could throughout a hard cold winter, taught myself to mount those elite horses, to ride seated in an English saddle and guide a horse with ball-headed spurs touching at the belly. It wasn't my job to ride, but rather to feed, brush and bathe the horses, to clean their straw-bedded stalls and to saddle and bridle them for the ladies. But a few of the club members asked me to exercise their mounts at the outside arena to keep them in shape. They didn't often ride in cold weather; so much of the winter would pass with horses languishing in stalls. Any horse regularly fed protein-rich alfalfa and high-energy oats goes quickly out of its mind when confined to a box stall and not exercised, like people on endless rainy days who succumb to cabin fever.

In retrospect, I valued less my experience with the horses than the interaction with a set of society I'd previously known only by having met Lorraine's mother: the aristocratic, cultivated, and rich. Male members of the club were doctors and lawyers and business executives.

Female members were the kind of women who marry that kind of man: attractive, slim, having been raised to take special interest in style and etiquette. Though just a humble groom and stall cleaner, I was treated with respect. Still, being so distinctly differentiated as a stable boy and objectified as such, I did not exist in those people's minds as a distinct person, was not of their world, and could share nothing with them but horse care. I came to know before long that a young girl's horse-craziness, before it metamorphoses at age fifteen or sixteen into boy-craziness, can reflexively re-emerge when a mature woman rides spreadlegged atop a pulsating leather saddle on a spirited horse at a fast trot. I was not as innocent as my eyes may have looked in theirs. On more than one occasion, I was flirted with unmercifully, to a point of shaky knees and hyper-ventilation, by a grown woman who found herself alone with me in the barn after she'd come in from a ride, who looked upon me as a real live boy to be toyed with. I still puzzle over what thoughts they had afterwards, if I was a picture in their minds when under the laboring bodies of husbands. History cannot record the whole truths of such intimacies.

W orking with horses aroused my nostalgia for farm life. After completing the eighth grade in June 1942, I was about to turn fourteen, old enough to hire out as a farmhand rather than take some stockroom or bicycle-delivery job. My father was sympathetic to the thought that I spend the summer working on my Uncle Gifford's farm near Brunsville, a few miles north of Sioux City. Hiring out was a respectable thing to do back then, at least for members of my social class.

Uncle Gifford was a decent and hard-working man. English-blooded but American-born, his ancestry on the sire line dated way back to the mid-eighteenth century when an indentured servant, John Sawin, was imported from London aboard the Neptune to serve out his bondage in Watertown, Massachusetts. As a freeman after 1751, John Sawin worked as a shoemaker. After aging, he committed suicide in 1790. How his genes made the trip to the late nineteenth century and thus to the farm I was standing on, I haven't the faintest idea.

Uncle Gifford was forty-eight the summer I worked for him—a lean and sinewy man, with chisel-cut features, darkly tanned, leathery skin, tightly wrinkled after years under the sky. His wife, Bertha, then thirty-nine, was my mother's sister, and like my mother, fleshy-featured with a goitrous neck. A strong-willed woman, her bones, she said, could predict storms, and she could feel thunder an hour before hearing it.

Three children completed the Gifford household. The older daughter, Corletta, whose seesaw hips and lilac-talced angel face and cherub lips still haunt me, wasn't around much. She worked in town as a housemaid. Later that year, two months pregnant, she married a young farmer, Raymond Faust. Clara Ellen at fifteen was a year older than me. Chester was eight, short and pudgy. I can't remember much about either of them, although saucy Clara Ellen's maturing body must have captured my thoughts and imagination. I recall one evening when I was sitting on the porch's swing-seat in front of an open bedroom window, secretly listening to her and a sleeping-over girlfriend, their bed next to the window. They became aware of me out there, got to giggling, and one or the other of them reached through the raised sash, took a grip on my arm, and drew it back through the window. I was old enough not to resist. My hand was pressed to a naked breast, more developed than my sweet Lorraine's, then rudely pushed back out as the window sash came down with a bang, followed by a pulled-down shade.

The Gifford house was a typically white clapboard balloon-frame structure with a front porch that was never used and a screened porch on the kitchen-entrance side furnished with a few chairs and a cot for outdoor sleeping. The grassy yard surrounding the house was ornamented with dandelions and white clover; in the back, near the chicken yard, was a rhubarb border and a scattering of peonies, day lilies, and Dutch irises; off to the side of the screened porch, a tub of petunias; further away, some low evergreens. A gravel path to the door was edged with bricks, long ago painted white.

The farm was only an eighty-acre spread—about as small as the least farmstead in Iowa—and too hilly for cash crops. The livestock was common, the equipment old and always breaking down, so Gifford's production was prone to more disasters than bad-tempered weather and drops in hog prices. Yet, over the months that I worked beside this gentle uncle, not a word of despair did I hear from him, not a sound that was not kind or useful to performing daily tasks, though I never felt sure that his soul and body were in the same place at the same time, or that his thoughts were connected to his actions. He liked me and was very kind, but rarely spoke to me. When he did it was to say what was on his mind for only a short moment. Over the entire three months, I felt at times as if I were working beside a ghost.

Gifford had eight mixed-breed milk cows, fifteen or so brood sows and a feedlot teeming with weanling pigs scheduled for the winter market. Because normally he worked the fields alone, with Aunt Bertha and Clara Ellen kept mostly to the house and the chicken coops, he had only two harness teams and a couple of other horses still green. One of the teams—grays named Queen and Bird—was the gentlest to handle and most often used. Bird was blind, having lost one eye to an infection and the other to a whiplash delivered by a neighbor farmer to whom Gifford had loaned her. That farmer had hitched this mare to the wrong side of the tongue, her blind eye inward, causing her to veer out of line because her partner was on her blind eye; for that misdemeanor he'd lashed her head; an errant tip of his whip cut her good eye. That dumb farmer could have corrected her alignment by just switching her to her usual position: like milk cows coming to the exact same station each time they are to be milked, each horse knows its position in a team of two or four abreast. Even when completely blind, Bird worked well when hitched with her sighted partner, was a willing horse that had long before stopped paying attention to anything but a tug on the reins and the sound of Whoa! and Back! I've not forgotten her.

When I arrived at the Gifford place, about ten acres of alfalfa were ready for cutting. My tenderhearted uncle had found a pair of kingbirds nesting in the open toolbox of the two-horse sickle-mower he'd left to winter-over in the field. Babies were still in the nest; his concern for their survival moved him to borrow a sickle from a neighbor. Over two days he guided the mower round and round the field, winding from the first pass along the fences towards the middle, stopping the team now and then to raise the blade a bit to clear the teeth of impacted fiber. While he worked out there, cutting around Meadow Lark nests when alerted by a frantic parent, leaving a dozen almond shaped islands as nest sites he would cut with a hand scythe when the babies left home, I did routine farmyard chores: fed livestock, cleaned stalls and the hog house, herded milk cows out along the road to graze on wild grasses and yellow-flowered sweet clover that lined the road bed like floral hedges.

After the alfalfa had been cut and laid flat under the boiling mid-summer sky for a few days, drying out, my fieldwork started. Gifford's horse-drawn dump-rake was put to gathering the downed hay into rows, about twenty feet apart, across the length of the field. Then began the task I most disliked: hand-forking the hay onto a flat-bed wagon and packing it down, then at the barn forking it overhead from atop the wagon through the hay-loft door. When dry, leafy alfalfa is flaky and dusty, like crushed autumn leaves that pranksters put down the shirt-backs of the unwary. The lint settles into one's neck-sweat under the collar and up one's shirtsleeves and pant legs, itching like jigger bites. So I tied a twine noose around each of my pant leg cuffs and buttoned my sleeves and the top button of my work shirt and wore a narrow ban-danna knotted around my neck. In the July sun, then, no cooling relief came from evaporating neck-sweat, and my pale blue eyes got seared by the harsh sun and invaded by hay dust when I looked up to lay a fork-ful of alfalfa onto the wagon. By the end of each workday my arms and shoulders were exhausted. After getting his team out of harness, haying and bedding them down for the night, I could at last remove my cloth-ing and plunge my itchy body into the horse tank, recovering in freshly pumped cool water from a sun-induced headache, then help my uncle and young Chester with the milking.

This sort of labor to earn one's daily bread was the only work Uncle Gifford had ever known, so when up at the house for mid-day dinner or post-milking supper, with Aunt Bertha shuffling about, tuned in to the battery-powered radio, nothing was said at the table. Not much can be said about what just repeats daily or seasonally and is never dif-ferent enough to make conversation—plowing, cultivating, haying, milking, shoveling, and pumping. There wasn't a book anywhere to be seen, and neither one in the household played cards.

The house interior was steamy hot when the outside air was thick, when the August sky was too exhausted to rain and daytime breezes were warmed by heat-radiating soil. After a typical supper of fried or baked chicken, boiled potatoes with white gravy, peas, beans, or beets, watermelon pickles and rhubarb shortcake under a mound of whipped cream, Gifford, Bertha, and their children took turns at the outhouse, washed up at the pump, and retired to their bedrooms. I would follow suit under a million stars one cannot see over a city, simulated by glowworms courting over the lawn and copulating in the grass, then flop onto a cot on the breezy porch, and be lulled to sleep by screeching bats and night-hawks taking insects on the wing, cicadas playing tedious music on the ridges of their saw-tooth legs, while thinking through gauzy dreams of what God had put me on this earth for—not to be a farmer I was coming to know, yet I felt no other force of direction.

The weeks passed with my doing sundry chores with Chester helping and learning from me a thing or two, while Uncle Gifford and his two-horse breaking plow tried to add a few acres of hillside pasture land to his cornfield. Those acres of wild grasses, daisies and buttercups had been my nature preserve the summer before when visiting the Giffords. Then I was not working but wandering over that prairie-like spread with my field books. I knew the birds that nested in its wildness and in the shrub borders piled up with tumbleweeds and undermined by rabbits and a colony of badgers. Wildflowers with animal and insect names, that few farmers bothered to learn, made me wonder how things get named: dog-toothed violet, turtlehead, crowfoot, wake-robin, goosefoot, snake-mouth, hog peanut, gopherberry, butterfly weed, moth mullein, cow wheat, fox-glove, fleabane, bee-balm, goat's-rue.

Late July and August were the weeks for cutting oats. Gifford couldn't afford a combine that both mows and threshes in the field, and his acreage was insufficient to join other farmers for cooperative harvesting. So the oats had to be mowed with a horse-drawn binder that cuts the stalks at the base, leaving only stubble, wraps them into bundles with a machine-tied loop of sisal twine and drops them lifeless onto the field. The sun's hot rays dry the milky moisture in the seed-heads that otherwise would mold and rot, so each bundle, laying flat on the ground with half its body in its own shade, must be stood upright, heads to the sun. And because a bundle cannot stand on its own feet, it must lean against another stood-up bundle, like two drunks on a sidewalk; and because two bundles leaning on each other for support can easily fall sideways, it takes four bundles leaning inward from the cardinal directions to keep each one of them stable. Configuring these four or six bundles was called, why I don't know, «shocking.»

I might have died that August had Uncle Gifford not seen me collapse like an unbuttressed bundle onto the stubble, had he been working not nearby but over the crest of a hill, or napping under the big-leafed mulberry trees that densely shaded one corner of the field where we ate lunch and slogged down water from a gallon can after crunching rock-salt. The high noon sun had gotten through my straw hat and was cooking my brain. I suffered sunstroke and passed out. As later he told me, Gifford dragged my still-breathing corpse to the shade of the mulberry trees and doused it with jug-water. We were a ways from the house but he managed to carry me part way, then drag me along with a grip under my armpits when his leg muscles got rubbery. At the house, I was laid out on a sofa in Aunt Bertha's parlor, stripped down to underwear, my head, neck, chest, and ankles layered with towels that Uncle Gifford had soaked in cold water from the well outside the house. In relays, he re-soaked the towels my body heat warmed. How long this went on I don't know, and whether the ministrations were medically sound I don't know either. Common sense tells one that anything overheated—whether a car radiator or a feverish brain—is in need of cooling down. At some hour of the night, I awakened in the dark space with a monstrous throbbing headache and tried to sit up but was too weak to more than lift my head and upper torso on elbow supports. Aunt Bertha had fallen asleep in a nearby rocking chair, not leaving me unattended for a moment.

I spent two days in that window-draped dark parlor. The house was not electrified, so without a fan the daytime temperature was high enough to slow roast a chicken and the night hours were not much cooler. Over this incarceration, I ate canned fruit and applesauce, drank a tin cup of water every hour, aspirin tablets with each cup. The headache retreated and I gained back strength enough to move about the room, shifting locations from one seat to another while listening with earphones to a crystal radio. On the third day of being invisible in that cabbage-wallpapered oven that smelled cloyingly of furniture wax, Uncle Gifford stopped in to suggest that, when I was up to it, we should work the fields by night, after supper and after milking, and into the morning until the sun got high, then sleep during the day. So when the sun had set that evening, and the moonlit air was level on the gray-scale with the darkened parlor, we stepped out toward the almost night and straight to the fields.

Time came around for my return to Sioux City. School was about to start, a month before corn picking. It would be the last time I saw the Giffords. Less than two years later, Aunt Bertha died a slow death of stomach cancer at age forty-one. Tragedy struck again in December when Clara Ellen, then sixteen, with four other teenagers was killed in a car crash against a moving freight train—crushed and burned at an early morning hour after a Saturday night party in nearby Brunsville. No one could be sure how the accident happened. The teenage driver wasn't necessarily racing to beat a train to a crossing. In those days no flashing lights were at rural railroad crossings and no warning lights would be on the train, other than the engine's single swiveling headlight, perhaps already a quarter mile up-track, and a single red lantern on the caboose's back porch a ways down-track. Automobile headlights were dim and yellowy—low-voltage bulbs behind glass covers invariably dirty from country-road driving. If the teenage driver saw anything as he approached the crossing, it would have been a moving blur through a clouded windshield. He crashed headlong into the side of a passing flat-car. After Aunt Bertha and Clara Ellen's deaths, Uncle Gifford gave up his acres, and with Chester, who was coming to a workman's age, hired out to other farmers. Gifford lived out his life with his widowed daughter, Corletta. I lost track of Chester.

Chapter 15

She wandered through the door
sat down on my cot, looked up and
said, Are you dirty minded?

In early September of 1942, shortly after I'd turned fourteen and while on the Gifford farm, my restless mother instigated another move, this one to 715, 33rd Street between Jackson and Jones. Bethel and Fern were living with their mothers-in-law, so I was housed with one older sister, Esther, and the younger ones, Alice and Avis, and little brother Harold. The new house was less crowded but by then I'd updated my phobia about living in a house. I took over the garage my father had no use for. It wasn't his habit to park in a garage, even over snowy winters. I installed out there a spring cot for sleeping, a kitchen-type chair and another chair salvaged from a heap of junk set out in an alley for collection, with lion claw feet and a crackled leather seat secured by button-headed nails. I built a bookshelf and a writing table long enough to hold a mass of clutter around a pale blue blotter pad, nailed up a row of clothes hooks for my wardrobe of jeans, shirts, and jackets, and banged a couple of 30-penny spikes into the wall as a rack for my squirrel-hunting rifle that lusted after rats like a terrier when taken to town-edge flour mills.

The walls above my cot were soon collaged with photographs of big band musicians, vocalists, film actors and actresses—Veronica Lake, the one-eyed beauty, red-haired Maureen O'Hara, Betty Grable's legs, air-brushed Vargas Girl pin-ups from *Esquire*, a reproduction of Tintoretto's *Rape of Lucretia* cut from *Life* magazine. My study desk and a laboratory bench were backed by shelves of explosive and corrosive chemicals, and artifacts of natural history—stuff I'd collected: bird nests, crystals, garnet stones, fossils, land snails, bug carcasses, butterflies and Cecropia and Luna Moths, a tarantula given to me by the kid across the street whose dad imported bananas from South America that often included among them a few giant spiders, some ground squirrel skins on which I'd practiced taxidermy, spare parts of demised radios swiped from a junk yard, books on nature, writing paper, scrapbooks, pictures I'd drawn, and plans for inventions. I had electricity out there, two bare bulbs suspended from ceiling cords. From Gifford's farm I'd brought in a few barn pigeons, selected pie-balds and rust-winged checkers captured one night in the cupola. I needed some non-human company and had no interest in dogs or cats. At one end of the garage I built a floor-to-ceiling coop for the birds, with orange-crate nesting boxes and access to an outside fly-pen through a hole sawed in the wall. The cooing and wing flapping broke up the silence of my remote habitat, which was off limits to the family.

My father was visible to his children mostly on Sundays. On the other days he closed his beer parlor after midnight and arrived home at one or two in the morning. Most nights the engine of his car had awakened me when he pulled into the driveway and parked in front of the garage. Some nights—if my light was on that late—he would knock on the door and without entering say: «C'mon in the house and let's eat some graveyard stew.» His only objection to my garage setup was that it didn't look good to have so many pictures of enticing women tacked up, that it might give people the wrong idea. But when I reminded him that he had pictures of really naked women hanging in the toilet at his Place, he just smiled and said «Yeah, but those customers of mine are grown-ups!»

His graveyard stew had evolved over the years into toasted white bread copiously buttered and drowned in a bowl of salted and peppered hot milk. Sometimes, when the fishmonger would come by his beer joint with raw oysters in cartons, the stew was the same peppery hot, buttery milk but poured over slimy gray oysters and topped with oyster crackers. He would slurp up his liquid stew and chew the oysters, but as a rule—he said it was a rule—only with two or three quick chomps before letting them slide down his gullet, and the crackers had to be downed before they became sogged. I hated the feel of an oyster in my mouth but liked the flavor in the hot milk. I pretended to chew but swallowed the oysters whole, while adding crackers to my bowl and oysters to his. He would grow serene and hallowed while eating. My mother said that was because of his upbringing in Denmark where even farmers ate oysters raw. But she wouldn't allow one in the house, saying they were unsightly and disgusting and caused stomach poisoning. So eating grave-yard stew was a man-to-man ritual. There was mystery to it—symboli-cally more potent than when offered the gizzard my mother reserved at chicken dinners for the man at the table, the muscular gizzard having something to do with virility.

Over the ninth grade all my resources would come together in this garage-hovel—my home except when taking meals in the family house and escaping extreme cold winter nights by bedding down with my crystal radio on a mattress in the house's rear second-story glassed-in porch. The women I'd pinned to the garage wall were pestering muses—ten of them, my Top Ten. With them I enjoyed the space of a fantasy at any moment I chose. On command—as I'd read in a book about pashas and harem girls—the one I desired would come alive and look directly at me. I'd positioned them that way, had selected each expression from the most coaxing and yielding angle. From time to time, I'd rearrange them or substitute a different girl, a new image of one I wanted to know. That kept the composition fresh and my atten-tion balanced between them. I would do the same with my pigeon flock—upgrading, evaluating, and always improving. I got that wisdom from reading Charles Darwin, who got his first insights into evolution by studying how pigeon breeders had developed over the centuries so many varieties that bred true. Darwin's was the true and natural way to evolve—by instinctual selection and recombination of the most surviv-able. A true fancier wouldn't think twice about destroying any bird that didn't measure up, or take down the picture of a girl who'd lost her bewitchments.

My favorite pigeon was an archangel, though I'd seen one only in a book—reddish with much fluorescence, like the red-haired, green-eyed, positively lovely Deanna Durbin. She'd look down from her strate-gic place on the wall, anticipating my attention. With tired eyes in can-dlelight, slipping in and out of focus, I could hold her image in mind and force my eyes to overlay her head with an Archangel's—tossing in slow, hypnotic motion, lips moving but not speaking, pursed. A lovely cowl of reverse hair would then form around her head, copper-gold, fluorescent in oranges and red-violets and purple, taking the shape of a halo that shot rays of colored light against the darkness like a Fourth of July sparkler. Then in patterns of gentle arcs and whorls, the darting colors would gather into flocks of performance pigeons, tumblers and tipplers and rollers that would come falling out of the night sky in waves and regiments. I would flatten myself to receive their impact, give up fighting against sleep, feel devout and peaceful, and let a heavy weight of blackness press me into the ground.

Two houses away, at the corner of 33rd and Jones, lived a family with three boys and a girl my age named Jennifer who wore knee-length dresses and orange lipstick and panicked me when she passed too closely or waved hello. Her older brother Luke had a loft of purebred homing pigeons. And across the street on Jones, in a house high up on the shoulder of a clay bank lived Sioux City's weatherman, whose only daughter Shirley was the temptress assigned by the Devil to bring about my moral downfall. She was fifteen, a year older than me, a Catholic who attended the Blessed Sacrament parochial school at 31st and Jackson, so I hadn't seen her around North Junior High. She wandered into the open door of my garage late one afternoon, hovered for a while, looking around, asked a few questions about what I don't remember, plopped seated on my cot on which I'd not drawn the covers back, looked up to me, and said, «Why do you have all these girls hanging on the wall?» I'm not sure that even saying, «I look at them,» was an answer I might have dredged up before she giggled and said, «I'll bet you look at them when you're playing with yourself.»

«You are dirty-minded?» she said emphatically, looking askance.

«I don't know,» I said, jarred by her bluntness. «What do you mean?»

«I mean...well, just dirty-minded, that's all. All these girls pinned up on the wall. You like them?»

I wasn't breathing right. Shirley fussed with things on my desk. «You like science?» she asked. If I responded, I would have said, «Yes.»

«I think science is sad,» she said. «Everything in my science class at school is dead. Scientists are always killing and cutting up things, dissecting them. These things you have in jars are all dead.»

«They're specimens,» I said.

«They're dead ones!» she said. «I like living things.»

She leaned back on her elbows and turned her head sharply to peer at my pin-ups.

I didn't want her to look back at me. I tried not to look at her. She said without turning her head: «I know why you have these girls pinned up here...» She giggled just once, then fell serious: «I know most of them. Which one's your favorite? No, don't tell me...I'll guess—it's this one. D'ya know how I can tell?»

I couldn't answer. I'd backed up to the edge of my desk, leaning away from her, feeling dizzy and out of tune. «You like her because she's got big breasts. Yes, you do...I'll bet you do. You like girls with big breasts. I'm going to have big breasts, just like my mother's. Mine are pretty big now...do you want to see them?»

«What d'ya think?» she asked as she pushed out her chest and looked down from one cone to the other.

«Yeah, they're pretty big,» I think I said.

«How big are you?» she asked.

«I'm tall,» I said,»...taller than most kids my age, and I'm strong.»

«That's not what I meant. I mean, are you growing up like I am? Getting bigger? You're Scandinavian, aren't you? So am I.»

«I'm Danish.»

«Do you like blond girls or red-heads?» she asked. «I'm half-way...I'm sort of reddish-blond. My mother uses henna—she says it's more sexy when a girl's hair is sort of reddish.»

I looked up to the wall. «Deanna Durbin has reddish hair. She's right there above your head—maybe she's my favorite. She reminds me of a pigeon...an archangel.»

«A pigeon!»

«Yes, like a pigeon I had for a little while—an archangel with reddish feathers and all iridescent in violets and purples. One day I'm going to get another pair just like them.»

«Why don't you get a girl? You got a girl?»

«Not now.. But I talk a lot with a girl I know at school.»

«Do you like to fool around?»

«Do what?»

«Just fool around. Smooo-tch. You know what I mean—kiss and fool around with a girl?»

Life wouldn't be the same after that encounter with Shirley. From this distance and with a certain knowledge, I now understand that she'd gotten stuck in infantile sexuality, needing to see and to touch, and that she would never in a lifetime need sex education to kill her curiosity, as if playing with a boy's penis, inviting it between her legs, was still answering her infantile question of what differentiates the sexes. And this was coming to me not in a sex education course but live, with only fragments of truth to support my going astray in such grotesque fashion. I suppose that my infantile sexual impulses had been converted by then to bashfulness, to rushes of blood that heated my body, shorting out nerves and crippling my tongue. Unable to be aggressive against Shirley's massive experience, I was submissive, my vaporous state then re-solidifying like Jell-O cooling off without any shape, concrete poured without forms. Submitting to God must be something like that, giving over one's infantile omnipotence to the Almighty, not throwing caution to the wind but meekly rising to the occasion.

Shirley became a frequent nighttime visitor, coming at an hour when her trusting parents were asleep, even through brittle air or howling wind. I shot out the street light at the intersection of my alley and Jones Street so she could dart from her house like a slippery dim shadow. Sometimes, even when there was snow on the ground, we would meet atop the clay bank that rose up steeply behind her house to a flat top, a remaining plot of buffalo range close to the sky from when the city's hills were cut down, up where on cloudless dark evenings the old man in the moon half way up the sky had an unobstructed view of our performance. The moon saw as much of Shirley as I did, for we never fooled around except at night and in dark places, in candlelight or night-sky light, talking in whispers.

During the year of this particular ninth grade, the Iowa school system introduced into junior high schools what would be today a sex education course. Then it was called «The Next Generation,» how the species multiplies rather than today's lessons on gender confusion and how to prevent infection and teen-age pregnancy. The course featured bees pollinating flowers and frogs laying eggs—the frog eggs fertilized by a male frog outside the female's body, becoming tadpoles on hatching that would grow into frogs for the sole purpose of going through the same process. Our teacher for this course was young and beautiful, and she wore pink lipstick and an unpleated skirt so tight at the hips and flat at the front that in raking light from the windows one could detect the slight bump of what, in my poetic mind, would be her mound of Venus—easy enough for me to see, seated up front in the first seat near the window. She wore a wedding ring, so we knew she'd done it, maybe the night before or that morning just before coming to school. Her lower lip quivered noticeably when speaking about pollination and breeding, and her voice broke when on occasion she rashly deployed the word «copulation» in a sentence and over-pronounced it as if trying not to say it. She must have known—I'm sure she did—that half the boys in the class were breathing through their mouths. After class, most boys left the room in haste and walked in silence down the hall with a notebook held awkwardly over their groin.

Chapter 16

Church leaders would look upon
dancing as a grave moral problem

S
ex and music tend to engender each other, like ancient Greek sheep-tending and reed flutes. Music came my way during the seventh grade. Marius and his wife Eileen were then living in a duplex adjacent to a family with a high school boy who was taking saxophone lessons. To earn money to pay his teacher, the boy took to heart my brother's suggestion that he give lessons to me in turn. My father was in favor. Musicians played regularly at his saloon, being paid whatever the sit-up cardboard kitty took into its open mouth. So with my father's gift of a C-melody saxophone, for which he paid eight dollars at a hock shop, I started on a music career that would last until January 1948, when, at age twenty in the infamous Phoenix City, Alabama dance hall, Beechy-Howard's, which was also a brothel, I drank my last glass of whiskey-spiked strawberry pop, played my last job, and called it quits.

The 1930s Jazz Age had seeped into every stratum of Midwest society, shoving aside most of the fiddlers and accordionists. Big Band ballrooms, even in small towns, had put an end to the barn dances my parents and rural relatives enjoyed during the twenties and early thirties. Southern blues lingered, and western music—promoted by cowboy movies—was occasionally heard in the Sioux City area, but Iowa was not cattle country and Iowa farmers didn't ride the range but sat on tractors and machinery pulled by horses. Across the state, in Davenport, the jazz cornetist Bix Beiderbecke (Leon Bismark Beiderbecke) was adding his own river-traffic blues style to New Orleans jazz moving up the Mississippi and the Missouri on paddleboats. Bix was born in Davenport, Iowa, in 1903, got his inspiration from Louis Armstrong, and when just a teenager, played to jazz enthusiasts, and anyone within range, such memorable tunes as *Riverboat Shuffle, At the Jazz Band Ball,*

Louisiana. He died an alcoholic at the age of 28 in 1931.

My Uncle John—the uncle who operated a pool hall and bar in nearby Correctionville—had five children who became musicians. The first-born Richard and his friend Roger Mead were known in the area as the Saxophone Twins. Richard, as I mentioned earlier, died of pneumonia at the age of fifteen in 1931 (since then, and still in 1998, Roger Mead has put flowers on Richard's grave each Memorial Day—sixty-seven years of remembering). The second son Moss, at age twenty, and Harley at sixteen, became successful swing band musicians in the 1930s. The youngest son, Bunny, took a musicology degree in college and became a music teacher and bandleader in Storm Lake, Iowa. The daughter, Norma Jean—my age to the day—aspired to be a vocalist, and by age sixteen was singing in clubs with her brother Harley's combo; at seventeen and eighteen, she would sing with Lawrence Welk's big band whenever he was playing in the area. Those years were before Welk honey-coated a dumbed-down television audience in the 1950s.

From its beginning, Sioux City was a music hub. Its first street concert was held in July 1857 when the city was only two years old and Pearl Street was the main street. It was fifteen years old when its municipal theater, the Academy of Music, was dedicated in January 1871 (just a decade after Paris had completed its Opéra). The Academy building was between Douglas and Pierce, with a 90-foot facade on the south side of Fourth Street. It seated 800 persons before a 22-by-50-foot stage equipped with gas footlights that could be raised and lowered by an off-stage hand crank, and two trap doors for creating unusual dramatic effects. The elaborate stage curtain was hailed as an «artistic specimen» representing a sunset in Venice—silhouetted gondolas on the Grand Canal. The opening performance was a double billing: «The Serious Family» and «A Day in Paris.» Although strictly an urban institution to cultivate taste rather than crops, on March 3rd and April 2nd, 1875, this «finest theater west of Chicago» performed to a packed house an oratorio, *The Beautiful Queen*, promoted as *A Benefit for Grasshopper Sufferers*.[36]

After a decade of utility, the Academy of Music fell into sporadic use by traveling stock companies, becoming in 1889 a ten-cent museum and an amuseatorium, a forerunner of the cheap variety-show theaters which would center on Pearl Street along with pool halls, saloons, and other unsavory joints as more respectable enterprises moved to newer commercial streets. The building was razed in 1918, its original function taken over earlier by an auditorium built on the corner of Seventh and Douglas. In July 1909, this auditorium was dedicated over a three-day celebration. The Grand Opera Singers kicked it off with a concert of pieces that included Johann Strauss' *Variations Carnivals* and the popular *Hungarian Rhapsody, No. 12*, by Liszt. The final day of the festival opened with a grand ball and closed with a vaudeville performance.

With the advent of the Peavy Grand, the truly marvelous opera house that supplanted the Academy, Sioux City sustained its place at the forefront of midwestern culture.[37] By then, every city and small town had an opera house, most of them serving a variety of uses, from Medicine Man shows to repertory theater, with stock traveling stock companies traversing the state, playing in tents when an opera house wasn't available. *Uncle Tom's Cabin* had a run from 1893 to 1928. Sioux City's Morgan Wallace Stock Company performed throughout the state from 1915 to 1921. Touring companies performing the latest Broadway hits, great productions, including Bronson Howard's *Shenandoah, Ben Hur*, and *Quo Vadis*; William Gillete's *Sherlock Holmes*, and such star players as Ethyl Barrymore, Henrietta Crossman, Julia Marlowe, James Herne in *Shore Acres*, Joseph Jefferson III in *Rip van Winkle*, and Sarah Bernhardt featured in *Camille*. These grand performances trickled down when played by local companies in small towns, where whole families would be the audience. Then the plays played to a lower culture:farm and hamlet dwellers attended such performances as *Down on the Farm, Our New Minister*, and *The Katzenjammer Kids*.

The 72-by-200-foot mixed-use Peavy Grand, fronting on Fourth Street at the corner of Jones, was dedicated on September 24th, 1888. It was the work of the extraordinary architect, Oscar Cobb, whose innovations did much to revolutionize theater design in the United States. Cobb abandoned the traditional horseshoe curve for the straight line of sight and rejected the orchestra pit in favor of the parquet and parquet circle. He placed the royal boxes away from the proscenium arch to include them as part of the auditorium, and was the first in America to use the French *nacelle* (hanging basket, or gondola) private viewing boxes. The interior doors were ornamented with stained glass; the entire floor covered with Bigalow-bodied Brussels carpet; entrances off the foyer were draped with blue and gold Templeton silk curtains, doubled with red plush draperies lined with damask. The volumetric interior, sparkling with gold trimmings and brass fittings, seated 900 on the main floor, 300 in the balcony circle, and 500 in the gallery. The stage had 26 sets of scenery with solid rather than the usual canvas side-flats. «It is the literal and absolute truth to say,» proclaimed the Sioux City *Tribune*, «that in the United States there is no city the size of Sioux City which has so beautiful and perfect a theater, and some features that no other structure in the world can display.» But all too soon, with the advent of motion pictures and their cheap admission tickets, live stage productions across the country declined. By the time I was born, the Peavy was in disrepair and the grand stage was an indoor parking garage. In November 1931, the entire building burned to the ground.

My youth traversed from folk dancing to jazz coming up from New Orleans and to swing music from Chicago. The Academy, the Auditorium, and the Peavy Grand were not part of my family's culture. I was not born to a world of opera and classical music, silk hats, white gloves, ivory-handled black umbrellas carried tightly under one's arm when it hadn't rained in a month and most likely wouldn't that evening («Was that Mozart?» asked a lady who'd come in from the farm in her finery to hear a concert, wanting to impress a lady next to her at the very moment the conductor brought a concerto to a resounding close. «I don't know,» said the lady she'd asked, also a farmwoman in disguise. «He hasn't turned around yet»). If Iowa had any historical background for my kind of music, it would have been to the coal-mining towns of south-central Iowa between 1900 and the 1920s, when the coal mining town of Buxton in Monroe County had a huge population of blacks—5,000 or more. In Buxton's big auditorium, like most opera houses built for meetings and entertainment. Booker T. Washington sometimes spoke on education, and W. C. Handy once played *The Memphis Blues*. New Orleans jazz, Southern Blues, and Dixieland bands played on Saturday nights.

Every town supported community dances during the Prohibition years when alcohol hadn't yet set age limits for dancers. If a barn or a vacant store weren't available, a tent would be set up. Over time, most of the small towns built dance halls: at Correctionville was The Blue Eagle, a few years later The Opera House, where about everything but an opera was performed; at Danbury one danced at Uhl's Pavilion. Lawrence Welk got his start at a dance hall in Fielding. Along with potluck dinners and church socials, barn, street, and parlor dancing was the rural form of socializing and neighborhood bonding.

Age was not a factor: pre-schoolers hardly able to walk danced with grand- and great-grandparents, who sometimes were also hardly able to walk. On the farm and in every rural hamlet and town, street dances were held during fair-weather months on festival days and whenever a traveling fair or gypsy circus was in town. When barn lofts were cleared of last seasons' hay and not yet filled with new hay, barn dances were in season, the music usually supplied by an accordionist and violinists. Jew's harps, zithers, violins, and guitars were popular in folk bands, and every barn and street dance needed a square-dance caller, something my father would try doing on occasion, only to entangle the dancers like dropped spaghetti. We had a barn dances on our farm in Hinton. Even today, I remember at age five helping my sister Loretta sweep the loft free of chaff and hammer down flooring nail-heads that had worked their way up. It was her eighteenth birthday and she wanted it to be jolly and festive. My father contributed his homemade brew and guests brought along refreshments: cookies, cupcakes, taffy, fudge, and cases of soda pop.

The Danish Christmas Tree dances were popular in such farming communities as Ida Grove, which had a large population of Danes. A decorated conifer would be placed in the center of the dance floor and danced around. Such family events were locked in a tradition of asexual social dancing, when men made sure they had asked every woman they knew to dance, not wanting to be impolite to any one of them, when parents danced with their children and children with each other, girls with girls but not boys with boys. Back then, old folks taught toddlers to fox trot—two steps forward, one to the side—from the day they managed to stand up. Lacking baby-sitters, children came along to the street and barn dances and to rural houses where parlor rugs were rolled up, the furniture lined along walls, and a cranked-up phonograph played the stack of records on its platter—*Indian Love Call, The World is Waiting for the Sunrise, Oh Johnny*. Little ones when petered out would be laid across the grain on beds to sleep. mixed in with coats. Men not dancing smoked cigars and told jokes, congregated in the kitchen or on the screened porch. Women chitchatted and traded gossip in the dining room or sun parlor. Sometimes the rural revelers would fall into group singing— «There is a tavern in the town, in the town...», or hear a teasing solo by a lusty man or woman: «Yes, we have no bananas,» or «I've got a lovely bunch of coconuts,» without the least inkling of the phallic suggestiveness. In town dances, in streets or halls, it was customary for a long intermission to be called at about 11:00 P.M. By then, most of the tots had fallen asleep on benches or grandmothers' laps and dancers were free to hit the cafes and saloons for refreshment before returning to the floor, which typically stayed alive 'til the cows came home, when the band would play its shutting-down strain, «Good-night Irene, I'll see you in my dreams.» No woman in history has ever had as many good-nights sung in her ear as that anomalous Irene.

When swing music came along in the mid-1930s, territorial dance bands worked the Midwest, ranging from combos to big bands of fourteen or more—four saxophones, three trumpets, three trombones, piano, bass, drums, and sometimes an accordion or guitar. Close dancing and jitterbugging were more compatible with the dating age of singles and young married couples. A transition from family-type, or folk dancing, came about when country music gave way to New Orleans and Chicago-style jazz, and then to romantic swing music with lyrics aimed at lovers—*Teach Me Tonight, Alone Together, Body and Soul, What Is This Thing Called Love, Tangerine, Yours Is My Heart Alone.* While ice-skating and indoor roller-skating remained favorite activities for Iowa youths, more than any other activity for paired sexes, dancing supported dating. Then church leaders would look upon dancing as a grave moral problem for young people—an excuse to hug, wriggle, and rub, and come home at daybreak with grass in one's hair and a lost earring. One of my favorite cartoons still in mind from an early 1940s girlie magazine depicts a naked man and woman standing before the officer-of-the-night in a police station, the man holding a car's rear seat under his arm, saying, «We'd like to report a stolen car.»

In rural areas and small towns, the transition from folk dancing, sanctioned by the church as a family activity, to close dancing associated with sex, came to the foreground in the 1930s. After forty years of banned dancing at Sioux City's Morningside College, the College Board authorized the first campus dance on January 13th, 1933. It wasn't that the College's board was prepared to condone dancing, but that quite a few unrepentant coeds had been sneaking out nights to attend dances in downtown Sioux City. Not chaperoned, they were fated to meet strangers and get into trouble. The first college dance was held in the gymnasium with music by Verne Hoshal and his orchestra, a popular local band. Students of either sex were required to get advance permission from the dean to invite someone from off-campus, and faculty members, obliged to act as chaperones, had to resist taking to the dance floor themselves.

Morningside College's rules for the proper behavior of young adults were typical of those enforced by most midwestern churches and parochial high schools and colleges. In earlier decades, and still generally in force in the 1940s, coeds had to be chaperoned when visiting downtown Sioux City or dining in a hotel. If out motoring, at least three people had to be in the car. Strolling at dusk, dancing, and card playing were rigorously forbidden. At entertainment affairs to which men were admitted, the girls were required to wear bloomers and ankle-length skirts (this was the decade when excited crowds jammed Wimbleton to see the first women to play tennis in knee-length skirts). When Morningside College established a women's athletic program, the girl's basketball team—scantily dressed, bare below the knees and elbows— was not allowed to play if men were in the spectator stands. This rule aroused much protest among the male students. One young man brought the matter down to fundamental biology, saying, «How can we make a decision about someone we might marry if not allowed to see what's real and what's padded?» The protests came to a high point of boisterous mirth when a group of boys were caught in the viewing gallery one afternoon dressed in women's clothing.[38]

Our school dances were rigorously chaperoned. Cheek-to-cheek dancing was not permitted. Air space was required between pelvises; couples were not to exit the room together or hold hands when not dancing; an alert teacher or volunteer parent escorted girls to the toilet. On more than one occasion, I was cautioned not to pump my pelvis when jitterbugging. Girls from the more affluent families would regularly invite a circle of friends to dance at their home where, depending on their parents' state of mind, the rules were less strict. The more socially advanced girls might combine dancing with parlor games, such as Musical Chairs, Pin the Tail on the Donkey, or Spin the Bottle. Many boys kissed a girl for the first time by being in the right place on the floor when the quart milk bottle stopped spinning. If it stopped and pointed at a girl, it signaled her turn to go out in the hallway and await her fate at the bottle's next spin. Spin the bottle separated boys from men in my early adolescent youth—shy boys preferred being safely outdoors playing Kick the Can, a more complex hide-and-seek game that incorporated a posse chasing a villain.

Church-led protests could not check the 1940s tidal wave of club and ballroom dancing. Arthur Murray dance studios were proliferating throughout the country, and musicals coming out of Hollywood, such as Busby Berkeley's productions, fed a craving for dancing in the least amount of clothing. Girls at finishing schools, while learning poise, manners, cosmetics, and the art of flirting, also learned to dance, and many of them fancied they'd become dancers or models rather than typists and wives. And as high schools continued turning out musicians, most of the players preferred performing in dance bands rather than playing marches in a military-style band. By this time I was playing swing-beat music and some Chicago-style jazz. Yet, to accommodate my father's wishes, I joined a newly formed concert and marching band fostered by the Sioux City Scandinavian Club, of which my father was a founding member. But on entering Central High School, I would refuse to join the school band. Marching in parades, rooting for a football or basketball team, was strictly for squares.

Scaled-down dance bands and three- or four-piece combos led by major musicians employing local side-men played clubs in Hinton, LeMars, Correctionville, and other towns on either side of the Missouri, all the way down to Council Bluffs and Omaha. Sioux City and Omaha were centers for the larger swing bands that were less known or halfway to the big time. The Rigadon in Sioux City drew the name bands and was most everyone's favorite dance hall. For the more moneyed classes, it was the Skylon Ballroom. At one or the other, one could hear Jan Garber, Horace Heights, Tommy Dorsey, Jimmy Dorsey, Harry James, Gene Krupa, Chet Fields, and Lawrence Welk. In addition to big-band adaptations of romance ballads, one danced to waltzes, Scottish jigs, polkas, the Cake Walk, the Charleston, and by the mid-forties, jitterbugged to the brisk rhythms of *In the Mood* or *Muskrat Ramble* or *Let Me Off Uptown*—favorites that brought everyone onto the floor. For enfeebled romantics there were the likes of *I'm Forever Blowing Bubbles*, and Kate Smith's *When the Moon Comes Over the Mountain*—mawkish songs I hated to play—and Lawrence Welk's version of *Clarinet Polka* that enraptured a middle-class audience as deftly as *The Flight of the Bumble Bee* bewitched middle-brows in concert halls.

At North Junior High, I had connected with the one boy in class who by choice would have no other friend but me: Jimmy Kliever, the son of an entrepreneur who'd moved from Chicago to Sioux City to convert a flour mill into Sioux City's first soybean pressing plant. Vegetal oils were coming into their own as city folk turned against lard and farmers were being told of soybean's nitrogen fixing value to corn production when alternated as a crop. Butchers across the country were demanding more meat and less fat on pork as soy and rape seed oils replaced lard in home use and hydrogented in manufactured shortenings.

Jimmy was of a non-physical medium height, movie star-handsome, and a well-schooled drummer with the air of someone who'd never in his life touched a live animal or plant or the bare earth; if he'd ever experienced farm life it would have been through an automobile or train window. He was the opposite of everything I'd been and mostly still was, with many of the personality attributes of what I would become. Nothing about him or his parents would suggest that they lived in Sioux City. When I think back from any distance to the time I spent with Jimmy, I still feel awkward. He was so neat and polished. He enjoyed going hiking with me out into the country, to Stone Park or to the oak hollows where squirrels abounded, but he remained remote from nature. I gave up teaching him how to shoot my rifle; he would get so nervous with it in his hands, afraid it would go off accidently When, on occasion, we went fishing at the Big Sioux, I had to put the worms on his hook. He was too conversational to keep his eye on the bobber; when he managed to hook a bullhead or catfish, I had to take the victim off the hook for him because he feared the fin-barbs, and then obliged to throw the fish back because Jimmy insisted it was too ugly to eat.

We occasionally dropped in on the disk jockey at radio station

KTRI, and we hung around KSCJ, wanting to know first-hand what broadcasting was all about. And when a name band was performing in town at the Rigadon or the Skylon, we would sneak in through fire-exit doors that were invariably cracked open to ventilate cigarette smoke and sweaty dancers.

Jimmy's father had bought him a full set of Radio King drums: snare, bass, three tom-toms—chrome and white pearl, with three spun-brass Schnelling cymbals and a trap. So connected was Jimmy to his plan to be a big-band drummer like Gene Krupa, who'd split from Benny Goodman to form his own group (the first drummer to lead a major band), that he refused to drum in the school band; the thought of wearing a school-band uniform, marching in daylight, rather than in a tuxedo under stage lights, put him in feigned convulsions when the topic came up. He would eventually go east as a jazz club drummer, although I don't think he ever realized his dream of leading his own band, for I never found his name in an issue of Metronome. He'd fixed in his mind a name for his band, King Karl Kliever, though I'd warned him enough times that the monogram KKK on his base drum and music stand fronts would not endear him to black musicians. As fate would have it, the year Jimmy played his first New York gig at the age of nineteen, I was the drum major who led the 287th military band down the streets of Birmingham, Alabama—the first occasion, I recall, when whites and blacks marched together. The spectators were segregated, too, and not just by neighborhood, so when I would see a line-up of blacks ahead, I'd put the band into a boogie beat and we'd march through a crowd wildly dancing in the street.

Like my elementary school partner, Lorraine, Jimmy was an only child. His father wasn't around any more than mine, but his mother was an unbroken presence in Jimmy's life. Like Lorraine's mother, she was sexy, slim, dark-haired, with mascara-laden eyes above rouged lips, who seemed to dress only in kimonos and consume nothing but black coffee at her kitchen table. Her housekeeping was so neat that I felt displaced in her house, never knowing where to sit when not in the kitchen—towels in the bathroom so perfectly folded over a bar that I dared not wipe my hands except on my trouser legs. Everything about her was noticeable. When her eyes looked towards me I could see that they were intensely blue like lapis lazuli—not brown like Jimmy's. That didn't surprise me because among pigeons brown eyes are subordinate to blue. Her long black hair fell down over her shoulders to her waist like poured tar. I hadn't thought that any grown-up woman could look as pretty and ornamental as she did, esspecially when she tossed her head when talking as if she had something stuck in her ear. Her nervous preening, hair fingering, nail-filing, connected her in my mind with young hen pigeons that preen wing-feathers nervously just before squatting for the cock to mount, and again after he gets off. They act as if nothing had happened in case other birds had taken a glance her way and caught her being awkward and submissive—the usual problem when performing a private act in public view. I would feel despicably sinful thinking that way about Jimmy's mother, so when mesmerized by her I would shift my mind to the image of Lorraine in a glossy silk kimono with Jimmy's mother's blue eyes but with clay-colored hair—the eye and plumage color of perky Dun Modenas.

I must have learned music quickly, although I'd stopped taking lessons after just a few sessions—enough to know how to finger the saxophone's mechanics. By the spring term of the ninth grade in 1943, I was playing bassoon in the school's string orchestra and tenor sax in the band, having shifted from the C-melody to the tenor, using a school instrument with permission to take it home. Outside of school, with Jimmy drumming and another friend on piano, we played popular dance ballads and upbeat pieces inspired by records played over and over: Glenn Miller, Tommy Dorsey, Coleman Hawkins, Louis Armstrong, Jack Teagarden, Dizzy Gillespie, the singing voices of Anita O'Day and Peggy Lee.

Emerging sexuality is lured out of dark places and into the open by erogenous music—Pan's pipes, Sirens' songs, the call of the wild. The preachers were right. But Jimmy and I were still adolescent schoolboys with a veneer of maturity. He was smart enough to achieve grades without being noticed by teachers and to avoid extra-curricular activities that would prolong a school day. A letter acquired by his mother from an accommodating physician freed him from physical education and set him up to be excused for sickness whenever he felt like playing hooky and drumming in the cork-lined, sound-proof basement room his father had a carpenter build for him. I was not as committed to music, sharing Jimmy's fantasies but not his dedication. In the absence of desire there was no need for me to struggle toward an achievement I wasn't sure I wanted to aim at, so my practice sessions were random and usually short, and music theory didn't interest me. I learned to read scores but played by ear when not reading sheets, making up songs as I went along, and resisted memorizing scales, chords, and progressions. By contrast, Jimmy correctly followed his drum teacher's instructions and practiced not less than two hours a day.

Few lives in music record what swing bands were like in the Midwest, what environments they helped to generate, because books on the period are only about band leaders that made the big time—only two or three of them represent Midwest culture. True history, like a mountain range, is not just lofty peaks and statistics; if it were, I would not be writing this book as if only about myself. My cousin Harley Andersen was perhaps the most well known tenor sax player in the Sioux City area. He had taken it up in 1931 when I hadn't yet learned to whistle. Still, we had rather parallel lives in music, even the same middle name, Vesti, and performance name, Whitey. Harley was typical of a vast number of musicians whose lives passed on and left behind no worthy fossils. By the year I began playing the saxophone, he was in the army, having been inducted in 1942. He, too, had started with a C-Melody saxophone and failed to get down to fundamentals. He had a knack I didn't have—the ability to hear a tune and play it from memory while not knowing what chord he was moving through or what key he was in, if any. His first tenor sax cost him fifteen dollars. The previous owner, who'd taken it apart for an overhaul and couldn't get it back together, delivered the pieces to Harley in a flour sack.

Music was all around us in those days—nickelodeons, church music, piano-playing in silent movies; every town had a municipal band and road shows came with musicians. Traveling salesmen, hawking their wares from cases that folded out to become display trays, always had a few impulse-buy items, mostly for children, as kids were easy to seduce into begging their mother to buy them something. Among the most popular were tin flutes (my first instrument at age six), nose-whistles, Jew's harps, and ocarinas. Children easily memorized simple tunes without knowing the words, and sometimes pranksters taught youngsters to sing words and play ditties that horrified their mothers. Harley recalled a snappy tune he'd learned to play on a tin flute. He played it repeatedly until a man stopped him on the street one day and told him it was a very dirty song that he should stop playing. The words were, «She's got the clap and the seven-year-itch. She's a syphilitic son-of-a-bitch.»

Radios hadn't come around until the mid-1920s, but before then Uncle John had provided his family with a piano that no one in the household could play any better than a cat walking on it. He also bought an Edison cylinder phonograph. By the mid-1930s, most families had radios. Ours was a Bakelite, battery-powered, four-tube Atwater-Kent that could out-squeal a pig if you didn't get the three knobs synchronized. Radio technology was moving along quickly, so as people rushed to purchase the latest, most powerful models that could bring in Omaha and Chicago, radio parts became available to those who today would be called hackers. As boys learned how radio stations sent signals, and how radios pick them up, every town soon had one or more five-watt stations fabricated with discarded radio parts. The first station affecting my extended family was in Correctionville, concocted by a group of garage mechanics. They called it «The Voice of Little Sioux Valley.» It could reach as far as ten miles.

Small-town stations made it possible for anyone with any degree of talent to be a radio artist. Jimmy and I played with a remarkably awful small band on Sioux City's station KTRI in 1943—the result was that the station's owner who'd just happened to tune in during one of our maladroit sessions decimated the studio's sole technician. We'd hardly played through our first set that afternoon before a telephone call from his boss brought the DJ to his senses and we were cut off the air. The most popular live music station in the 1930s and early forties was at Yankton—across the river in South Dakota. Daily concerts featured bands and soloists that would go on to various levels of fame: Lawrence Welk, Jimmy Barnett, the Leo Terry Swing Band, Little Joe Hart, the Rosebud Kids, Happy Jack O'Malley, the Bohemian Band, the Verne Wilson Band. One of the earliest dance and radio bands to succeed, at least in the Omaha and Sioux City area, was The Bluebirds, organized and led by a woman, Alyce Uehle.

The first of my cousins to play dance tunes was Uncle John's oldest son, my cousin Moss, whose practice sessions drove an across-the-street lady out of her wits. She counter-attacked by putting her radio out on the front porch, tuned to the station that played church music loud enough to blast Moss to kingdom come (from such incidents, which must have been commonplace, the FBI may have gotten the idea that ear-splitting blasts of rock music would lead the holed-up Branch Davidians in Waco to surrender). The theme song of Cousin Harley's first band was *The Sheik of Araby*, the ditty made famous later by the antics of Spike Jones and his City Slickers. (In running through connections with Harley, I can't pass up saying that my first girlfriend when living in Hollywood in 1951 was one of the blonde twins who danced regularly in scanty attire with Spike Jones' band. When Gloria and I went jitterbugging at the Palladium, dancing couples would clear out all around us, as if we required the whole floor. She was a great dancer and we had unlimited endurance).

Over the 1930s, Cousin Harley had many adventures playing with road bands from town to town.[39] My string of comparable adventures didn't come until I was in California playing most anywhere, in big bands, combos, at Al Davis' Silver Log Tavern at Clear Lake, California, at the Vallejo Hotel, at the Presidio in San Francisco. Those years were between 1944 and 1946, when I was sixteen and seventeen. One night, playing with Mike Primo's band at Clear Lake where I bunked on the club owner's yacht, I fell off the dock into the lake just before the band was to start up one evening. Jimmy Durante was the featured performer and I had the lead for playing his background. My tuxedo was soaked and muddy from crawling out of the water on a dirt bank, and Mike Primo was as furious as a wet hen. Al Davis rushed to his private rooms and came back with a suit fitted for a man half a foot shorter than me, so that night I played in gray business attire with wet hair, wrist cuffs halfway up my arm, and pant cuffs so close to my knees that I had to belt the trousers below my hip bones. A few nights later, having been called by the musician's union to rush down-state to Modesto to fill in for a tenor sax player who was ill, I got to the dance hall a few minutes before the first set. The band was full sixteen pieces, the music sheets hand-scored and messily annotated. Knowing that the saxophone section rises at times to stand and play, I urged the 3rd Alto player next to me to signal when the section was to rise. All went well until into the second set when the alto man turned towards me, his mouthpiece still in his mouth. I thought he was indicating that the section would rise on the next phrase; what he was actually trying to tell me was that I was dragging the beat—understandably, because I was having one hell of a time following the hand-written notes. Anyway, when the next phrase came along, I jumped up standing. But at that very moment the trombone section on the raised tier behind me reached for a very low note. A trombone slide-thrust poked me hard in the back. To keep from falling forward onto my music stand, I reflexively countered the thrust. The trombone and trumpet sections were on chairs with hind legs precariously close to the back edge of the platform, about five feet above the floor level behind them. When I jerked back against the slide thrust, the trombonist who'd assaulted me toppled off the platform. As he fell, he grabbed the trombonist next to him, who then grabbed the trombonist next to him, and that trombonist grabbed onto the shoulder of the trumpeter at his side, and so on down the line. The entire seven-man brass section disappeared overboard like a string of roped-together mountain climbers falling into a crevice. A good laugh was had by all.

Harley's favorite story came from playing for a dance in Cody, Nebraska, which was cattle country. His band found themselves playing behind a screen of chicken wire. On asking about it, he was told that fights usually break out during the dance, and that the favorite target of beer bottles is the band's bass drum. «It's one of the biggest sports in town,» the proprietor said, «so we have to protect you fellers from getting banged up.»

Harley never made the big time, nor would I. His best job was playing at the Figueroa in Los Angeles in 1940. Coincidentally, I performed in that same theater in 1951, not as a musician, however, but as the «apron man» for a variety show. After Harley returned from Los Angeles, playing a few one-niters en route, he went back to high school. Soon after Pearl Harbor, he found himself in the army. After discharge at the age of twenty-nine—married, and needing more out of life than being on the road with no roosting board to fly home to—he and his wife Betty took up a new career. They bought a small-town newspaper and entered the publishing business. His older brother Moss had taken over his dad's pool hall and no longer played music, while younger brother Bunny became music director for an Iowa high school. Norma Jean occasionally still sings with visiting road bands in Omaha and Council Bluffs, her voice at the age of seventy as strong and sensual as when she was eighteen.

189

Chapter 17

*That year the American Legion
canonized a good citizen caught
red-handed playing hooky*

M usic offered continuity from one semester to the other during my junior high years, but I had other irons in the fire—too many, my mother often warned me, too many sunflowers in my head facing different suns. My investments of time were as diversified as a subsistence farm, my mind in constant struggle between devotion and negligence, caught between what interested me and in what I was supposed to be interested. Every thought entering my head took over my brain for a spell, like the vagrant colors of a chameleon's skin. That diversification of cerebral capital would torture me all through life. At every turn there was something in front of my nose to keep me moving, even when resisting the lead of desire. Over the 1950s at the University of California in Berkeley, it took eight years to complete a bachelor's degree, having changed majors so often that at one point as a junior, where I'd been stuck for two years, I was required to obtain a psychiatrist's approval before readmission. As if impatient to get rid of me, at a Dean's Committee meeting in May 1959, convened after I'd refused a degree in any specific field and pleaded—not on my knees but with stand-up oratorical sagacity—for personal academic freedom as to career choice, I was granted a special degree in the General Curriculum with majors in Anthropology, Biology, Art History, and Speech. At the same meeting the Dean's Committee abolished the General Curriculum degree, never again to put up with someone like me. The Cal Tech student newspaper featured my case in an issue under the heading, *Cal's Last Freewheeling Intellectual.* Later that month, at a pathway intersection on the campus, I encountered my favorite biology professor, who'd projected a stellar career for me in genetics, and told him

191

I'd decided to go on to graduate studies, not in biology but art history. In disbelief, he stared into my eyes, wrinkled his nose into a sneer, and uttered the single word, «Art!» then turned his back on me and walked away.

Although that variability of interests came later, it started in Sioux City. Off and on, over the three years at North Junior High, I overlaid attraction to art, music, and writing with nature studies undertaken on my own at the public library where a small natural history museum was housed: specimens of rocks, minerals, fossils, stuffed birds and animals. I made self-guided field trips over country-land to observe birds and butterflies, and seined in Perry Creek for larvae that looked like primordial monsters under my microscope. The Missouri River was a natural migratory flyway, but from this temporal distance I'm not sure if I was as interested in the birds as in the sound of their names: scarlet tanager, indigo bunting, crested fly-catcher, ruby-throated hummingbird, rose-breasted grosbeak, lark bunting, red-shafted blackbird, brown creeper, white-breasted nuthatch, tufted titmouse; or that I was fascinated by butterflies other than in their colors and patterns and their Latin names found in Holland's etymology of winged insects. Why else would I kill them before admiring their strange beauty?

Outside of school I read Darwin's *The Origin of Species* and every book on natural history in the school library. I memorized the basic insect anatomy from antennae and mandibles to ovipositor. Under my microscope, I studied the fly's compound eyeballs, the varied shapes of butterflies' wing powder, and the metabolism of the amoebae. Years later, when learning French, I read for vocabulary enhancement not the literary texts of Molière, Balzac, or Flaubert but zoology books: *Animaux de tous les pays* and *Le Monde étrange et fascinant des animaux*. Yet I was not destined to be a biologist, although I ended up at the highly scientific Massachusetts Institute of Technology rather than at a humanistic Harvard or Yale where I taught on occasion as a visiting lecturer but never felt comfortable, and one of the books I wrote was on Freud's mishap confusing hawks with vultures, leading to his spurious analysis of Leonardo da Vinci's life-style. I've always managed to bring some aspect of biology or science into my later work. My book on Èdouard Manet's art of the 1860s started when I noticed he'd added a bullfinch flying through treetops in his *Déjeuner sur l'herbe*.

Interest in art started in my second year when I was thirteen, and it was never far from my attraction to writing. Both were fueled in copious spurts, I recall, by my emerging sexuality. In my garage, I spent many hours studying a huge illustrated Webster's dictionary that a door-to-door salesman had talked my mother into buying. I took to memorizing an array of words and their meanings, but won't now disclaim that the words catching my attention were those that brought me to euphoria, got my head spinning and my pulse racing. I hadn't yet read those dirty stories so richly endowed with affective vocabulary that passed around among men and high-school boys. My only access to erotica, when the underside of my morality began taking command, were such sizzling Bible stories as Lot and His Daughters, Jacob and Leah, King David and Bathsheba, the Song of Songs; and monthly displays of barebreasted women in *National Geographic* and pink-bodied nudes by Venetian and Flemish painters—Titian, Rubens, Veronese, Tintoretto, Giorgione, even Rembrandt—with which *Life* magazine periodically tortured young boys while enhancing circulation among men with photographs of war violence and clandestine erotica in the guise of high culture. Few men and boys who bought copies of *Modern Photography*, with its many nudes, had any interest in taking pictures.

I was also fascinated by the dictionary's miniature illustrations. I studied words, practiced spelling, and copied certain pictures over and over until effortlessly I could render them in line and photographic shading without needing exemplars in front of my eyes. My favorite images to copy were the American flag hanging loosely from a pole and a three-mast ship with sails billowing. Hardly lifting my pencil from the paper, I drew them repeatedly at school, publicizing my skill, arousing the attention of the art teacher, Miss Boe, who recommended that I take supplementary art lessons at the Sioux City Art Center, the Center founded in 1938 as a WPA-funded project through the efforts of the Sioux City Fine Arts Society that originated in 1914. It was located in the basement of Willigess, a fashionable ladies' fur store at 613 Pierce Street—now a department store. At thirteen I attended a class there one or two afternoons a week, where I worked in transparent watercolor and, to the bewilderment of those who were trying to appropriately teach me, painted not from still-life set-ups or by copying, as had been my habit, but from imagination. My subject matter was typically far from Iowa: exotic jungles of livid greens under a cadmium-yellow sky, while outside the windowless basement, gray winter raged in its usual blustery fashion. Perhaps Tarzan and scanty-clad Jane, living in sin in a tree house, were on my mind: the colors I deployed were as intense as those seen in fresh comic books. At school art classes I was less passionate, restrained by Miss Boe's strict assignments, mostly based on media. She had us work in colored chalk and colored pencils; we painted in tempera, then water-soluble crayons; made a linoleum cut, modeled a bear in white Ivory soap, a seal in unfired clay; over one term we joined with the drama class and fabricated marionettes of hinged wood joints and lead-weighted feet. For our mothers we carved a brooch in walnut wood—mine just a swollen lozenge shape that took an hour of polishing with linseed oil to bring to tactile perfection. For our fathers we made a tooled calf-leather wallet. The notion of giving a self-created gift to one's parents as loving thanks for one's gift of life was operative: our parents had made us, after all, had given us form; we were supposed to thank them with something we in turn had formed: a globular brooch to pin near the nurturing breast, a wallet to pocket near the generative organ. But I doubt if Miss Boe or anyone in that class, including myself, had an explanation of this sort in an accessible state of mind: compensatory gift-giving was instinctual.

I was appointed school artist, responsible for hallway murals and decorations for Christmas, Easter, and Halloween, and for designing stage sets and lighting. I worked intensely on projects, shoving off helpers like a Michelangelo atop his Sistine Chapel scaffold, displaying such arrogant individualism that Miss Boe didn't have the heart to object when over the final year I segregated myself from the class in a rear corner of the art room to fabricate my own studio. Protected from intrusive eyes by a solid wood screen, I could work there during lunch hour and recess and as late after school as Miss Boe hung around. During ninth grade she saved me and the entire school from a horrid embarrassment on the day when an American Legion delegation arrived for a ceremony to hand out the 1942 junior high school level citizenship award. Unknown to me, I was to receive the award. During the assembly, after speeches were heard and anticipation had swept over the audience, the chief of the Post announced my name as the recipient. Surely everyone expected me to jump up, or at least to rise with the dignity of an exemplary citizen and walk, not run, to the stage. But no Wayne Andersen responded. Eyes from the stage scanned the audience. Miss Boe rose from her seat saying, «I think I know where he is.» She rushed to the art room, grabbed me by an upper arm and led me down the corridor to the auditorium. As we came through the door with me in her grip, the audience broke out in applause but mostly in laughs and hoots. So that year, the American Legion canonized a good citizen caught red-handed playing hooky.

W alter Jones was my second mentor. He was an inventor and manufacturer of stage illusions. Magicians from throughout the country patronized his factory in Sioux City, even Houdini, Thurston, and Blackstone. I stopped by his place one afternoon, having found one of his catalogues in the public library. I had hopes of securing a part-time job. Jones was very talkative and responsive to my interest in his workshop. He took a shine to me and without charge gave me an assortment of traded-in illusions that were in need of repair too costly for resale. He invited me to lunch at his home the next Saturday when the world-renowned Blackstone would be staying with him over a weekend. I took him up on it.

White-haired Blackstone was a very jovial, friendly man. At the luncheon table, he and Mr. Jones told trade stories that enthralled me, like tales by adventurers would; they talked about theaters in distant large cities, compared ideas for new illusions, always attentive to keep me in the conversation. After lunch, Blackstone took out a pack of cards and tricked me several times before telling me why I was easy to fool. So eager to catch him in the act of deception, to defeat him, I couldn't resist watching for what he cleverly lured me into looking for while he did something altogether different, as when standing very close to me he held his left hand high in the air and shook it to make me suspect he was working a playing card down his sleeve, while his right hand was down at my hip slipping the card into my jacket pocket, to be amazingly found in there moments later. He gave me an hour of lessons in patter and timing, on how to deceive the audience with words—a veritable Sun Tzu example of the ancient art of war as not just aggression but deception: intelligence will always overwhelm ignorant physicality.

He advised me never to shuffle cards with flair, or deal as if I were a pro, but to display awkwardness, be clumsy with the deck. After that lesson, it would take me hours of practice to handle cards with deceptive skill while appearing to be heavy-handed and inept, like a tightrope walker who expertly fakes slips and falls. I still guard as Blackstone's personal gift an astonishing card trick with infinite variations he taught me that afternoon at Jones' house. I've deployed it a thousand times and not once been caught. Just take a card, memorize it, cut it into the deck. *Hand me the deck and in two or three shuffles and one cut I will have placed your card as deep in the deck as the number of letters in your combined first and last names That's where you will find it. If your name is Thomas Equinus, the card you selected will be the thirteenth from the top. Here, look for it yourself. I'm not touching the deck.*

After that happy occasion at Mr. Jones', I didn't bother to learn prestidigitation—manual magic it was called—that takes as many hundreds of hours to perfect as playing a piano without visualizing the keys. Stage illusions that depend on ingenious mechanical devices, not the art of conjuring, was to be my style—illusions, deceptions, falsehoods to fascinate bright eyes: white pigeons disappearing and reappearing, an entire pitcher of milk poured into a small drinking glass, a cut-up rope made whole again. People want to be fooled; that's what they pay for, like masochists who pay to be whipped. As with the impersonations I'd perfected and performed at school assemblies—a frenetic politician, Hitler in a raging speech, an idiot teaching a blind man how to drive, a school boy delivering an oral report while desperately needing to pee— stage magic required the performer to control an audience, as I would have to do several thousand times in adulthood as professor, public lecturer, and presenter of architectural projects—keeping an audience at risk of being hoodwinked, never knowing what strange idea I would pull out of the hat: rabbit, plucked chicken, or skunk. Within weeks, I was skilled enough to do a complete program for school assembly and house parties.

Should this text get beyond the Sioux City years, you will find me in vaudeville by the age of sixteen. Somewhat later, in 1951 at age twenty-two, I would quit performing stage magic as abruptly as two years earlier I'd stopped playing in bands. At that time I was bouncing around California theaters and clubs, at first in a variety show, then partnered with the horror-show and illusion magician Arthur Bull, a protégé of Houdini, with the stage name «The Great Francisco.» A high school friend, a tumbler, who went on to perform as a comic acrobat, introduced me to Bull, then in his late-sixties, a gracious and ordinary fatherly man who lived with his sweet wife in a modest wood-frame house in Oakland and drove a conservative blue Plymouth sedan, a new one every year because he couldn't risk breakdowns pulling an equipment trailer.

Our extreme age difference served our acts because most of what we did involved reversals—him showing up where I had just been, or the other way around, as when my hands would be cuffed behind my back, and I'd be put into a canvas mailbag, the bag's neck tied tightly by a volunteer from the audience, entombed in a trunk on castors with knees drawn up and head bent down (a regular attic-type steamer trunk), the lid then lowered, padlocked, encircled by three ropes tied by another audience volunteer, the trunk stood on end. With the volunteers on stage to assist, a four-sided curtain, supported by a simple steel frame, would be placed around the trunk. Francisco would step into the enclosure, draw the front curtain closed, leaving only his head and right hand extended through a slit, and say to one of the volunteers, «Take my hand, hold it tightly, and when I count 'three,' pull hard.» Francisco's head would then disappear and he would call out at close intervals: «One... two... three.» The volunteer would pull him out. It wouldn't be him but me! For by the time the curtain assembly had been installed around the trunk, I was out of the cuffs and out of the mailbag. By the time Francisco said «two,» I was out of the trunk, standing beside him, ready to slip my right hand through the curtain slit as if it were his. A second after he'd closed the curtain over his face, Bull was entering the trunk; before I pulled back the curtain, he was getting into the mailbag. Then, with the audience astonished at the switch and the volunteers helping, the ropes would be removed, the padlock unlocked, the trunk opened, the mailbag untied, and out would emerge Francisco in handcuffs. The audience would rise with applause and appreciative whooping. They'd gotten their money's worth, which is all a performer has to offer. That trick was Houdini's invention, and the first one he performed when taking to stage work.

Francisco and I were one of six acts chosen to perform in 1951 before the annual convention of the Magic Circle in Los Angeles. Our audience was entirely professional magicians—three to five hundred from all over the world. The criterion for appreciation and applause was the expertise and novelty of the performance, for no one in that privileged audience would be fooled. Doris Day, a celebrity magnet, was there to receive the Circle's annual award for promoting magic. She hadn't promoted it at all except by singing *That Old Black Magic*, which had topped the sales charts that year. I had a moment to chat with her backstage. She was a few years older than I, her face, with its flashing smile, terribly pocked from years of stage makeup, her bleached blonde hair as coarse as broom-straw. Only a few years later did I come to appreciate her role in music—the last of the great love balladeers. By 1952 the most popular singer would be Patti Paige, whose contrived and saponaceous *How Much Is That Doggie in the Window* topped the charts for record sales that year, and her rendition of *Tennessee Waltz*, which sold ten million copies the next year, spelled the end of 1940s music. Paige was a mechanical singer, like a wind-up tin bird, all technique and no soul; she sang from the brain. And by that time Charlie Parker and bebop had moved music out of the blue-jazz and swing era. Soon there would never again be a Dizzy Gillespie, Stan Kenton, Coleman Hawkins; never again a Peggy Lee or a Doris Day. Great ballad singing wouldn't come again until Bobby Darin did *Mack the Knife*. With Patti Paige's *Tennessee Waltz* came a crossover of Western with popular songs, a neutered blend of popularity that would move along with the asexual aging of the jazz generation and leave a vacuum for rock bands to fill.

Francisco retired after the summer of 1950, when I was twenty-two and after we'd done a few television shows from a station atop Knob Hill in San Francisco. Vaudeville and variety shows, too, were finished. Ken Murray's Blackouts in Hollywood would soon close down after years of running. Laurel and Hardy, The Marx Brothers, Jimmy Durante, were dissolving, and after Clyde Beattie retired, circus lions and tigers would be tamed, not trained.

At that point I stopped performing. The season was changing and stage work was not opening up to a big enough world for me. After a few months at Hollywood's National Telecasting Corporation in 1950, mostly designing sets, and a few sessions as a script reader, I knew that I would never be a professional comic or a legitimate actor. As it had been with music, I was not sufficiently trained and not inclined to become so. Natural talent has its limitations, and in just about everything I'd tried to do, I'd found my limits far short of professional competence. I was not motivated to push on. I thought about things too much. I talked too much. I needed a larger mental platform, and after a performance more than coffee and a grilled-cheese sandwich in an all-night greasy spoon, followed by an early morning-to-noontime stay in a motel room smelling of cockroach spray. I didn't yet know that I was an intellectual. I didn't own a single book. I didn't even wear glasses.

Chapter 18

Arrested for driving while sober on a drunk driver road

Music, art, and stage work dominated my junior high school years in Sioux City, but by ninth grade, I was also writing seriously. I'd taken second prize in state poster contest warning against drunk driving. My poster read—how corny it now sounds, «Put alcohol in the radiator, not in the operator.» Restraint of drunk driving was not a new topic for the Iowa school system. Almost every year students in art classes were set to poster competitions alerting people to the dangers of drinking and driving. In May 1935, following repeal of the general prohibition law in 1934, the Des Moines *Register* printed a long article on the history of Iowa's engagement with liquor, and recommended that schools assign essays on the subject of driving and intoxication.

At North Junior High, I was the English teacher's star essay writer and prime stand-up actor, so I followed up on my competition poster with one of my best monologues at a school assembly. By then I had absolute confidence in my contrary nature and was determined to exploit it at each and every chance. My disposition had become rivalrous. Just being better than others—brighter, craftier—came too easily. To justify my efforts, I fabricated obstacles, took risks of screwing up, bit off more than I could chew and swallowed anyway. Dazzling disagreements drew attention to me, which is what a performer craves. My speech before the assembly would imitate a politician pleading in fine oratorical fashion for a solution to a grave social crisis: how to eradicate drunk drivers from streets and roadways.

A committee of three teachers previewed my act to assure it was appropriate entertainment. My approach was not wholeheartedly endorsed, although I'm sure that not one of the referees had taken into account that a percentage of the drunks in our town were patrons of my father's saloon. Although charmed by my wit, I recall, and sympathetic to my stage art, the committee was rather disdainful of me for taking drunk driving so lightly, as they had been the semester before when I gave a Hitler impersonation—my speech titled «I Want Peace—a piece of everything: a piece of Poland, a piece of Czechoslovakia, a piece of Romania, and so on,» cribbed from a radio show I'd heard. (Only that year had the full scope of Nazi atrocities been noted in the press. We knew a little about deportations and concentration camps, but not about the gas chambers, and Germany was a long way off). My presentation was approved, nonetheless, with admonition that I keep it stringently comical.

Drunk driving killed a lot of innocent people when automobile tail lights and streetlights were dim and no colorful traffic signals controlled intersections, just stop signs under incandescent and short-lived light bulbs suspended on arms stemming from telephone poles—easy targets for a BB gun or fractious gusts of wind. To prevent innocent people from being killed by drunk drivers, after insisting that neither posters nor punishment would stop drinkers from driving, I proposed a scheme by which only drunks would be killed. This involved construction of a special road, exclusively for drunk drivers, running around the city and with lots of sharp curves and bumps. Signs would be strategically placed along it: *Drunk Drivers Only*. Any driver on this road whose car did not appear to be swaying erratically would be chased down by the Highway Patrol and arrested for driving sober on a drunk driver road. There would be many fatal accidents of course—drunks piling head-on into each other—but no innocent people would be maimed or killed. Over time, the high death rate for drunk drivers would drastically decrease their number. About ten years, I had figured, would be all it should take for them to wipe each other out—a self-destructed species eradicated as efficiently as dinosaurs were for having become so big and ugly and failing to keep in step with an esthetically aimed evolution. The last surviving drunk driver would roam the dedicated road in search of a car to crash into. But before he had time to sober up, the Highway Patrol would apprehend and summarily execute him, his corpse to be embalmed at the city morgue and put on permanent display in the natural history corridor of Sioux City's public library, right next to the stuffed gorilla.

In addition to comedy, I made a few attempts during the ninth grade to write poems and short stories, but my natural tendency, whether due to gift or flawed personality, was to write disputative essays. Not much was to be gained by being agreeable. And not until the mid-1950s, when reviewing one of my adolescent essays with a physicist friend in Berkeley, Oliver Johnson, a basic science researcher for Standard Oil, did I recognize that every piece I wrote or performed at age thirteen and fourteen involved coming to terms with Darwinian theory. The key essay that I recalled when talking to Oliver was one with which, in 1942, I won the Iowa State Essay Contest for the junior high school division. This happened during the last term of the ninth grade when the Iowa school system was a model for the entire country, with writing stressed. (In 1915 the Iowa novelist John T. Frederick had launched a literary magazine, *The Midland,* meant to encourage young writers. In the 1920s, Norman Foerster's School of Letters was established within the university at Iowa City. The Iowa Writer's Workshop remains the most acclaimed writing school in this country).

The competition theme for the year I entered was typically righteous: *Why We Must Conserve Raw Materials.* I was selected by the principal to represent our school. The rules stated that I could receive no help from anyone; the thoughts and writing must be entirely mine. So when I handed over my pre-submittal contrarian essay to the English teacher for her blessing, she fell into a conniption fit, for my essay was titled, *Why We Should NOT Conserve Raw Materials.* She was shocked and furious, and not about to listen to reason, but the competition rules allowed her only to beg me to reconsider. She could beat her breast to keep down her blood pressure but not change anything I'd written.

The principal hadn't scolded me for the gross deviation from the rules, as Miss Burke thought he should have, even though she'd told him she'd been embarrassed to tears by what I'd written. The only way I could redeem myself in her eyes was to write a new essay. I went at it for a whole week, tried several versions at my desk in the garage, taking different angles: why we should restrict lumbering, burn less coal, save water, plow contours, limit hunting and trapping. I managed to write the ordinary essay that Miss Burke wanted, took it to her office after school one day, and without uttering a word—not sure what to say—handed it to her. She read it while I stood next to her chair. She marked a couple of misspelled words, circled out of habit a verb out of tense. She looked up at me once she'd read it all the way through, her face smilingly pink and ardent. «It's just perfect,» she gushed. Then she jumped up abruptly, hooked her right hand around the nape of my neck and pulled my face right into her pillowy bosom.

In planning my original essay, after listing reasons why natural resources must be conserved, it was plain as day that every pupil bright enough to be a selected contestant would list the same reasons. What then would distinguish one essay from another other than how well it was written? I didn't have enough faith in my writing to feel confident that, on a level playing field of literary competence, it would be good enough to score. So I thought hard, rather than agreeably, about why natural resources—raw materials: coal, minerals, oil, forest trees, fur bearing animals—should be preserved. I thought about people saving things, which wasn't difficult at the time because, in the midst of World War II, hoarding was a widespread affliction and rationing was the law. I thought about the pressure put on little kids to save pennies in a piggy bank, for older kids to save dimes in a contraption widely used then that automatically counted dimes into dollars and could be opened only with a key held by a parent or the bank. After running those and other examples through my mind, my conclusion was that people who save for rainy days must be very depressed during fair days. On rainy days one should stay cozily at home and read an exciting book; on warm sunny days go out and spend money and have a good time. Nature was joyful and profligate in abundance; its only depressed aspects were deserts, such as Death Valley and the Sahara, and anything frozen stiff or lifeless—permafrost, fossils, skeletons, and the despondent masses in India.

Late one evening, having gone to bed for a while and then gotten up because I couldn't fall asleep without dreaming guiltily, I thought that if every person in the world were to restrain every process in the world, the globe might stop spinning. But mostly, I decided, everybody would become depressed. There would be no more crises! No motivation for scientists to discover new things! No new technologies! Industries would be stuck with burning old primeval swamp gunk and dinosaur carcasses for the rest of eternity. If the problem of diminishing natural resources really became serious, scientists would aggressively work to relieve it—not by conserving oil or coal, or being content with mud huts and wood houses, but by forging ahead like passionate explorers to discover new sources of energy, alternative building materials, and synthetic furs for ladies' coats. In the absence of peril there would be no scientific advances, complacency would lead to boredom and evolution would brake to a halt.

I didn't mail the approved essay. Miss Burke really blew her lid when she found out that I'd slipped the original one into the envelope that got mailed to Iowa City, rather than the one she'd read and surreptitiously approved. She didn't know about it until it was too late. Miss Burke showed me a letter she'd received from some supervisor at the Board of Education who was one of the judges. In heavy letters, as if shouted, was written: «What are you teaching these days? What does this pupil mean? That we should deplete all our natural resources as rapidly as we can burn them up to avoid social depression and restraint of science?» Still, my essay was awarded First Prize. But after the principal had been informed of the results by letter, he was told by phone that the jury had been subjected to protests, considering that I had not obeyed the title of the theme. My essay was disqualified, my prize reduced to Special Mention. By then the principal had confessed to me that after he'd read the essay a dozen times, and discussed it with several people, he had come around to agreeing with me and made an effort to have the decision reversed.

The disqualification had undervalued my intelligence. I was angry at the world, and for the first time felt disillusioned about school. I was having enough trouble maintaining a functional level of self-respect and self-worth, considering that my doubting mind was always at risk of coming up short. And my morality was floundering in a quagmire of deception—stage illusions, my off-limits garage, and secret notebooks, not to mention Shirley. I couldn't have known at this time, and wouldn't know until looking through aged Sioux City records in preparation for this book, that graduating from Central High School on June 11th, 1902 was a girl who would have been my soul mate, had her soul not existed a quarter-century before mine was born. Her name was Grace Pierce (perhaps a descendent of John Pierce whose love note to Sioux City is a priceless piece of lore: «There burns within my bosom that

youthful first love that knows no death»). Grace Pierce read a valedictorian essay titled *The Dangers of Contentment*::

> «Contentment has been extolled by great men and philosophers of
> all ages; the Bible, even, classes it as one of the greatest blessings.
> Yet, contentment is dangerous. Had men always been contented
> the world would have no civilization. Men are ever searching after
> something they have not, and this search is what saves the race
> from sluggishness into which contentment would surely plunge the
> world. One of the greatest difficulties in improving the condition
> of laboring people is the fact that they are too generally contented
> with their lot. They have no ambition for better. One of the best
> signs for the future would be a general sign of dissatisfaction.»[40]

Chapter 19

Having spent all my school years
in the first seat of the first row, I would
at last be safely out of range

The final semester of junior high school was, for a few years to come, my final term as an accomplished student. It remains on my mind that, after three years of straight As, winner of essay contests, being voted most popular boy, winning the American Legion good citizen award, playing the lead in the class play, taking about every honor the Iowa school system offered, I would graduate three years later from a California high school, singled out by the principal as the student least deserving of a high school diploma.

How this least-deserving status came about, I now comprehend, but I recall that I understood it back then too. The first year of high school coming up in Sioux City would be a disaster. Then, midway through the eleventh grade in Richmond, California, I would be expelled for truancy and for being caught with a loaded pistol in my pocket. The following autumn of 1945, I would register for the fall term of the twelfth grade at Berkeley High School but would be expelled after an act of justifiable violence that I'd perpetrated on someone, and the principal's discovery that I hadn't attended the eleventh grade. So I stayed away from school until mid-year when I met a girl, Jackie Evans, who attended Oakland Technical High School. That school had weak academic standards and for that reason attracted the best young East Bay musicians who didn't give a rat's ass about education. I enrolled at the opening of the spring term of 1946, and over the entire months of attendance, took five music courses and one course in mechanical drawing. My dismal high-school record, with no previous grades after the tenth-grade year in Sioux City, came to the principal's attention only when he reviewed students slated to graduate that June. Horrified, the worst he could think of doing was to call me to his office to tell me that, of all the students receiving diplomas, I was the least deserving. He had to graduate me because I was approaching the age of eighteen and the draft laws were still in effect—no high-school boys were allowed not to graduate. So I achieved the distinction of absolute worst in the principal's eyes—the absolute best among the worst, not just an ordinary bad pupil, such as one who had tried but failed. I thanked the principal profusely and departed his office as a triumphal boy of distinguished valor, saying to myself, «I can't help but win.»

Years later, in 1962, I was awarded the $5000 William Bayard Cutting prize from Columbia University as the most outstanding graduate student that year. The award meant a lot to the Columbia Graduate Faculties in the Humanities; in all previous years it had been awarded to a graduate student in the sciences. For me it also had special meaning. I had forsaken a career in science for one in art history, and yet had won that award in competition with candidates in the various scientific fields. But the thorny path that would take me from worst student in high school to best in graduate school that led to becoming a tenured professor at a place like MIT was not a sentimental journey that anyone would want to set to music.

The downslide started in the last month of junior high school. Teacher expectations during the final term of the ninth grade may have been more than I could bear. Playing the lead in the class play was the straw that broke this farm boy's back. The drama teacher had insisted that I take the role of Mister Hargrove in a silly drama called *Mister Hargrove Takes a Holiday*. I had mature stage presence, she said, and my voice had overcome its adolescent squeaks and crackles and was low and adult-like. Moreover, she said, I was the only pupil in the school capable of memorizing the entire play, which was imperative because Mr. Hargrove never exited throughout the three acts.

I had made a great effort to avoid participating. The first letter of my family name, an «A», had throughout the school years confined me to the first seat of the first row, forcing me to recite first and feel obliged to be the model. On the day when a roster of students was assigned to show up for the class play try-outs, I took the last seat in the auditorium, high up and in a corner, as invisible as I could make myself, safely out of range, I thought. Down in front, eager to be noticed, were those who lusted after a part. But when the drama teacher called for the first student to try out, she pointed right at me, saying, «We will start with those in the back row.»

I could have fluffed my try-out for the part. But it was not yet my nature to fail, so instinctually I rose to the occasion like a cornered animal doomed to its fate. I was assigned the lead role. Rehearsals took place over the homeroom hours and on two afternoons a week when I wasn't suffering catechism at the church. Jimmy and I were jamming in his soundproofed room that semester and needed the time to practice, and Shirley was taking up too many late hours. Because she was Catholic, she was handily forgiven every Sunday, if not whenever she crossed herself, while my unforgiven Protestant sins were piling atop one another like shovelfuls on a manure pile.

And I'd gotten in trouble by helping the neighbor boy, Luke— more than a boy, he was almost eighteen—steal six pairs of fancy show pigeons from a breeder's loft. This caper would be the most expedient way to upgrade our flock, Luke had said. He had a particular pigeon loft in mind—the owner not a member of the pigeon clubs and not an exhibitor, but an Indian from India, who, being a foreigner, wouldn't report the theft to the police, so he thought. Luke said he'd planned everything carefully, and if I agreed to go along and help pull off the heist we would split the loot.

Luke lived two houses away on the corner of the same street. It wasn't until mid-winter that I'd met him. I'd seen his birds in flight and on roofs, and had watched him work his homers, training them to hit the trap on return and not dally on the roof wasting racing time. He was the oldest of four kids, four years older than me. He smoked pre-rolled cigarettes, drooled from the sides of his mouth like a bulldog, and habitually spit sideways through tight lips as if shooting gnats on the fly. His thick lenses doubled the size of his eyes. When I looked at him straight on he always seemed too close. I was wary of his family; they were city-types, the father a professional man in some sort of business. When anywhere near Luke's house, I felt out of sorts. His younger sister, a bit older than me, had taunted me earlier on when I'd just moved into the block. She was awfully good-looking, with thick but not fat legs, and she wore short dresses. She attended Blessed Sacrament School nearby but, being younger, wouldn't have been in Shirley's class. All those Catholic girls, even Shirley, were mystical and unnatural.

Luke would stop by my place now and then. I didn't mind inviting him in because we would talk about pigeons, or sometimes about becoming rich, which was Luke's theme, not mine. Unlike other boys I knew from school, he had the aspect of a grown-up. He was down-to-earth, as factual as a toilet. He never played games or told jokes, never talked about school or sports. He didn't seem interested in anything. And when I wasn't with him, I had no idea what his thoughts might be. He would come over just to stand around, sit in a chair or on the edge of the bed, smoke, drink a Coke or a glass of Kool-Aid brought out from the house, look around and sometimes stare for long silent minutes at some object or image on my desk or work-table, on the floor, on a shelf, or tacked to a wall, but wouldn't ask what it was or why I had it there. Once he showed signs of curiosity in something I'd made: a magneto of six induction coils in series that could deliver 600,000 low-amp volts to any cat preying on my pigeons. I showed him how it worked by firing a bolt of lightening through wood an inch thick. Luke was impressed but warned me that his mother would get really upset if I electrocuted her cat.

Luke had decided that for our caper we would steal six adult pairs, three pairs apiece. Earlier that day through binoculars, he had reconnoitered the loft from atop a clay bank across the alley. The India-man's flock was composed of eight true varieties, he'd told me: Dragoons, Trumpeters, Fantails, English Pouters, Carriers, French Muffed Tumblers, English Clean-Legged Tumblers, and Archangels. Among them were some crosses, which Luke cautioned we must be careful in the darkness not to steal. He described the scene: the loft's fly-pen on the shed roof of a garage, the loft inside. He set the role I was to play, his features turning gangster-like, his face skewed and grimaced, as if he were laying plans to rob Sioux City's National Bank. He could create a real put-on face when in this gangster mode, and had adopted a high-pitched, narrow style of delivery like Peter Lorre.

Moments later we were headed to a distant neighborhood on the northwest segment of Sioux City, about a mile off. The air had become dark, the yellow streetlights attacked by bugs. It took a long half-hour to get to the pigeon loft. At the entrance of the alley we climbed the clay bank and waded through tall grasses and willow shrubs to the edge overlooking the loft. There we lay down on our bellies to peer over the edge, careful not to crumble it. The loft was a balconied upper story in the gable of the big garage. Attached at one end of the garage was a flat-roof shed surmounted by the loft's fly-pen. We could easily make out the alley windows by the light of a bare bulb on a nearby power pole. Luke said he should have brought his BB gun to shoot out the light.

Luke produced a roll of white surgical tape from his pocket. «This is what the pros use. You crisscross the window glass with strips of tape, then you break the glass and it all comes out in one piece—doesn't hardly make a sound, just a thunk.»

At that Luke smiled straight at me, then spit down the side of the bank and rolled over to lie on his back, hands on his chest, one hand grasping a pack of Lucky Strikes, the other the roll of tape. And that's the way we were bivouacked until the lights in the India-man's house went out and an extra half-hour had passed for good measure. On the highest level of the clay bank, in autumn dried grass, we lay in wait like tigers near the water hole, night-sighted timber wolves threatening the valley creatures—the Clay Bank Mob.

Stars were overhead with an ordinary moon that night, and crickets were sawing away at their legs like demented cellists. Autumnal forces were in progress—too late in the year for anything to breed, time for day creatures to go to sleep, for the summer ones to lie down and die. Lying there looking up at the sky, I thought about night sounds when sleeping outdoors on the farm: cicadas chirping, frogs croaking, the shrill radar calls of night-hawks, skunks chattering at the garbage pit, badgers arguing at the drainage ditch, a rodent the hoot-owl'd just pinioned, shrieking; dogs all across the county baying. In the city, the alleys at night—tomcats wailing over a female in heat, hoboes scavenging trash barrels, terrifying sounds in the rail yard downtown where in heavy darkness, risking hobo assaults and club-weilding guards, I would sneak into empty boxcars to glean soybeans and Canadian peas that had leaked from ruptured gunny sacks—pigeon food I couldn't afford to buy at the feed store.

Everything is more real at night. One hears everything in the world exactly as it is: a streetcar a mile away, train whistles as far off as Leeds, the Loadstar airplane flying a mile up, coming from Chicago, going over Sioux City about 10 P.M. every night. One wouldn't hear that airplane in the daytime when nothing at a great distance is heard except thunder.

That is what I thought about lying in the grass next to Luke. He felt real, not part of anything but himself. Nobody in the world except Luke knew where I was, and he wasn't the type to think about such things. He just lay there, flat on his back, puffing a cigarette, blowing clouds that drifted overhead. He hadn't spoken a word since he'd rolled over. I asked, «Luke, what if we get caught?» He was contemplating the cloudy sky he'd made out of smoke puffs, and now he spit straight up to make it rain. «We won't,» he replied, «we won't get caught.»

We stole the birds. The fancier's garage was unlocked—a ladder from the garage floor to the door of the loft was in place. And as Luke had predicted we found carrying-crates in the workshop attached to the garage. Luke climbed up into the loft to select the birds, judging each one in turn in the glare of his flashlight, while in the dim light coming through a window from the alley's power-pole bulb, I readied two crates and shoved them up the ladder. As swiftly as we could we completed the heist, then got out of there and headed down the alley towards home, each carrying a crate with six birds.

Luke had paired them, sexed them male and female, a breeding pair of each kind, just as Noah had when selecting couples to repopulate the earth he'd washed of sin. Now, with ark-like crates and doves in hand, we flowed silently through a mile-long network of alleys until we reached our own. I split off to cut across the orchard behind my family's house, passing between two giant box-elder trees, careful not to trip on their surface roots looping along the ground. It was close to midnight and very cold. Dead twigs and dry leaves beneath my boots were frosty and brittle; each step I took toward the garage sounded like radio static. Lights in the neighborhood were out; my entire family was asleep in the house, except for my father who wouldn't come home before two in the morning after closing his beer parlor or cashing in after a poker game somewhere in the county.

Luke had selected for me a pair each of Dragoons, Trumpeters, and Archangels. I released them one by one into my loft. The birds were startled, transfixed by the light turned on them. They posed with only their heads in motion, as pigeons do when confused. I gazed from one to the other, seeing them for the first time—the magnificent Dragoons that I'd seen in book reproductions at the library but never in real life: three times larger than barn pigeons, twice the size of my largest homer, an incredible wattle surmounting their bills, and eye ceres an inch in diameter! They were mystical—like Druids. And I had never seen an real Archangel; the one I thought I had was just a common bird that happened to rust-colored. I had read about Archangels and memorized their type: small, bright copper-colored, each feather of their wings outlined in black, fluorescent neck feathers, an elegant small cowl of reversed feathers at the basal arc of their head.

Hardly two days passed before the cuckolded fancier, having toured the town and located his birds in plain sight in our fly-pens, showed up at school with two detectives. I was seated at that moment in the rear of my homeroom class. The principal entered the classroom and walked to the teacher's desk at the head of the class. He said something to her, and then, with every pupil's face focused on his, he looked straight at me. At the same moment the teacher pushed back her chair, came around her desk on the American flag side, and approached me. So as not to disturb the class, she leaned down to get very close to my ear and said in a half-whisper, «Mr. Billings would like you to go with him to his office.»

I was interrogated in cold blood. Flagrantly I lied, told the detectives that my friend and I had bought the birds for twenty-five cents apiece from two boys at the Catholic school who'd had them out on the sidewalk in a cardboard box, saying they had to sell them because their family was moving west. The principal defended me, promoting that I was not the sort of boy who could possibly have committed such a crime. Convinced for the moment by the principal's heartfelt affirmations of my honesty and bolstered by my silver-tongued lying that they were barking up the wrong tree, the detectives let me off, saying with my mother's permission they had already recovered the birds, as they'd been identified by their registry bands (which an accomplished crook would have cut from their legs). When released to return to the classroom, I bolted out the back door of the school and headed out to find Luke and make sure that when questioned he would tell the same story.

I was racked with guilt. If I had lied with the courage of a lion, I had displayed the scruples of a thief. Never before had I felt such a loss of self-esteem; perhaps it was only then that I realized what self-esteem was. I could blame no one, not even Luke who'd talked me into doing that deed, so wickedly contributing to the delinquency of a minor. In retrospect, I know that at age fourteen a boy has a precarious hold on life. When reality bears down hardest, and childhood recedes too quickly for adulthood to take its place, crime slips into the vacuum. Adolescence is a hell on earth of deferred gratification when one hasn't yet learned to want sensibly. After two weeks of hating myself, I had no choice, short of blaming my Vikinging instincts, but to seek redemption through confession, not to the church preacher who, on hearing my unbosoming would mortify me if not cast me straight into hell, but to the man from whom I'd stolen the pigeons. I went on the next Sunday afternoon to see him, knocked on his door. When he opened it, a scowl on his face, I said, «I came to tell you I stole your pigeons.»

«Of course you did,» he snapped. «You were lying through your teeth.»

«Yes, Sir. I was.»

What else could I say? There couldn't be the least gap between what I'd said and what I meant—couldn't have both stolen his birds and claimed I hadn't.

I cannot recall the entire conversation that followed my confession and receipt of forgiveness. Maybe it was the cute cowlick atop my blond head that Brilliantine couldn't put down. Maybe my endearing blue eyes liquefied the India-man's heart. Perhaps he was startled by my confession. Rather than retaliating with some grand dressing-down, after a few befuddling words he took me to his back yard to see the birds in his loft that a few days before I'd helped to plunder. He sat with me on lawn chairs around a garden table spiced with pigeon and sparrow droppings, asked who I was and what my life was like, and after the least response came forward with a surprising offer. He was Indian on his father's side, he said, his mother was British, and he was about to go to India to marry a girl his father had provided dowry for. He wanted to rent out his house for a year, but most likely no one would take it with a pigeon coop in a foul-smelling garage. He'd sold some of his birds, he said, but would give me his remaining collection if I'd trash his coop and fly-pen and put the garage in an impeccable and odorless state. Less than a week of after-school labor passed before his garage smelled like a ladies' powder room and my coop housed several show-quality fancy pigeons: Tumblers, Dragoons, Archangels, Trumpeters, Pouters.

In spite of that crisis, the performance date of the Class Play came along, as dates typically do. I'd managed to memorize the entire play and had designed and built the stage set, which was, for Act II, the fuselage of an airplane, while Acts I and III took place in an ordinary living room and needed only furniture. I played my part as expected, but near the middle of the second act made a dreadful error. Two of my lines had a similar ending; each was a cue. I uttered the wrong one first. The girl playing opposite me, playing Mr. Hargrove's wife, took that cue and skipped a section of dialogue, neither of us realizing at the time what we'd done. I took up my lines where, in turn, she cued me in. The blooper cut out one of the bit-part actors waiting in the wings to enter and say her few lines, the only lines she had. When the act was over, the curtain down, and I'd exited to get ready for Act III, the erased girl was behind stage, hysterical, screaming at me through pulsating sobs. She'd been practicing for a month, her entire family was in the audience, she was emotionally devastated, she hated me, the entire cast was wrought up; their leading man had failed them. I felt decimated. For the first time in my entire life, I had made a public mistake! I managed half-consciously to get through the final act and the bows and curtain calls, then escaped through the stage's fire door and fled for Grandview Park where I washed off my stage makeup in the birdbath and snuck home through alleys to my hovel in the garage. I wound myself inside my quilt and lay awake, cocooned, over the rest of the night.

The final weeks of junior high school life went from bad to worse. At Grace Lutheran Church, where the Reverend Jancke presided over a dozen or so adolescents born into sin, I'd been almost expelled from catechism class a couple of times. I'd promoted natural origins and refused to disavow evolution. Nor would I agree with the pastor that Eve's desire for knowledge was the cause of thorns and thistles, which I dared attribute instead to bad farming. I had over-argued that point and pumped up the Reverend's blood pressure to a life-threatening level. Catechism class was held in the basement of the church—an appropriate place, one level below the terrestrial church floor and two levels below the sky's mantle, like the descending layers of Heaven, Earth, and Hell. Reverend Jancke was obsessed with sin down in that hellish basement room, he in his black-crow robe and shiny patent-leather shoes, battering us with his heavy-handed omniscient preachiness. Behind the desk, at which he sat for the hour, was a pull-down oil cloth sheet on which was pictured a colossal tree with many branches. On one side of the tree's trunk each branch was labeled a sin of commission; on the other side were the sins of omission.

I had thought that when Moses met with God atop a mountain all worldly sins were negotiated down to ten manageable ones. But Reverend Jancke must have had twenty on each side of the tree trunk. While he ran through his branchy roster of sins, skipping over adultery which wouldn't apply to our ages, I occupied my detracted mind with such practical acts as counting loops in the twin braids at the back of the girl's head in front of me to determine if they were equally woven and balanced. Surely God had made Adam and Eve asymmetrical and caused Cain and Abel to behave asymmetrically, and had set the North Pole intentionally off center. Nothing that is symmetrical or balanced can be in motion or alive. One had only to look at an empty teeter-totter to understand that universal principle. Or at a girl's paired braids. If evenly woven, she would still be a virgin, I assumed.

I didn't like Reverend Jancke. He had insulted my father. After one special Christmas Eve candlelight service when he noticed my father pushing in with his big Danish smile through the departing congregation to shake his hand and say Merry Christmas, Jancke turned his back on him. My father tried a couple more times to get his hand in, but Jancke made it obvious that he wasn't about to shake one as sinful as his. Janke had also threatened to excommunicate my sister Fern because she'd refused to confess that ballroom dancing was sinful.

This Reverend wasn't showing any of us the right way. To go his way was to deny every other path, to give up, to sublimate, to repress all desires and my own omnipotence. We were lost children, he said, but I knew at all times where I was, even if he didn't. I was more factually unlost than he; he couldn't even know where God was, for if God is everywhere he's nowhere, as I once told the Reverend, but he didn't understand what I meant. I didn't believe in ghosts, so no Holy Ghost dwelled within me, and if Jesus died on the cross for all of our sins, why did I have to die for my share, and why should I deteriorate to cannibalism and drink of his blood and eat of his flesh? It wasn't that I didn't believe in a supreme being named God. I didn't believe in the preacher.

On Confirmation Sunday, when we novitiates in white robes were seated piously in a semi-circle facing the congregation, each of us were to respond to three questions from the pastor. My name, starting with an A, put me in the first chair to the congregation's left, the first to be subjected to the inquisition. Reverend Jancke asked me to recite the first, fifth and tenth commandments. I stared at him, trying not to look insolent. I hadn't planned not to respond, but at the moment he asked the question, I froze. He repeated the question, but I'd become as hard as stone and as resolutely silent. He shifted his eyes to the next kid, asked her to name the two animals in «The Sacrifice of Isaac»—that dreadful story of a man who would have plunged a knife into his own son's heart just to prove his willingness to obey the Lord. The girl responded without hesitation, «the donkey and the ram.» Reverend Jancke glared at me before moving on to examine the third kid, and so on down the line. When my second turn came, Jancke paused over his question list, looked toward me threateningly over his glasses, his brow arched like the church ceiling. As if aiming a weapon, he asked me to explain a certain passage from Luke: «For no good tree bears bad fruit, nor does a bad tree bear good fruit; each tree is known by its own fruit.»

I wanted desperately to answer that one because he'd aimed it at me like a thrown dagger. I could have talked on the subject forever while upsetting him with a Darwinian explanation for fruit crop improvement. The Reverend repeated the question, his quality of teaching at stake. My revenge would be in control of my failure. I could see my mother and sisters just a few rows back in the congregation. I thought I saw my mother wipe her eyes with her handkerchief, crying over my abstention. I was getting dizzy from holding my breath; if I were to breathe I might speak inadvertently. The Reverend scowled and passed me over with a short wave of his preaching arm, like an umpire calling a strike. The inquisition passed on to the next child.

I was beginning to feel awful about what I was doing up there, embarrassing my family in front of everyone. I decided to respond to the third question with fullness and brilliance, for there wasn't anything the Reverend might ask me that I couldn't use to redeem myself in astonishing detail. But I didn't get the chance to reconstruct my ruination. He skipped over me the third and final time around.

I was confirmed anyway. The preacher would be rid of me. The reception at home after the ceremony was like a funeral wake with me as a living corpse. My parents and sisters were kind enough not to bring up my failure to respond. I managed to keep on my robe, look pious, and hold in folded hands the Bible my mother presented to me after she'd inscribed it with family names and birth dates. I still have that Bible—a red-letter edition with a zipper, the imitation leather cover now cracked and crinkled but the paper still bright. In 1970 when, at the age of 42, I had about completed my book *Gauguin's Paradise Lost*, I added a chapter entitled «The Calvary of Eve.» At the time my psyche must have been still coping with that confirmation trauma. As source material for some parts of that chapter, I used the begifted confirmation Bible. I had defended Eve in Reverend Jancke's class and would defend her again, charging God for using her as a defining device to set sin off from grace, and for disgracing grain farmers by preferring Abel's sacrifice of a lamb. In my text, Jesus and Eve meet on Calvary Hill, each bearing their crossweight of grievances: Eve caused to bear children in pain and Jesus to bear the weight of earthly sins.

Chapter 20

The white woolly mass flowed
like a glacier under a summer sun

So ended my junior high school years. A pigeon thief, a liar, an excommunicated sinner; cleaning a saloon when I should be in church, going to blue movies with Leona; my red blood cells being drained by an incorrigible nymphet, softening my brain and turning my blond hair as white as a Swede's. Still, not everything had failed me, and I'd kept up a good front. My grades were high, and to my face no one disliked me. I presented a good-looking exterior—popular, smart and clever, a smooth talker and dancer. Any number of girls would have welcomed my invitation to the prom. I invited as my date a pretty Jewish girl named Marcia, who was so sophisticated that an ordinary boy wouldn't dare walk down the street with her. As had Lorraine, she lived in a house built not of straw, not of wood, but of brick, the sort of house a wolf cannot blow down. Arriving at her house to pick her up for the walk to the dance, I was invited in: «Come in, come in. Marcia is not quite ready,» her mother, whom I'd not met before, said melodiously, and she directed me to a seat on her living room sofa. I'd hardly had to say a word to her mother before Marcia came tripping down the stairs, barefoot and covered only by a black lace shift. That shocked me, for I thought women's underwear was supposed to be white in the country and pink in the city. Not flustered in the least by her indecent exposure, Marcia tossed me a cheery hello and after getting something from the kitchen, came over to accept the corsage I'd brought her, a white gardenia decorated with red rosebuds, then raced upstairs, leaving me in a dense cloud of perfume.

But inside me was a distressed central self, a core that was rotting. I needed an environmental change The best escape would be out of the city and onto a farm, dragging a thick eraser behind me to eradicate the past. Hardly a week had passed after school let out for the summer than my father came up with a proposal, a job on a sheep farm, far away from urban iniquities, where perhaps like shepherd Abel, who was commendatory in God's eyes, I would find some peace and quiet.

This time I would not be working for an uncle for no pay but the Supervisor of County Roads, who owned a farm about twenty miles north of Sioux City and a mile east of Le Mars. I would be paid thirty dollars a month plus room and board with Sundays off. The farmer's name was Charles Riggs. He was one of my father's regular customers, and as I found out soon enough in one sense, but too late in another, an alcoholic. He frequented saloons in every town within his district while out inspecting roads, leaving me to work his sheep and serve the daily needs of his aged and ailing wife, condemned to finish her life in silence and exile.

My father drove me to the Riggs place. After having coffee with the Riggs, he headed back to town. Mr. Riggs sat me down at the kitchen table to hear an outline of my job. As County Supervisor he would be away from the farm most every day. First thing at sunrise, I was to open the feed-lots and drive the sheep to designated fields, alternating pastures every few days as the forage was nibbled down (unlike cows, sheep cut grass close to the root); feed the horse and pick its stall, bring cobs and a day's load of firewood to the house, where Mrs. Riggs would give me breakfast and a packed lunch. Twice daily, saddle the mare and ride fences to check for sheep that had gotten their heads caught in the fence's wire rectangles designed to keep in pigs who don't harbor thoughts that grass is greener on the other side. Late in the day, before bringing in the sheep for the night, haul sacks of grain-pellets and cracked corn to the feed-lots, distribute the feed along a couple dozen twenty-foot-long feed troughs, pump fresh water into a very long sheet-metal water trough.

Riggs was a large, square-jawed man about sixty, stout as a bull yet fat as a sow, sandy haired and brown-eyed, well-groomed hair, looking like he could have been a city banker. My father had assured me he would not be a bad person to work for. A responsible man, he said, and good for the county, with sympathetic ears and a firm handle on the county budget. Road building and maintenance contractors could come to terms with him. They needed his help and he needed theirs, for farmers controlled county politics and had friends at the state capital.

Late each morning Mr. Riggs would drive to the county seat at Le Mars and long about dark return from somewhere in the county. To keep in touch with his constituency, he circulated from one to another farm town where locals gathered. He'd ask about their families, listen to complaints about rutted roads, wash-outs and plugged culverts, sagging power lines, shorted-out transformers. He probably took a few beers at every town he visited. Many were the time I would see his headlights immobile at the farm-lane gate off the gravel county road. He could make it to the gate but was not always sober enough to get out of his car and open it. I would leg it down to wrestle his dead-weight from behind the wheel to the passenger side, drive him the last hundred yards to the house and leave him propped in the seat to sleep it off enough to wake up and turn in for the rest of the night.

Mrs. Riggs looked older. White-haired and sallow, near skin and bones, shaky, her thin purply hands warped by arthritis, and she spoke with a tremor. Her chest was leveled and her floral print dresses hung loosely to mid-calf above mousy house-slippers. Her dry flaxen hair, tightly combed and gathered at the back in a braided knot, must have flowed once upon a time in golden ripples around moist ochre eyes and pink cheeks, her narrow face then powdered pale, her body lithe and firm, corseted like a wasp's. I knew her figure in youth from a tinted wedding photograph I spied on her dresser one day when she and Mr. Riggs were in town and I'd looked into their bedroom—lavender satin sheets under a white chenille spread, throw-pillows in blue velour cases, a purple flannel bathrobe studded with bunny-rabbit tails

The Riggs' place was a different sort of farm than any I had known. It would give me a taste of what a gentleman's farm was like— not a diversified subsistence farm but orderly and for profit. No work horses, cows, or pigs, and except for a few acres of alfalfa, no field crops, just grazing pastures in every direction, uniformly green and fenced. On my survey of the farm a shepherd dog hung in close, look-ing me over as severely as I was sizing up the buildings and grounds— a low-slung yellow-eyed Alsatian farmhand, gray at the muzzle, who would soon give me some tips about sheep-tending.

The sheep sheds and board-fenced yards were empty. Off in a dis-tant pasture a large flock was scattered like white caps on a grass green sea. In the farmyard, I saw a tractor in a lean-to shed no bigger than a single garage, a small rubber-tired Ford, unscratched and polished, that didn't look like it could pull much of anything. In a stable of sorts that didn't have the look of a horse barn, I found a well-groomed sorrel mare in a box stall. Astride a rack was a single western saddle, decoratively tooled. The mare hadn't been turned out, I assumed, to protect her from horse flies that hang out in sunny air. I entered the stall and gave her a few pats, figuring we'd soon get acquainted. Other than a scattering of hens and roosters running loose, and a couple of mouser cats, no other animals caught my eye.

As a hired man approaching age fourteen, I wasn't a viable statistic. The youngest age bracket classified by the Iowa Agricultural Experiment Station was sixteen to nineteen. That bracket comprised twenty percent of Iowa's farm laborers, of which ten percent had not finished the eighth grade. By 1942 the figures may have changed, as many of the eighteen to twenty-five-year-olds had been inducted, and by 1943, Iowa was making use of German and Italian war prisoners to work the larger farms. But at the time I wasn't aware of any such statistics. All I knew was that over the next three months there would be about 450 sheep to tend, weeds to keep down with a scythe, wood to chop, fences to keep in repair, water to pump, and that in a few weeks I'd be weaning lambs born in April and May that would be ready for market in early Fall, about when I'd be returning to school.

Never before in my life had I seen a sheep farm—hadn't even seen a sheep except at the Plymouth County Agricultural Fair. Riggs' pastures looked like vast city lawns—timothy and brome grass mixed with Ladino clover. Ordinary pastures, like those on our Hinton farm, were made from acres not suitable for corn, seeded with prairie and orchard grass and nature's weedy contributions: peppergrass, bindweed, red sorrel where the turf was thin, and along fences and in scattered clumps that the cows hadn't cut down, daisies and buttercups, ragweed, wild mustard, wild carrot, thistles, cockleburs, and reed canarygrass where soil edging a creek was soggy. But other than a few clumps of clover blossoms, daisies and buttercups, Riggs' sheep pastures looked as if they'd been mowed. And I had thought that sheep belonged to good shepherds in the Bible and on the grasslands of Montana, Idaho, and New Zealand. It wouldn't have occurred to me that a serious Iowa farmer would raise sheep. As I came to know later, mutton was a capital industry in Iowa, third to dairy cows and hogs. But unlike out in the Wild West where sheep herds roam freely over boundless ranges, Iowa sheep graze in fenced pastures from spring to autumn and winter-over in feedlots and under sheds.

Moving sheep from shed to pasture turned out to be a simple task. Just open the gates. My helper, the dog named Shep, would get the flock moving through fenced channels that led to alternate pastures. Once underway, lead ewes pulled the flock along like magnets dragging iron filings. With the old girls in front following my brisk trot, and Shep in the rear, barking and nipping straggler's heels, the white woolly mass flowed like a glacier under a summer sun. When the last slowpoke was in the designated pasture, and the sheep up ahead were fanning out to graze, Shep would turn and look at me, perhaps saying in his head that could think but not talk, «Don't just stand there, shut the gate!» Bringing the sheep in at day's end was even easier, for by then they needed to drink. Bored with grazing all day, they lusted after grain and were waiting impatiently for me to send them home for supper. I didn't have to lead them and Shep had an easy time as the driver.

The 1940 farm census identified 19% of Iowa farms as having a substantial number of breeding ewes. That would figure about 41,000 farms out of a 212,500 total—an awful lot of sheep, 1.3 million in fact, but not so many considering that in the same year, Iowa farmers supported about 10 million hogs and 1.2 million horses and mules. By the 1920s, sheep wool was not a commercial product in Iowas. In the nineteenth century, the government had subsidized woolen mills to reduce dependence on imports. In 1875, in Iowa alone, were 85 mills, but Iowa's sheep farmers couldn't produce enough to keep them going. By 1880, the number of mills was reduced to 50; by my time there were none with commercial capacity.

The hog-to-sheep ratio was an economic factor, a sort of balanced investment fund. Hogs and sheep are prone to different diseases, so when a year or two of hog cholera lowers a farmer's income from pork production, the mutton income rises to help offset the loss.

I gleaned these statistics from sheep-farmer reports, finding answers to what puzzled me about the sheep I was tending. It wouldn't have done any good to ask Mr. Riggs, because he didn't seem to like me, and Mrs. Riggs wouldn't converse with me at all. I was, after all, a hired man, which too often in those days was just a notch above a slave. Accounts that I've read by others who farmed-out at youths tell the same story—both boys and girls often treated badly, and girls subjected to sexual teasing, mauling, and rape, and too bewildered and humiliated to expose their assailants. It was of course true that farmers had to be careful about not getting family-like with hired boys or men, leading them to feel part of the family and expecting privileges, such as dating a daughter or borrowing the car.

I took my meals on the porch, not at the table; used the outhouse, not the modern toilet in the house, and hand washed my own clothes on a wash-bench in the houseyard, even though Mrs. Riggs had an electric washing machine. No conversation took place between her and me, just work orders and grievances: the stove kindling too green, tracked-in dirt on the linoleum floor when I came in to take out her trash, and she said enough times that I left behind an odor in the house. She loathed the thick scent of wet sheep wool, the creosotic vapors of sheep-dip and tick-spray that bonds to one's work clothes like smoke-house smoke to meat.

I couldn't avoid physical contact with the sheep, had put my arms around more sheep that summer than any lover around different women—sheep with their heads caught in the fence, kneeling down beside their fat bodies, their creamy subcutaneous tallow melting from exertion in the hot sun, clasping them with an elbow at each shoulder, pushing them forward in the hog-wire noose, my fingers clawing back the bunched-up thick wrinkles of neck skin until their short-haired ears were at the wire, pressing down the skull with the left hand while through the fence pushing up the muzzle with the right, extracting the head. The denoosed ewe would race off in leaps and with backward glances as if she'd been mugged and violated by the good shepherd.

«Didn't see much of you around this afternoon. What were you up to?»

«Just working, cleaning up things, currying the horse.»

«Well, you have plenty to do, so keep busy.»

One evening after supper Mrs. Riggs spied me from the kitchen window sitting on the bench scrubbing socks in a washbasin. «Get on your feet!» she screeched. «A good man does not sit down while working.» She was the first person to call me a good man, if that was what she meant—a good man when vertical, upstanding, erect, but she wouldn't have been aware of that meaning, so instinctually buried.

One of the few evenings Mr. Riggs came home sober for dinner, he said over the meal I was invited in to share because it was raining, «A good man would have cleared that windfall in two days.» He was the second person to call me a man, although not a good one. A ferocious windstorm had mauled the woods and toppled three cottonwood trees. I was told to saw them into wood blocks, piled up to dry for next year's splitting. Between sheep and fieldwork I had been at that chore for a week, lopping off limbs, sawing and chopping. I felt inclined to mention that he'd forbidden my use of dynamite sticks to split the logs lengthwise— «Too close to the house, you might blow out windows,» he said—and that it was as hard for one man to cross-cut tree trunks into splittable blocks with a two-man saw as it was for a kid to teeter-totter by himself. But I held off trying to explain it away.

He wouldn't have had the good sense to thank me for rushing up the windmill hill during the middle of a night-time storm, in driving rain and lightning striking all around the place, to brake the whirling fan blades that would surely have shattered had they kept turning so wildly. He would remain oblivious to the amount of destruction I'd saved his farm by acting so swiftly and at risk to my life. Nor was he emotionally affected over weaning lambs having been attacked by marauding dogs the night before. The shepherd sleeping nights with alert ears and a ready shotgun was I, not him. He must have been aware that the sheep-production problem in Iowa was in good part laid to dogs, something I'd learned first-hand when coming to the weaning pasture in the early morning and finding two prime lambs dead on the ground, a few more chewed up but alive, and three entangled in a fence they'd tried to climb in their panic.

Had I been in Montana, the culprits would have been wolves, but wolves don't kill for fun and leave uneaten carcasses on the killing field. The genes of domesticated dogs are entirely screwed up, having lost the neural connectors between hunger and killing, like serial killers of any stripe. In the nineteenth century, farmers rebuffed the federal government's push to increase the production of wool, saying it wouldn't be possible unless dog breeding were outlawed. In 1862, the Iowa legislature had passed a measure taxing dogs one to three dollars a head, ordering county police officers to kill dogs running loose without collars and tags, and making dog owners responsible for the cost of livestock their dogs destroyed. That law was still in effect, but I wasn't satisfied that a county sheriff had any more rights than a good shepherd does to protect his sheep, so I deputized myself, and with Mr. Riggs' 12-gauge pump-action shotgun decimated two buccaneering dogs while lying in ambush at the most likely path to the weaning pasture. The path crossed a small creek, which in August was more like a string of shallow pools lined with small willows and moisture-loving brushwood. I had old Shep with me, and a good moon to see by. I hunkered down—Shep on his belly, too, my right elbow on his neck so he'd stay in place—and listened to the frogs croaking, knowing that should they stop it was because something was threatening.

Frogs are sentries, a good thing to know when alone in a wilderness. An hour or two of frog music passed, then Shep emitted a low rumbling growl. Whether the frogs had stopped croaking at that moment, I don't recall. Shep raise his head. I whispered for him to stay, and readied my aim in the direction his nose was pointed. My aim followed the line of his nose as he slowly turned it. Two large dogs soon trotted into view. Shep let out a fierce growl. On hearing it, the dogs froze in their tracks—a fatal hesitation. My gun exploded four or five times. The dogs were whirled about by the impacts and in a jiffy were dead. When Mr. Riggs saw the carnage the next morning, he seemed a bit more respectful of me.

At the time this was happening, I didn't know that the sheep I was tending were descendants of stock imported from Sussex, England in the 1880s by a Captain Moreton, a retired British naval officer. Over that decade, sons of British aristocracy, wearing fashionable London clothes, had arrived as emigrants, lured by the Iowa Land Company listed on the London stock exchange with capital stock of $5.5 million—half a billion by today's money. Promotional literature promised a 50% profit to investors, and a safe Iowa environment «where no one carries revolvers or other arms, bowie knives and such playthings.» Captain Moreton started a farmer's training camp on one thousand acres near Le Mars, where inexperienced gentry-bred settlers were taught how to farm. An English correspondent who visited the place wrote of aristocratic boys doing most of the work, while pointing out as well that he'd found Lord Hobart mowing grain, and the honorable Captain Moreton, himself, feeding a threshing machine, assisted by two of Lord St. Vincent's sons. The settled-in gentlemen imported foxhounds, polo and steeplechase horses, constructed a racetrack and polo grounds, and formed a polo team competent to play against established teams in St. Louis and Chicago. The gentlemen and ladies rode to hounds over hundreds of grazing acres, and dressed impeccably for dining and dancing. The men shaved every morning, honoring the motto that the sun never rose or set on an unshaven British chin. Their favorite tavern was called the House of Lords. Le Mars was no doubt the only town in the Midwest with a church in which prayers were offered to Queen Victoria as Head of State.

But by the early 1890s the fun and games were over. As the young men aged, they married imported girls and started raising families. Then fanciful reality got entangled in hard facts. With cheap land still available, there were no landless peasants to do the hard labor. Peasant-types worked their own acreage. And after a few years of severe droughts, grasshopper invasions, and bitter winters, the colonists lost their élan. Many returned homesick to England. Some re-settled in more civilized Minnesota. Their land was subdivided and bought up by Germans who were not aristocrats but ordinary farmers. The cattle and sheep herds were divided and sold. Genetic quality fell off rapidly when no longer fortified by bulls and rams imported from England or British-type farms in the eastern states. The polo and cricket fields were plowed over. Pub-like taverns became rowdy beer halls, dancing regressed from courtly waltzes and minuets to family-type square and circle dancing.

With the sun having no more say in seasonal matters than I did, the summer on the Riggs farm managed to pass. At the end of my last day, I didn't wait for Mr. Riggs to come home and offer me a ride to Sioux City, but packed my canvas bag, chained Shep so he wouldn't follow me, and took off walking, bemused by the fact that the next day, beer-bellied Riggs would have to haul his own feed sacks in an early September sun still hot. Twenty miles at a farmer's stride would take only half the night. Maybe I'd get to Fourth Street before the last street-car headed up Jackson, or to my father's saloon in time for a ride home. But I hadn't hiked more than a mile or two before a trucker stopped and offered me a ride to town, so I was home long before midnight. And I saw that Shirley's bedroom light was still burning.

Chapter 21

I wouldn't trade any bird in my
loft for that young cock of yours

In mid-September 1943, after the summer on the Riggs farm, I enrolled in Sioux City's Central High School. This famous «Castle on the Hill» was then fifty years old, built in 1892. The American flag was raised atop its pole on February 22nd, 1893, with the first commencement held in June. A three-story building, constructed of large blocks of prentisse brown sandstone with a 102-foot tower, was a fit and enduring monument to Sioux City's confidence in its future and dedication to progressive education. The first impression it gave, however, was that of a fortification, and more than one out-of-town visitor, not aware of the building's purpose, was puzzled as to why the city would build a prison in the midst of a residential neighborhood.

That June, my mother had moved us again, this time to another rented house, at 1014 27th Street, the fourth domicile and fourth neighborhood in Sioux City we would inhabit. I had to forsake my garage, and with no place to meet nights I also lost Shirley, who by this time had no need of me anyway. In 1942, a military airbase had been established across the river. Shirley had turned seventeen and started dating men from the base, much to the displeasure of her parents, but by then she was more than ever out of their control. Over the summer, she'd attended a girl's finishing school and been practicing walking in spike heels with a book on her head and applying make-up. Her mother had a drawer full of silk stockings that Shirley's father got at one of the only places one could get anything made of silk, the airbase PX (post exchange), where airmen would say they were buying them for their wives. «Mostly they give them to girls they get sex from,» Shirley said.

«Silk's a war material,» I recall saying. «We can't get it from Japan and China anymore, and what we have we need to make parachutes for the paratroopers.»

«It's needed for girls' stockings too!» Shirley pouted. «If a girl wants to show off her legs, she can't put them in cotton socks.»

My allotment of the new family house was on the second level, a closed-in rear porch with a single iron-spring bed and three-drawer dresser. The house had no garage and hardly any yard. I built my new pigeon house across the street on a vacant lot backed by a steep clay bank, without concern over who owned the property. My father provided the lumber and wire, delivered from a used-lumber yard where we'd gone together to pick what I would need. This loft would be the largest I'd ever had, roomy enough to divide nesting pairs from unmated youngsters, and for me a compartment where I could hide out when needing to be alone with my thoughts and fantasies.

Jimmy and I had put together a five-piece band—the two of us plus a piano, trumpet, and bass fiddle. We played school dances and wedding parties around town, earning fifteen to twenty-five dollars per engagement, three to five dollars apiece. But over the entire first year of high school, feeling different in ways I was sure no one else was, I made no effort to come close to anyone. Jimmy was too good a friend for any other boy to measure up to. So not much could be gained by socializing with anyone else.

Day-to-day school life focused on activities. In classes, I tried to keep up without standing out, as again I was on the bottom rung and not inclined to fight my way up. As a first-year pupil I couldn't hope to perform stage work, so my interest in stage magic and impersonations trailed off. Only the English and art classes aroused my attention, the other five or six taken over the year, dull in their regularity—history, civics, geography, and such—have blended over time into soluable abstractions.

The art room was huge, the classes amorphous, not organized by grade level but by any student's available time. One could work in the studio whenever the school doors were open. Commercial art was emphasized, media and technique, the sort of art that leads to employment rather than life in a garret. Mostly I worked at silk-screening posters for the drama department. Near the end of the spring term I demonstraed to the art and drama teachers that I could design and operate stage lighting for the senior class play. With their permission, I created utterly fantastic and bizarre effects to go along with the spooky drama, the theme of which I've forgotten. Having noticed that the lighting designer was not acknowledged in the program, the art teacher wrote a remedial review for the school newspaper, headed, The Magician Behind the Scenes.

Central High was progressive and had been from the start. Back in the spring of 1893, its Civics Club scheduled formal debates on compulsory education, capital punishment, the annexation of Hawaii, and the issue of Whites versus Negroes in the South. The science laboratory was equipped from the start with one of the first voice recording instruments available in high schools; at a special Sioux City Educational Exhibit at the Chicago World's Fair, recorded voices of Central High's students were heard by an incredulous public. Sioux City girls, attending that fair and seeing eastern girls there, returned with the first reformation idea appropriate to the new school: the right for girls to wear knee-length dresses during muddy weather. Of this, a local newspaper, the *Record,* said in an editorial, «The high school, as well as the world at large, awaits with breathless interest the debut of the young ladies in knee dresses, but it's dollars to cents that when the next rainy day comes they'll either wear their old dresses or stay at home.»

Writing, particularly essay writing, was being stressed in all of the Iowa schools. At Central High's first commencement, the salutatorian made an oratorical speech, the valedictorian read an essay, and two or three other graduating students took their turn at oral delivery of an topic on some social issue. The school newspaper reported an unusual incident at a graduation ceremony. Louise Rees, with «Ceaseless» as her topic, stepped up to the platform and opened by stating that, in justice, she should have received the highest honors because her standing was the highest, but that she wanted to take the opportunity to openly forgive all those who had committed the injustice and diminished her status. Louise had been ill for a good part of her first year. Although given grades for that year and earning the highest grades over the next years, the selection committee insisted that the top honor could go only to a student in full attendance for every year. While her audience sat motionless, struggling to discern whether she was being jocular or sincere,

Louise then proceded to deliver her essay. I identify with Louise Rees. One should be rewarded on the basis of one's accomplishment, not by adherence to rules over which one has no control.

A story I wrote in the first term, read by the teacher to the class, was depreciated by fellow students' accusations of my having copied it from somewhere—from where, nobody would even speculate. In biology class, my laboratory book was downgraded because the cells I'd drawn in it while peering at specimens in a microscope looked exactly like what I'd seen, including dirt particles on the old slide and cell walls that had ruptured when the plant tissue was sliced for mounting. My teacher was very upset. He said I'd drawn the slide and not the specimen; he showed me the difference between my ugly drawings and those in the textbook, saying, «Don't draw what you see but what the cells actually look like.» To that I responded, «Then why don't I copy from the book rather than look into a microscope?» From then on, in my biology teacher's eyes, I was pond slime.

As the weeks passed in English class, eager to write essays, I also looked forward to writing short stories like Ernest Thompson Seton's *Wild Animals I Have Known,* and eventually long stories emulating Jack London's *The Call of the Wild* and *White Fang.* But in writing class the academic world came apart during the essay-writing phase early in the year, when creative writing supplanted the previous weeks of focus on grammar. After a month spent composing literary sketches—plot set-ups, character descriptions, two- and three-person narratives—the graying-haired teacher, who'd published a few stories in *Reader's Digest,* assigned the first story we were to write as homework. She gave us a plot: «Suppose you had only 24 hours to live—what would you do?» We were granted one week to author a response.

I hadn't the faintest idea what I would do if faced with imminent in class would say they'd do: confess their sins, apologize to all the people they'd offended, and like Miss America contestants, who say they are going into teaching the handicapped or nursing in an orphanage or old folks' home, would do sugary things, such as distribute their possessions among the poor and buy candy and an ice-cream cone for every kid in the neighborhood. The themes would flow with bleeding-heart sentiment. This was, after all, the high school from which the Friedman twins, Abigail Van Buren (Dear Abby) and Ann Landers (Dear Ann), graduated in 1936, going on to Sioux City's Morningside College, where they perfected their gossip columns and married well (Esther Pauline and Pauline Esther were their personal names, cleverly symmetrical. «Stuck-up Jewish girls» they were systematically called, according to my sister Bethel, who was one of their classmates).[41]

Since any notion of me dying couldn't anchor thoughts about what I would do were I about to die, the character couldn't be me but would have to be someone else. I decided to write the essay in third person and overreach for the sake of exaggeration and theatricality. Obedient to my natural propensity, an appropriate title came quickly to mind: *The Man Who Could Not Die.*

I fashioned a fictional character: a wicked old man living in a rooming house who'd just been told by his physician that he had only twenty-four hours to live. The distraught man couldn't think about anything but an abiding vulture perched on his shoulder—the horror of it, like a death-row prisoner on Alcatraz condemned to count days, then hours, then minutes, then seconds, to the moment the warden would take his eyes off the red telephone and pull the switch. Left alone in his room—an attic room, of course, the hours deep into winter and with darkness falling—the old man layers anger on dread, enraged that he'd had no more choice in the matter of dying than when being born. And now his last hours will pass in guiltiness and pain, with grimacing devils lying in wait for him, fanning the coals, heating their pitchforks and torture irons. Having years ago forsaken the church, knowing he'd failed his last hope, the old man tries but doesn't know how to stuff all his deadly sins into one confession, not having dealt with them timely in portions a priest could digest. He fixes on suicide—will take charge of the situation and challenge death on its own terms, downing every pill he can find in his medicine cabinet, the medley of over-doses washed down his throat with gulps of water spiked with rat poison. With a razor blade, he slits his wrists.

But the pills have no effect, as if they had neutralized each other. The rat poison burns in his stomach. Blood from his wrists is not flowing, only leaking. He grabs a butcher knife but in his weakening condition can't drive it through the ribcage that protects his heart; he plunges it into his liver and again and again into his guts. So much blood on the floor, he slips and slides but doesn't fall. Suddenly a rapping at his door.

He staggers, opens it. No one there. No one. But he hears voices ... or was it the sound of singing? The calling is coming from the foot of the stairs. He is drawn down, out the door, into the night. Hand over hand, clutching at air, he gropes through blackness, following the singing voice that leads him to a church, an empty church, but with doors open and candles burning on the altar. His now bloodless body white as a sheet, this ghostly man stumbles through the church door and up the aisle— the singing now coming from the altar, lifting in great crescendos, while the altar candles burns more and more brightly until the entire nave is dazzling, the choir deafening. The man cups his ears in bloody hands, pressing fingertips into his eyes, bellows a shattering appeal, an ejaculatory confession. He disintegrates—not dead, just gone. A stain on the floor the janitor will mop up in the morning.

After the stories had been turned in, the teacher at the next class meeting asked two pupils to come to the front and read aloud. Their stories were as expected: soppy, tear-jerking, nauseating. Then she took up another manuscript, looked my way, and said something like, «Here's a story written by Wayne, and if he doesn't mind, I will read it myself.» Because she was also one of the school's drama teachers, she read it with profuse dramatization. When she'd finished, she had tears in her eyes. After class, she held me back for a moment to ask if she could make a copy of my story and I agreed.

On going down the hall to my next subject, a boy from the writing class called out to me: «Where'd you copy that story from?» Three or four others from the class were walking near him, and before I could react to his noxious insult, I noticed they were of the same mind. We came to a confrontational stop. They accused me of plagiarism and needled me to admit it, convinced that no one my age could write that well.

This acid-in-the-face assault against which I couldn't defend myself burned deeply. Influenced by the class accusation, the teacher suspended my grade. Thereafter, there would be no in-between; papers and my test sheets would be handed in pre-graded—an A when I felt like it, otherwise an F. The distraught teacher became alarmed over my alternating grades. «Why are you doing this?» she asked. I responded that I wanted to control my own life, be my own judge; no longer would I trust anyone to determine the least iota of my fate.

She couldn't know what was going on in my head. School was not

allowing me anything to be proud of. From then on, no one but myself would be permitted to evaluate me. She begged me to see the school psychologist, and had asked my biology teacher to take me under his wing, not aware that I despised him for having accused me of switching my sick baby squirrel for his healthy baby squirrel when we'd caged them together for observation to determine if having companionship would cure my squirrel's ills. On the morning after this malfeasance was supposed to have happened, the biology teacher came up to me in class, fuming: «You took my healthy squirrel and left your sick one with me, and it died overnight.» I insisted that I hadn't, and told him my squirrel had died too. From then on, we never spoke. He went his self-righteous way through the semester contemptuous of me while giving me an opportunity to learn how revulsion felt.

This sort of discrediting humiliation extended even to my pigeons. The reason was not that I was out of sorts but out of scale. By high school I had moved off from fancy birds and taken up New-Type White Kings, a variety being brought to perfection by top breeders across the country as a squabbing bird—very large at the breast, short in the wing and tail, a robust and meaty breeder of exceptional deportment and beauty. With income from selling the fancy birds I'd been given by the India-man, whose strange sounding name I've forgotten, I'd bought two pairs of White Kings from Mr. Franz, a famous breeder of Kings in the Midwest who lived on the outskirts of Sioux City near Perry Creek.

Figuring that, because I was just a kid, I wouldn't know anything about Kings, Mr. Franz must have assumed I wouldn't pick any of his top breeders, so he offered me my choice among the many birds in his loft. He didn't know that I was the reincarnated shepherd Paris, with an eye for Aphroditean beauty. If naiveté was indeed the fault he'd assigned me, he had erred in my favor. At the preceding Tri-State Pigeon Show (Iowa, Nebraska, Kansas), I'd spent hours on end studying the three hundred or so Kings shipped in for the competition. Over the period of judging, I'd followed the judge's eye, and when winning birds were lined up in their individual show cages, had made sketches of their conformations, head-shapes, and eyes, memorizing everything. And Mr. Franz didn't know that I'd been going to a certain Reverend Burton's house off and on to talk about breeding King-type birds. The Reverend lived on the west side of town, and was preachy only on Sunday morning. He bred Blue Kings mostly, no Whites. Anyone who ate white pigeons, he'd say, risked being sent straight to Hell, for a white pigeon could at any moment be the Holy Spirit embodied. (It wouldn't have done any good to explain to the Reverend that in The Gospel According to Luke, the Holy Ghost was a white dove, not a white pigeon, and that Saint Luke would have known the difference). Not taking chances that he might behead and broil the Holy Ghost, the Reverend raised Blue Kings and Silver Kings, and he was the only breeder around who kept long-necked red and white Hungarians that had gone out of fashion maybe a hundred years back. He also bred Polish Runts, the biggest pigeons in the world but slow breeders. He liked the Hungarians and Runts, despite their worthlessness as show birds, because they were developed as breeding strains by monks in the Middle Ages—«...came right out of the cradle of Protestantism in Central Europe», he said.

One day when discussing religion with Reverend Burton, I told him that the so-called doves that Noah threw out to go scout dry land were for sure ordinary blue pigeons, like one sees in barns and on town squares, not white ones like Sunday School books show, and that all of the farm and city blue-bar and blue-check pigeons descended from them. Because they are social birds that had become dependent on human habitations, I'd said, the pigeons Noah put aboard would have taken the ark as a sort of floating island surrounded by cliffs, like their natural habitat. And the pigeon would have been the easiest kind of bird for Noah to catch and bring on board when it started raining—a lot easier than catching doves. Besides, I explained, Noah's pigeon was not bringing back the olive branch to show Noah that dry land had come up out of the water (even if that's what Noah thought). It was bringing back that little branch to start making a nest on the ark, where its mate was, in order to go about being fruitful and multiplying as the Creator had instrcuted. Anyway, the pigeon was the only bird Noah could count on to come home after it'd been sent out. If he had released any other kind of bird, his ark would have floated around in a vast ocean forever.

So when in Mr. Franz' loft, I judged each bird against the picture of the perfect bird in my mind, and bought what I determined were his two best mature cocks and his two best hens. The next spring in the Tri-

State show of 1944, I was the only boy competing in Kings against men, most of whom were long-time breeders.

At the registration desk I picked up my entries' cage numbers—White King / Young Cock, No. 27, White King / Young Hen, No. 16. The cages for the young White King cocks filled up the whole length of an aisle; the young hens occupied the next aisle. Beyond them, a double row was reserved for old hens and old cocks. Then came row upon row of cages for the color varieties—blues, reds, and silvers—most of them already filled with birds from Nebraska, Kansas, and across Iowa. I put my birds in their assigned show cages and set about studying the competition. My eyes roamed from one cage to another, taking aim at each White King.

The judge tossed half of the competition out of the running in the first round the next day, and most of the remaining birds wouldn't qualify for the finals. Each class would be cut from forty or so to twenty, then to ten. Like finalists in a Miss or Mister America contest, each of the ten would have flawless bodies and be perfect for breeding. But only a top judge could focus sharply enough to pick the ribbon-winners.

If either of my birds got cut on the first round, I figured I'd just say, «So what?» Even if one of them qualified but didn't win a ribbon, maybe no one would need to know I'd entered it except for the show secretary, who didn't know me anyway. I knew that I was not a true pigeon breeder. A true breeder breeds his own breeders. I had only two pairs of breeding stock, and they were ones Mr. Franz had bred and figured weren't worth keeping. He probably would have eaten them if I hadn't bought them.

«Mr. Franz doesn't make breeding mistakes,» I had said to Shirley when talking with her a while back about the show. «He's got the best eye in the business.»

«Oh yeah? What's his wife look like?» she mocked.

My young hen placed first in a class of over fifty. I was numbed by it, the fact of it was too real to fit to my hopes. And before I could deal with it emotionally, the judge was making the first cut of the young cocks, looking over the long row of qualifying birds and picking ten to be brought to the Top Ten table. I couldn't tell for sure if my entry was among them until the crowd around the judge thinned out and I could see that my bird's show cage was empty. The breeders pressed around the table to watch the judge select the winners: fourth place, third, second, first. The birds were then lined up in separate cages as stewards called out the leg-band numbers and the show secretary matched them to breeder's names: Second Young Cock— Whitey Andersen.

The crowd moved on to watch the color classes, allowing me to sneak up and see the red ribbon attached to my bird's cage. I looked hard at the First Young Cock with the blue ribbon—back and forth a dozen times between the two birds. What was it the judge saw? The cock's head was perfectly configured but no better than my bird's— rounder at the crest but mine had the slight flatness the male head should have...(not like the standard female head that's smaller and perfectly round with the eye dead center). My bird was a bit bigger than the blue-ribbon winner, higher in the shoulder but not longer-bodied. Point for point, each had every necessary quality: exactly shaped, true to type, standing up correctly—erect, balanced, steady. The difference might have been what I couldn't see: the flexibility of cartilage, the density of muscle tissue, and the spread of the wishbone. For the life of me I couldn't tell why my cock placed second.

At the show secretary's table I could see Mr. Franz sitting on a bench taking notes from the judge's cards. I thought he would be happy that the breeders he'd sold me had done so well. I walked over to say hello. He looked up just long enough to recognize me, then down at his notes, silent all the while as if I'd disturbed him. But I had to say something. «Those pairs you sold me turned out to be good producers, didn't they?» I said, figuring he would feel complimented. Mr. Franz shut his notebook abruptly, jammed his pencil into his shirt pocket, his pipe into his mouth, and rose from the bench. With a sideways glance at me, he turned away angrily, saying, «I wouldn't trade any bird in my loft for that young cock of yours.»

After the judging and announcement of awards, not one of the exhibitors made a complimentary remark to me, not even Reverend Burton. But as I could plainly see by then that the Reverend liked me not as a competitor but as a tousle-haired kid who was supposed to raise homers and fancy birds, such as fan-tails and tumblers, to only play at this competitive game and not beat grown men who were professional breeders with reputations at stake. Franz' best young hen had taken a third place and his best young cock a fourth.

His expression, «I wouldn't trade any bird in my loft for that young cock of yours,» had burned deeply, the hurt amplified by young cock of yours—mine not as good as any cock in his loft. Among the King breeders, I was no better than a predator who'd stolen a top ribbon, depriving grown men of glory. For what did my birds mean to the King Association of which I wasn't even a member? Why should any man who'd dedicated many years to developing the New-Type King variety give a pat on the back to a walk-on kid with only two pair of breeding stock in his loft that he hadn't himself bred, who claimed ribbons with the first youngsters hatched?

I will never know for sure whether pigeon judging infected my psyche when it came down to an optical choice of girls. Shortly after the Tri-State Pigeon Show, I spotted a girl in one of my classes whose appearance was dizzying. She was a Shirley-type in build but more beautiful than cute or pretty, taller, with longer legs not in stockings, shapely at the waist, and with well-developed breasts. In my imagination I lusted after her, not sexually but with spasms of rapture. After a week of catching me looking her way and softly returning the look, rather than causing mine to veer off, we walked down the hall together, getting acquainted. But when up close, I noticed she had one blue eye and one green eye. I was devastated. From then on I ignored her, and to this day feel contrite that such a small defect in genetic expression had turned off my burners, as if she had what breeders call a blemish.

I was obsessed with perfection. Not as a functional perfectionist, however. My preoccupation with perfection was limited to pigeons and girls. I had become Darwinian to the core. Natural selection improved the race. Selection relies on judgment, and judgment depends on having the perfect image lying behind one's discerning eye, so that what appears in front of the eye can be judged in comparison. Men of weak judgment end up owning ordinary birds and marrying ordinary women. Women, too, with an eye for men, make selections as nature urges: better-looking men don't necessarily make better husbands or fathers, but will be happier and sire better-looking children. This was enough to know at the age of fifteen.

One afternoon when school let out, I chanced to head homeward in the company of a diminutive and pretty brown-haired bookish girl with big green eyes named Christine. I had not noticed her at school. On arriving at her house yard, she said her mother wasn't at home and asked if I'd like to stop in for a cup of cocoa. Having found that saying yes is less stressful than saying no, I walked innocently into her web, carrying her books. In a cozy parlor, on a fat davenport, seated at either end with maximum distance between us, she asked me without inflection, without even a smile, if I would like to neck.

Other than Christine, I would make no other friends at school. Not yet sixteen, she was not allowed to date, could not even go to a movie matinee on a Sunday. It was unlikely that she saw anyone but me, or left the house without her mother at her side. So when we did get together, it had to be an innocent side-by-side walk from school to her house, a pot of cocoa or cola in Dixie Cups, and a box of Crackerjacks, doing our best without undressing, her mother off shopping or at the Women's Club where she was a volunteer bookkeeper. If her parents believed that by keeping her house-bound every night of the week they were guarding their daughter's purity, they'd gotten around to it too late, and would never know that their sweet daughter had lured a fox into their chicken house.

I didn't think of Christine as a girlfriend, nor did any notion of being a lover come to mind. And I wouldn't learn to overlay romance on sex until I was much older. At school, if Christine and I passed in the hall, we just exchanged smiles and a hand wave. She made no demands on me, and perhaps wasn't the type for whom I'd suffer a heart crush seeing her with another boy. I'd felt the same about Shirley, the type of girl who may have grown up without ever knowing love, having so often and when so young diluted its intensity.

The accusation of plagiarism aimed at my short story wouldn't have been enough grounds for the shift of endearment that turned my backside against school. When a balloon is fully inflated it doesn't take but a puff of air to explode it. It was clear to me that from then on anything I wrote in English class would be looked upon with suspicion. So I downshifted to banal writing. Never again would I be called upon to read anything in class. By the merciful end of that first high school year in Sioux City, I was close to adding my escape from the world to the statistics for teenage suicide. My contrariness had turned on me; defensively, my mind was looking out for its own survival, leaving me off to the side because I'd failed to keep up and had become a saboteur of its moral constitution.

Everything I valued was evaporating. The saloon had been sold. My father and Leona were in California. I'd concluded that all things are transient. We had never owned a house, just rented, and had moved every year from one neighborhood to another, planting but not harvesting,, and still adjusting at the same time we were moving. So life was constant reconciliation; never enough time at a new place to tie up loose ends from the previous place. Over my fourteen and a half years, I'd lived on a farm, in a town, and in a city; eight houses and as many neighborhoods; had attended four schools and worked on three farms and at a stable. Where on this earth would I have found myself had I not followed the sun west, for I didn't have much on which to build a life where I'd been standing. No solid ground beneath my feet and the future just blank air out in front of me. I wasn't even sure that I'd been born on the right planet. If my parents had given any thought at all about my prospects, becoming a truck driver, carpenter, mechanic, bartender, or any other tradesman would have been just fine. They were professional farmers. That's all they knew and all they could teach. Had my father not summoned me to join him in California that June of 1944, the tenth grade in Sioux City would have been my final school year. And even out west, what brought me a year and a half later to a diploma from Oakland Technical High School, an institution for non-achievers, was my interest in a girl, Jackie Evans, who attended the school and attracted me to it.

Graduating as the student least deserving a high school diploma—coming in last, rather than first, saved me from being middling. We farmers are accustomed to being regarded as the dirt from which everything grows. Dust to dust is the first and the last. All that's in between is transitory and ill defined. Anyway, no thought in my head implicated education. Those milestones were much further down the road.

Postscript

illy Nelson, who identifies with farmers, said of his musical
career, «It's not a good life but it's my life.» Well, it may have
been his life, and other musicians' lives, but it was not my
life. I wasn't good enough to play with complete confidence, or progress
beyond ordinary bands and pickup player for bands that traveled with
only key musicians and filled out with locals. Charlie Parker was the
Bird. Either you flew near his height or stayed on the ground like a
humbled Icarus.

My association with Jimmy Kliever broke off for a spell when I left
for California. On arriving—about to turn sixteen but soon furnished
with an ID saying I was eighteen—I worked as a laborer for a construction company and joined a seven-piece dance band that played for
wedding parties and school dances and put together a teenage vaudeville
troupe. After a few months of itinerant work, and due to circumstances
that may show up in a subsequent volume of this Life of Vesti, Son of
Vesti, I yearned to fly off and see if somewhere in the world I'd find a
roosting tree. It wasn't so much a case of adolescent depression as what
Germans call *Wanderlust*, and lust it was.

The family house was situated then in the Rollingwood appendage
to Richmond on the San Francisco East Bay. In the heat of an impulse
to remove myself, I packed a suitcase of sorts and without a word to my
parents walked to the Greyhound bus station in downtown Richmond.
Lacking the least idea where to relocate, I sat on a bench for a while trying to figure out where to go. Like an ancient Greek man in consulta-
tion with an oracle, I chose to let fortune decide. To myself I adminis-
tered an oath that I would go to the final stop of the next bus that rolled
into the station. I prayed to the oracle that it would be Portland, for I

felt a rush of sentiment to find my brother Marius up there. Chance disappointed me: the bus trusted to ascertain my fate was destined for Sacramento.

I was honor-bound to board it. Close to three hours later, on approaching Sacramento, the driver stopped at a crossroads on the edge of town to let off a few passengers. A short ways back, at the side of the road, I had spotted a Sacramento city limits sign. So I was there. I had gone there. My oath was satisfied. I'd not sworn to stay where the oracle sent me. Ahead was the highway running east, the cross-country route to New York, to wherever I would choose to travel. My friend Jimmy's image came to mind at the moment I jumped from my seat and exited the bus in time for the driver to recover my suitcase from storage in the bus's belly. With just a few dollars in my pocket—too little to take a train—I put out my thumb and within a few minutes was offered a ride.

The man who stopped for me had his wife in the front passenger seat and two young children in the back. Why he would stop to pick up a teen-age boy, I cannot answer other than saying that, if the result can explain the cause, it was because he had in mind a second driver, for no sooner had we exchanged notes on where we were each heading than he asked if I would spell him driving so he wouldn't need to lay over anywhere en route. Of course I agreed, not just to be grateful but because I didn't have sufficient money to stop at motels. He and his family were part of the post-war exodus from California, returning to the Midwest, to Indiana in his case, which would take me as far as Omaha before I'd have to dogleg north to Sioux City. Two days and two nights later, he let me off where the Interstate intersected the highway up the Missouri. I lucked into a ride all the way to Suiux City. By early afternoon, I was walking well-known streets, and in an hour or so had spotted a sign, «To Let»—the quaint British wording that pranksters often altered in the night to read «ToiLet.» I rented a room from a kind widow lady, and without taking off more than my shoes, fell into bed. Other than back-seat naps, I hadn't slept in four days.

The next day I would send a postcard to my parents, telling them I'd left home, that I was back in Iowa, that at sometime or another I would see them again. It wouldn't have occurred to me that they'd worry over my disappearance; over the months in California, I'd often failed to show up at the house for days on end. A sixteen-year old boy in their minds was no longer a child, no longer in need of concerned and protective parents.

I needed to find a job. The room with shared bath would cost eighteen dollars a week. I had enough to pay for one week's lodging and enough to eat for a few days. My first thought, however, was to find Jimmy. After awakening in the late afternoon, almost evening, of my arrival, after taking a bath and shaving, though at that age I had little hair on my face, I headed on foot to Jimmy's house. His mother answered the door. Surprised to see me, she said he'd just left for South Sioux City where he was playing with a band in the Grand Hotel.

After negotiating my way by streetcar downtown and catching a bus to cross the river into Nebraska, I found Jimmy in the hotel lobby an hour before the band was to start up. It had been less than a year since we'd seen each other, so a few minutes was enough time to make it seem that I hadn't been away. I asked about the band. Jimmy's face crumpled into a sneer as he admitted it wasn't much of a band and that he wouldn't be with it except he had to start somewhere. Then his face brightened as he asked if I had brought my saxophone, to which I had to say no, for I hadn't thought of doing that, wanting just to get away. He said the band needed a tenor sax man; the one they regularly had was off playing sideman in Omaha.

At about that moment the bandleader passed by to summon his players to the ballroom starting to fill up with people coming to dance. Jimmy introduced me and proposed I stand in for the missing sax man, providing we could find a saxophone. Lady Chance, who had gotten me safely to Sioux City, was still looking after me. The band's alto sax player had a tenor at his home a short drive away. He was dispatched to bring it to the hotel. So, within an hour I was on a bandstand again, with Jimmy drumming, earning eight dollars a night, four nights a week.

The gig lasted only two weeks. The regular tenor man rejoined, and besides, the bandleader was nervous over my not being a member of the local musician's union. I took a day job in the soybean mill that Jimmy's father owned—tying sacks and loading them onto trucks. After a couple of weeks of aching shoulders and bean dust down my neck, I looked up my sister Fern, who still lived in Sioux City, her husband off to war. When I told her I was returning to California, she offered me money for train fare. Too proud to accept it, a couple of days later I was on the road again, hitch-hiking. I made it to California in five days, sleeping when I could, wherever I could. Used car lots with most doors unlocked, offered an array of back-seat couches. On completing the last leg that started at Reno, I was but a half-mile from my parent's house. I rapped on the door about one in the morning. My father opened it, smiled broadly, and said, «Well I'll be damned. I never thought we would see you again.» His first move was to make some graveyard stew—buttered toast in hot milk, you will recall. We sat at the table and talked as we had many times when sharing a meal in the middle of the night. On awakening after a few hours on the living room couch, my mother said nothing at all about my absence, didn't question where I'd been or what I'd been doing. I could have come in after going out for a morning newspaper. Her immediate concern was that I wash up and come to the table for breakfast.

Shortly after that prodigal son's return, I formed my own combo and played summer-resort gigs at the Paradise Resort between Calistoga and Napa, sharing a cottage with a fifteen-year-old ballad singer I'd coaxed away from an Oakland high school band. I also played on occasion with a big band, Mike Primo's, at the Vallejo Hotel and Al Davis' Silver Log Tavern on the shore line of Clear Lake, about one hundred miles from San Francisco. Primo was about forty, a suave divorced Italian with Hollywood looks, reminding me of how Jimmy might look in time. During those troubled two years, I stayed out of school and didn't appear at the family home except for short periods. When in Vallejo, I had a spare second-floor bedroom in Mike Primo's house. To not invade his privacy, for he had a retinue of women befitting a harem, I accessed the room through a window he left unlocked so I could come and go using a ladder kept hidden behind foundation planting. At Clear Lake, I slept in a resort cabin when vacancies were available, at other times in a stateroom of Al Davis' 60-foot yacht, the Rubicon, that Davis had hauled up on a train's flat-car from the San Francisco Bay to accommodate special customers on moonlight cruises along the base of Mount Canopti, an ancient mountain, shaped like a reclining woman, that plunged down steeply into the north side of lake as if she were sleeping on a real water bed. Over this period I smoked and ate badly, but didn't drink much alcohol. Marijuana, the standard smoke of musicians when not on the stand, made me nauseous; the only drug I depended on was Benzadrine to keep me awake on the bandstand until two in the morning. Over those many months I remained unrooted. Everything I possessed could be carried with me: my saxophone, clarinet, and a stuffed suitcase. Another saxophonist, who'd recently joined Primo's band—an exceptional player on alto and the soprano sax—became a bit more to me than an acquaintance. He, too, lived out of a suitcase, but was into drugs, emaciated and crazy. Strangely, one night he was walking through the Marin County tunnel that leads into San Francisco, carrying his saxophone case. According to a disconsolate driver that hit, ran over, and killed him, he had suddenly leaped off the walkway and into the path of his truck.

Iowa stayed on my mind, for it was shaped by it. Not until many years later, in 1976 at the age of forty-eight, could I realize my lingering desire to own a real farm. After a couple of highly profitable years for the architecture firm that I founded in 1974—Vesti Design International, based in Boston and Geneva, but with most of my work in Saudi Arabia—I bought a 230-acre farm near Woodstock, Vermont, with the intention to establish an Arabian horse farm. I refurbished it, built a training barn with attached indoor arena, a mare barn, fouling barn, and staff quarters, and laid out the land with paddocks and pastures enclosed with four-board yellow pine fencing trucked up from South Carolina. Within a year and a half, I had forty-six horses and a staff of four to manage them and maintain the grounds.

It was a far cry from a dirt farm—the entire place impeccable, not a clod of dirt to be seen. I sent my best mares to National Champion stallions for breeding. Exceptional fouls, after being conditioned over their first months, were sent to the top trainers in the country, Gene and Ray LaCroix in Kentucky, and David Boggs in Minnesota. My horses racked up ribbons and trophies from one state to the other: in California: Pacific Slopes Grand Champion Stallion (with three-year-old Pomerol, who's still at stud); the Buck-eye Sweepstakes Champion Park Horse (with Bella Sahib), and trophies all across the country with two mares, Elitza and Sheer Elegance. I bred the high-selling filly of 1984 in the Kentucky Lasma Yearling sale (her name, Pacific Fleet), and the following year, the high-selling two-year-old in the Scottsdale Star-Stallion

sale (her name, South Pacific). After a few years of pleasurable success-
es, the stock market debacle in 1986-87 destroyed much of horse industry, so under the threat of bankruptcy, I sold the farm through Sotheby's
and staged an auction in Scottsdale, Arizona—the Vest Horses of the
Wind sale—selling thirty-two mares and fillies that I hadn't sold by private treaty. I kept two horses: one young stallion and an eventing mare.
I retired from MIT, spent a year dissolving my design firm, and after a
few weeks in India and Nepal, doing non-technical climbing to regen-
erate my health and confidence, I moved to France. Over four years in
Paris and one year in nearby Rueil-Malmaison, I wrote books and stage
plays.

Those epochs are not to figure in this book, which is, after all, a
history of a piece of Iowa over a short span of time, not a history of
how the dirtfarmer's son managed to fabricate a fairly wholesome life in
spite of himself. So I must end here, adding only one loop to bring this
book back to my Sioux City youth. That Second Young Cock award,
received in the Tri-State Pigeon Show in 1943, had lurked as a damaged
nerve ganglia in my lower brain. In 1984, while at my Vermont farm
reading the *Arabian Horse Times*, I noticed an announcement of a pend-
ing show in Iowa, the Iowa Fall Classic. At the time, I had in training
with David Boggs a two-year old stallion named Allert—son of the
multi-champion Aladdinn (horses' names are often intentionally misspelled). I called David, saying, «David, I have something to ask of you.
I want you to enter Allert in the Junior Stallion class at the Iowa Fall
Classic next month.»

David's response was quick and professional: «Why would you
want to do that? It's a minor show. Allert's already taken three Junior
Championships in major classes, and I'm getting him ready for the
Nationals.»

«I've got a reason,» I replied, «and it's important to me that you do
it. And I want you in the ring showing him, not one of your staff.»

David couldn't say no. In the horse business, the man with the
money gives the orders. About two weeks later, in the early evening, I
received a phone call from David: «Okay, Wayne. He won. He took First
Place and Junior Champion.»

And so it came to pass that the Second Young Cock of Iowa
became Iowa's Junior Champion Stud.

Pictures

T here was a life out ahead of me when youth gave way to adulthood. One's self, scaled to the world, expands to fill out a life
if allowed to move along by its own wits, unfettered, unbridled,
the body obedient to the mind. My adulthood was conditioned by my
youth. Youth is the framework within and upon one adulthood builds
its enhancements and elaborations Those who disparage their childhood, blame their parents for their calumnies, blame society for with-
holding nurture, are those whose adulthood is self-negating. I regret
nothing of my past that was not of my own doing.

Should anyone, whether by choice or by chance, read this book, I
owe them a sequel. My life didn't stop at the age of fifteen. Yet, to write
the rest of it would take several thousand pages. So, if a picture is worth
a thousand words, the pictures I've appended to this book will serve to
wind up the story, releasing the kid from his adolescence, like a moth
from its chrysalis—crawling to flying, drawn to the light.

My paternal grandparents, Mads Vesti Andersen and Marie Johansen.

The author at age three.

My parents, Henry Vesti Andersen and Marguerita Johanna Steinhagen. Their wedding picture. April 1912.

At age three. 1931. The upper barn on the Hinton farm. Our rodent terrier as staunchly posed.

The Hinton farmhouse, with big brother Marius and the hired man, Russell Hampton. 1933.

Probably at age three, in the beef-cattle feeding lot, standing next to a silage table. Straw-covered cattle shelter in the rear. Winter 1931-32.

The Floyd River at Hinton, flowing to Sioux City and the Missouri. At low water, looking peaceful; a raging torrent at flood stage.

The Hinton farm horses. *Left to right*: the riding horse Charlie, sister Loretta, then Blackie, Queen, Dan, Princess, Nancy, Topsy; brother Marius with the mules Jack and Jenny. Winter 1931.

My sister Loretta, the farm girl who called herself the hired man. Deadly pitcher for the Hinton Farm Girls baseball team.

Aboard Princess (*center*), with cousins Eldo and Everett Bollmeyer on Blackie and Topsy.

The disk harrow that cut off my father's toe and mangled Loretta's leg.

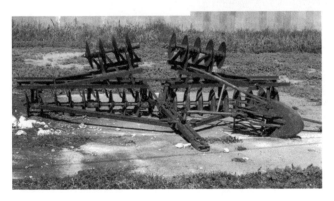

The ten children of
Henry Vesti and
Marguerita. *Left to
right, back row:* Esther,
Fern, Bethel, Loretta.
Center row:
Harold and Wayne on
either side of Marius
holding Nancy. *Lower
row:* Alice and Avis.
Sioux City, 1940.

At the age of
fourteen, with my
father, Henry
Vesti.

254

The extended family. Grandmother Steinhagen, my parents, uncles, aunts, and cousins. A farmer's social unit is the family, then the neighbors, then the county. You will find me in the front row, a bit in from the right, with hands folded.

At Perry Creek, Sioux City. 1942. Teaching my sister Alice how to shoot a rifle. I'm sure she's not aiming at a car passing over the bridge.

Uncle Gifford and Aunt Bertha. Their wedding picture, 1922. I worked a summer on their farm when thirteen.

255

What remains of the appearance of my father's Sioux City saloon. At age sixty-eight, I'm at the bar I knew so well at age fourteen.

The bar in 1943, my father serving and Leona entertaining. A typical social club for the rural and working class, much loved and enjoyed by its hardworking customers.

Sioux City's Peavy Grand Opera House on Fourth Street at the corner of Jones, dedicated on September 24th, 1888.

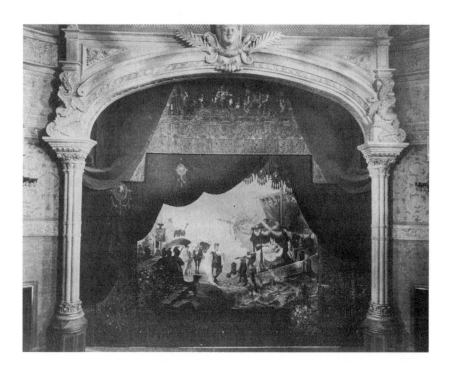

Sioux City's Central High School, built in 1892. The American flag raised atop its pole on February 22nd, 1893; the first commencement held in June. Constructed of large blocks of prentisse-brown sandstone, a monument to Sioux City's dedication to progressive education. It looks more like a fortification. When I attended this school in 1943, a huge howitzer cannon was on the terrace at the foot of a flag pole.

On being moved to California at age fifteen, one of the first things I did was to organize a six-piece dance band and a vaudeville troupe of talented teenagers. This photo is from the Richmond newspaper covering a performance given at the El Portal Club in the winter of 1944. I am standing at the magician's table. My sister Alice, almost fourteen and an excellent ballad singer, is standing at the far left.

258

At age seventeen in California.

On the far left. In the army. Enlisted in July 1946 for the airborne. To Camp Lee, Virginia for basic training. Entire regiment shipped to Germany, all but me. Was sent to Fort McClellen, Alabama, to hold until the next paratrooper training cycle at Fort Benning. Managed to join the camp dance band. Played the NCO and Officers' Club dances. When time came for the 82nd, was sent to Fort Benning, Georgia. Injured in training, put on limited service. Joined the camp's dance band. Played three nights a week at the Officers' Club and gigs off-base. Undertook learning to write. Discharged in February 1948.

At Fort McClellen, Alabama. The dance band musicians were permitted to wear civilian clothes, and, in consideration of their supple fingers, not required to perform mess hall duties or hard labor. Because of late night dances, not required to get up in the morning, or make up our bunks. We had our own kitchen.

At Fort McClellen, Alabama. The dance band had two formats: an eleven-piece band for the Non-commisioned Officer's Club, and a sixteen-piece band for the Officers' Club. I played in both. At the right, next to the leader.

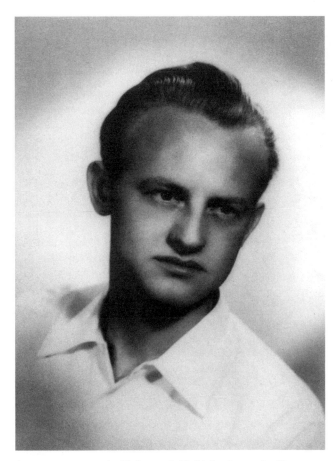

At age twenty-one, in Hollywood. Had joined a vaudeville company performing stage magic and skits. When not on the road, read scripts and studied directing and set design at the American Telecasting School in Los Angeles.

Early 1949 at my writing desk in the Fort McClellen musician's barracks. The picture on my desk is of Colleen, a beautiful brunette back in Berkeley whose father refused me to date (even though I had for quite some time), saying I was not the sort of man who would make a good life for her. At the time he was right.

Married Ebba Stoll in 1952. Ebba with our first of two children, Maja, born in 1953. (We were divorced in 1965). In Denver at the time of Maja's birth. I'd given up music and stage work. Adept at art, I was teaching at the Denver Art Center. In 1954, we were back in Berkeley. Enrolled in the University of California, on probation due to my lack of a proper high school diploma. Being a veteran, I could not be entirely rejected.

Awarded a $5000 prize from Columbia University in 1962 as most outstanding graduate student. With Ebba, Maja, and son Mark, sailed to France on the SS Rotterdam. In Paris for a year with side trips to Italy, England, and Switzerland. Then to Brussels as a Belgian-American Fellow. The stay in Europe was extended on receipt of a Ford Foundation grant.

My son Mark feeding pigeons in Trafalgar Square, London, 1963. A graduate of Art Center College, Los Angeles, Mark now heads his own product design firm in Los Angeles.

My daughter Maja, London, 1963. A graduate of Arizona State University, Maja is now an engineer in Pennsylvania.

Summer 1963. With Ebba, Maja and Mark visiting Egon Kormann
and his wife, the widow of Gustav Britsch, at the Britsch Institute
in Starnberg-bei-Munchen, Germany. Gustav Britsch's writings figured importantly in my intellectual development.

A day in the country with Maja and Mark, playing kick-ball in the
Fontainebleau Forest. south of Paris. Spring 1963.

An intellectual in Paris. On Jean Tingley's machine that does nothing in particular and goes nowhere at all, reading intensively. By this time I was involved with the Parisian art world and was the Paris correspondent for the Museum of Modern Art, New York.

Maja and Mark, studious as their father, thirsting for culture, reading Italian comic books at the base of Cimabue's *Madonna* in the Ufizzi, Florence.
Summer 1963.

At last, the dirtfarmer's son looks like a true intellectual. Photograph taken at the time of my appointment to the Massachusetts Institute of Technology in 1965. A presidential appointment as Associate Professor in the Department of Architecture, extended to full professor in 1968. During the twenty-year tenure, also taught one semester as Visiting Professor at Yale and two years at Harvard. Because MIT professors tend to be consultants, even practice their profession outside of the Institute, I also served as the art and design consultant to the Boston Urban Redevelopment Authority, the Federal Reserve Bank, AT&T, IBM, and a few other clients. At MIT, founded the Committee on the Visual Arts in 1965; with colleagues Henry Millon and Stanford Andersen, established the first PhD program in the History, Theory, and Criticism of Art and Architecture, a program that inspired many institution here and abroad to adopt.

Phyllis Sutton. We
were married in
1969. Phyllis is
Director of Cultural
Landscape Studies at
the Arnold
Arboretum of
Harvard University.

With Phyllis in Copenhagen, 1968.

With Phyllis at the Hotel Regina, Venice. 1970.

Phyllis with our 5-month old Belgian Sheepdog, Demon's Echo de Berger.

Phyllis with Echo at the age of two, and our Cairn Terrier, Foxy Lady. Echo was a top show dog, winning many ribbons and trophies in New England, with me as her handler. For Echo, the shortest distance between two points was a straight line; for Foxy it was as circuitous as she could make it, not wanting to miss anything on the way.

Phyllis and I took a four-week trip to France in 1972. We left Echo, not yet six months old, at Cape Cod with the renowned Belgian Sheepdog breeder, Mary Dilloway. On our return, on driving to the Cape to pick up our dog, we found Dilloway's property packed with cars, people, and dogs. The Cape Cod Belgian Sheep Dog show was underway, using Dilloway's show ring. Mary said she wasn't sure of the exact date of our return, but that Echo was so exceptional, she took the liberty of entering her in the Young Bitch Class. I asked Mary if she would handle our dog in the competition, which was coming up in a couple of hours. She was fully committed to a client but would ask around to see if a worthy handler was available for that class. As it turned out, all of the professional handlers were committed. Mary came up with a solution: «You'll have to handle her yourself.» My retort was quick. «I've never even been to a dog show!»

«Never mind,» Mary said. «I'll teach you.» And with that she put a show leash on her old brood bitch, Maud, who'd been many times champion, saying, «What I can't teach you, Maud will.» After a half-hour of lessons, during which I lost track entirely of which of my hands was the right or the left, if not both on one side, she had Echo brought to the ring. Echo had been previously trained to heel, sit, stay, and come, all with hand signals, so she knew more than what I'd just learned. I practised what I'd been taught, and in spite of me, Echo took first in the young bitch class and went on to beat the mature females, taking the Best Opposite Sex trophy.

Many years later, when I dissolved my Arabian horse breeding and show horse farm, out of 45 horses I retained one champion stallion, Pomerol, still at stud, and one champion Mare, Scientia. On moving to France in 1987, I gave the mare to a children's equine camp in western Massachusetts under the condition that she would be used by junior riders in competitions. Over the following years, many youngsters won ribbons atop Scientia at eventing and dressage. Scientia was so intelligent, so willing and well-trained, that even an average rider could place in tough competitions. Scientia corrected their mistakes. I owe this lesson to Mary Dilloway. Echo was so spectacular the judges probably didn't notice me.

Typical 1960s party style. At the opening of the Jim Huntington show, Hayden Galley, MIT, 1968. With Phyllis at the left, then Phyllis Rosen, Mary and Jim Huntington, Joan Sonnabend.

In Brittany near Carnac, studying dolmens and menhirs. 1969.

In 1971, received a $10,000 advance from Viking Press on my book, *Gauguin's Paradise Lost*. Bought a lot in Lexington, MA. With a construction loan in hand, designed and, with the help of two MIT architecture students, built a 3000 sq, ft. house. Two years later, not happy with suburbia, sold the house and bought a condominium in Boston's Back Bay.

Center, in light suit. At La Défense, Paris, presenting a site design proposal for Place Pascal to a committee of French architects and city officials. The proposal was approved.

With Cardinal O'Connor of the New York archdiocese. Phyllis to the right. Had been commissioned to stage a fund-raising exhibition of modern art in New York on behalf of the archdiocese. The turnout, a great success.

At Jimmy Rosati's studio in New York. Father Buck of the Boston archdioces at the left. Rosati center. Had been commissioned by the archdiocese to create a memorial to the late Cardinal Cushing. Rosati's bronze of the Cardinal is now in Boston at the Government Center.

With British sculptor Henry Moore at his Much Haddam studio estate, looking over my installation plans for the monumental bronze sculpture now installed in MIT's Killian Court.

With New York sculptor Louise Nevelson. 1975.

With Dizzy Gilespie aboard the aircraft carrier John. F. Kennedy, during a tall ships event in the Boston harbor.

In 1977, the Bay Area sculptor, Harold Paris, threw a «Welcome Home Wayne» party at his studio in Oakland. This event was to encourage me to return to California. «Honk» Anderson, a major art collector, furnished the champagne. Ruth Peizer (Taka), an exotic dancer from San Francisco, performed at midnight. Many of the artists and writers I had known and associated with in the 1950s attended. Still moored at MIT, I stayed in Boston.

At Elsinore,
Denmark, looking
across the sea to
Sweden.

With Phyllis in Paris at the Café Voltaire.

Born on a farm without a bathtub.
Now, so many years later,
he has a bathtub but no farm!

But that would change. In 1978, an aged and unused farm just down the hill from our summer home in Woodstock, Vermont, came up for sale. I bought it and brought it up to the level of a first class horse farm. Within a year, it was complete, with 22 mares, mostly purchased at Kentucky auctions. Bred to national quality stallions, the mares produced the Vesti herd.

Our Woodstock, Vermont house and guest house, with two fillies in the meadow. The houses are just above the farm.

With Phyllis in Walnut Creek, California, looking at the famous Russian stallion, Salon, recently imported from the Tersk Stud. Salon was the sire of our mare, Poviest, imported from Poland, who would give us the multi-champion stallion, Pomerol.

POMEROL, sired by the US and Canadian National Champion, Padron, out of the Vesti mare Poviest by Salon. A many times champion. Still at stud.

Advising the newborn colt, Cash, that if he wants to grow up as a showhorse, he must learn to keep his ears up.

Phyllis in the pasture for mares that have foaled.

A tour bus visting the Vesti Arabians farm. The farm was on the list of things to see in Vermont.

With stage and film director, and avid horseman, Mike Nichols, at the Lasma Arabian auction in Kentucky, discussing the sale horses during preliminary presentations. Looking on are two of the top trainers in the industry, Doug Leadly behind me, and Bill Bohl behind Nichols.

With a handful of Vesti broodmares, each with exceptional bloodlines.

Conducting a seminar at the farm for students from the veterinarian college at the University of Vermont.

Our formidable stallion, Barisznikov, sired by the National Champion Polish import, Aladdinn, out of New Fasion. He gave us many outstanding foals, one of which sold for $190,000 at the Lasma Yealing Sale. He is now at stud in Wisconsin.

All Three Wishes, a yearling filly sired by Barisznikov.

The mosque at the King Kahlid International Airport, Riyadh, Saudi Arabia. Interior and exterior features by my firm, Vesti Design International, including the stained glass clerestory, mosaic calligraphy band, stained glass windows, carved wood doors, carved wood minbar, marble and ceramic mirhab, and travertine calligraphic bands extending all around the interior and exterior. This five-year project was completed in 1986. In addition, my architecture firm designed and fabricated five ceiling domes for the Riyadh Community mosque, the entire landscape and interior design for what is now called the King Fahd International Airport in the Eastern Provinces, and as well the landscape design for the Royal Terminal and Royal Pavillion. These projects were completed over the years 1978 to 1986.

With Edman Avasian, Vesti's expert calligrapher and designer, at the Carrara stoneyard, Italy, verifying the stone carvings for the KKIA mosque mirhab.

At the Egyptian woodcarving studio in Jeddah going over our designs for the KKIA mosque doors.

With the ceramist Roger Capron at his studio near Nice, France, verifying ceramic colors and glazing for the KKIA mosque mirhab.

283

At the Carrara marble quarry in Italy, negotiating marble elements for the King Khaled mosque that was underway in Riyadh. Phyllis to my left. Across the table, Leslie Chabot, my vice president in charge of the Geneva office and project manager for the Middle East.

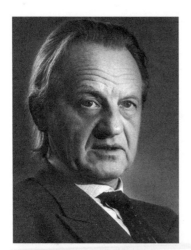

No longer a professorial scholar. Now a hardened businessman.

Below left: In conference with Leslie Chabot at the Boston office.

Below right: With Bechtel project manager in front of the mirhab of the completed mosque.

In 1986, the United States Congress revoked the five-year depreciation allowance on show horses. To make matters worse, the stock market collapsed. Most of the big-money breeders went bankrupt. To prevent that from happening to me, I sold my entire herd of horses in one grand auction, except for the young stallion Pomerol and one show mare. I also sold the farm. Because most of the work being done by my architecture firm, Vesti Design International, was in Saudi Arabia, the risk of taking on new projects there was becoming severe. Seventy-five percent of my gross revenue was from one client, the Saudi Ministry of Defense and Aviation. Over the latter part of 1986, and most of 1987, I completed all Vesti projects in the United States and abroad, and then dissolved the Vesti entities in both Boston and Geneva. I chose to abandon business and, like reformer-philosophers of yore, devote the balance of my life to writing. No more employees, no more flying all over the world on business, spending the better hours of my life in airplanes and hotels. The decision required a complete change. Not being the type to retire to a mountain cave, I went to Nepal, nonetheless, for two weeks of trekking, then came to Paris and acquired an apartment on Avenue Savignon de Brazza, one block from the Champs de Mars, with the Eiffel Tower outside my window. Phyllis would remain at her professional work in Boston, and come to Paris on holidays and when time permitted.

FREE AT LAST!

The apartment secured, my next move was to hire an assistant. Good fortune granted me Parry Jubert, an Persian milti-lingual dynamo, who, along with her husband, Jacques Jubert, remain dear friends. An excellent editor, trained in journalism, Parry was largely responsible for getting my writing on track.

With Jacques Jubert, at a café in Place Moufetard. Jacques teaches design at the Ècole Ètienne in Paris, and is one of France's formost postage stamp designers. He created the stamps and commemoratives for France's bi-centennial. He designed the first two books I wrote while in Paris, the autobiographical *MY SELF*, published by Èditions Fabriart in Geneva, in association with Presses Universtitaires de France, and *Scenario for an Artist's Apocalypse*, also published by Fabriart.

After a few months I was immersed in Parisian life. A soirée at my Paris apartment. The band is a genuine New Orleans-style creole combo.

With filmmaker Richard Leacock, my colleague when he taught at MIT, who'd also moved to Paris.

With friends Diane Wilson and Marie Berry, two jazz singers from Watts, California, at the restauant, La Muniche.

With Michel and Jacqueline Guèrin, two very dear French friends.

1988-89 New Year's dinner at the Paris apartment. With the writer, Silvia Sutton, and the MIT professor of architecture and my dear friend and colleague, Imre Halasz.

With Phyllis and Silvia, Imre taking the picture.

Writing and dinner parties still left time to join neighborhood kids at games.

With Karen Isgrig, Swedish-American-French *mannequin de la haute courture Parisienne*, my Paris companion and beloved friend.

With Nancy Spero and Leon Golub, two painters who figured importantly in my life from the first stay in Paris in 1962. This picture, from 1990, was taken on the occasion of Spero's major exhibition in Paris.

With Phyllis in Paris, the Château des Invalides in the background.

Paris would remain my second home town. But as an American in Paris, one is also a displaced person. In 1993, the time came to return to the United States. In Boston I still owned a large space in an early twentieth-century leather factory that I'd bought in 1987. Located in the Leather District of downtown Boston, between Chinatown and South Station, it was and still is a huge multi-layered open space, extending from the fourth up through the fifth and sixth floors, and onto the roof. I shipped everything from Paris to that space, but on my return, took an apartment in Boston's Back Bay, close to Phyllis' condominium. Rather than continue writing, I turned back to art making. The results of several months' work were exhibited at the Creiger-Dane Gallery on Boston's Newbury Street. Critical newspaper reviews of the show, which were not negative but ideologically driven by feminist reviewers, led me to write the booklet, *Forbidden Fantasies of the Straight White Male.*

I had not been forgotten in Europe. In 1994, I received a request to deliver the keynote address for a congress organized by the International Society for the Study of European Ideas (ISSI), the congregation to convene in Graz, Austria. Two years earlier, I'd given a talk at the ISSI conference held in Aalborg, Denmark. That talk became the core of my book, *Freud, Leonardo da Vinci, and the Vultures Tail*, published in 2001. For the Graz conference, I chose to offer a scheme I'd developed for a universal calendar to relieve nations from being bound to the ancient Roman calendar that, in modified form, became the Christian calendar in conflict with other religious and cultural calendars. My speech was covered by Austrian newspapers, and I was interviewed on Blue Danube News at Six (Central Europe's BBC). In 1998, I again addressed this congress when meeting at the University of Bergen, Norway. My topic was on the biological difference between need and desire, something that I, no more or less than you, perhaps, must cope with daily.

Having lived for a few years without income, to refurbish my financial state, in 1995 I moved to Scottsdale, Arizona, to take up architecture for a spell. This time I would work without a staff, other than one assistant, out of a large ranch house that I purchased and converted into a studio. I designed a small office building, and for very rich prople with houses under construction that needed individualizing enhancements, I designed main entrance doors, stair and balcony railings, stained glass windows, and a swimming pool. I continued making art when time permitted, and in the evenings translated Emile Zola's early letters, Paul Cézanne's early letter and poetry also. By the time of my return to Boston in 1998, my book, *The Youth of Cézanne and Zola: Art and Literature in Paris*, was almost finished. It will be published later this year.

On returning to Boston, I moved into the Leather District space and turned exclusively to writing. Shortly after that move, the entire third floor of the building came up for sale. In a swift move, I sold my space and on the same day bought the third floor. Over a period of six months, with a hired construction crew, I gutted the space, and built a large loft apartment. While the construction was underway, I stayed with Phyllis. When the apartment was ready for occupation, she sold her condominium and moved in with me. So we are once again together. The dogs having lived out their life expectancies, we bought two Bengal cats.

In 2001, my book, *Freud, Leonardo da Vinci, and the Vulture's Tail*, was published. A few months later the same press released my next book, *Picasso's Brothel: Les Demoiselles d'Avignon*. At the time of this writing, I have in press *The Youth of Cézanne and Zola: Notoriety at Its Source: Art and Literature in Paris*. This book, and the following three, will appear in 2003: *The Ara Pacis of Augustus and Mussolini, Cézanne and the Eternal Feminine*, and *Little Sister* (a novel written as a filmscript). In 2004, I will publish *The Picnic and the Prostitute*. My entire life is embedded in these books. When asked how long it takes for me to write a book, I respond, «Almost an entire lifetime.»

At the age of almost seventy, I took a trip to Iowa. The Hinton farm is still there, the remaining outbuildings not used and collapsing under the weight of time. No fences girdle the fields, as livestock no longer graze them. During the time I was there, I didn't see a horse, dairy cow, or pig, the latter now raised in climatized buildings, safe from germs, like babies in a nursery ward. Plow horses are now found in zoos or at fairs.It was soybean harvesting time, so I thought to join my still-farming cousins in Hinton and make a token contribution to the harvest. No four-horse team with eight reins in one's hands, seated on an iron seat, breathing in dust and chaff under a hot sun, but in the cab of a modern harvester with a bucket seat as comfortable as in a Porche, air-conditioned and sealed against dust, tape player and telephone, and a computer console to calculate what one is harvesting at the moment as to weight and its up-to-the-minute price per bushel on the grain market.

The bit of time in that harvester cab brought me full-circle. Once a farmer, always a farmer. Yet I must add, once a professor, always a professor. This year, over May and half of June, three hours each Tuesday and Thursday evening, I will teach in the Department of Art History and Archaeology at Columbia University. One achieves immortality by dissolving one's self in the minds of students, thus entering into the genetic flow of humanity.

Delivering the keynote address, «A Radical Revision of Historical Time,» for the International Society for the Study of European Ideas: *New Paradigms for the Next Millennium*, convened at the Karl-Fränzen-Universität, Gras, Austria. August 20, 1994.

The dirtfarmer's son's last harvest, 1998.

Adieu, mes amies. Adieu.

Notes

The nature of this book does not require the complete apparatus of an academic text. I would, however, like to recommend a few books on Iowa that the reader might enjoy, even though the best books on the cultural history of Iowa tend to stop short of the time period when this book begins, and hardly any deal with northwestern Iowa. An excellent general history is Joseph F. Wall, *Iowa: A Bicentennial History* (1978); for an admirable in-depth study of a single town within the context of Iowa up to the 1920s, one should read Thomas J. Moran, *Prairie Grass Roots: An Iowa Small Town in the Early Twentieth Century* (1988). For an unforgettable concentration of what Iowa represents as an agricultural state, nothing can tell one more than a few days at the Iowa State Fair held annually at Des Moines.

For more specialized books on Iowa, interested readers may wish to consult the following as my recommendations:

David R. Reynolds, *There Goes the Neighborhood: Rural School Consolidation at the Grass Roots in Early Twentieth-Century Iowa* (1999). Comprehensive and interesting reading.

William H. Cumberland, *Wallace M. Short: Iowa Rebel* (1983). Excellent coverage of the Milk War and Farmers Rebellion, in which Wallace Short played a significant role on the part of the striking farmers.

Growing Up in Iowa, ed. Clarence A. Andrews (1978). Fourteen Iowa authors tell their story of their Iowa youth.

John C. Hudson, *Making the Corn Belt: A Geographical History of Middle-Western Agriculture* (1994).

Lynn Marie Alex, *Exploring Iowa's Past: A Guide to Prehistoric Archaeology* (1980). A highly readable, authoritative study.

George Mills, *Rogues and Heroes from Iowa's Amazing Past* (1972).

George D. Glenn and Richard L. Poole, *The Opera Houses of Iowa* (1993). A book that tells you Iowa's opera houses were for much more than opera.

Mary Bennett. *An Iowa Album: A Photographic History, 1860-1920* (1990). A rich archive of photography, with excellent commentaries.

Cornelia F. Mutel, *Fragile Giants: A Natural History of the Loess Hills* (1989). Beyond the geology, an excellent reference book for northwestern Iowa's fauna and flora.

John F. Schmidt, *A Historical Profile of Sioux City* (1993; first published 1969). Most enjoyable reading, well illustrated. Available for purchase at the Sioux City Museum.

Douglas Bauer, *Prairie City, Iowa* (1979).

Heartland: *Comparative Histories of the Midwestern States*, ed. James H. Madison (1988).

Endnotes

1. Sioux City *Journal*, April 25, 1913.

2. C. C. Zimmerman, *Principles of Rural-Urban Sociology* (1929), p. 339.

3. The best place to experience the Loess Hills is at the Sylvan Runkel State Preserve overlooking the floodplain of the Missouri.

4. Bruguier's cabin has been restored in Riverside Park as a tourist attraction. War Eagle died in 1851 and was buried on a high bluff near the mouth of the Big Sioux River. Sioux City residents built a monument to commemorate him, which was dedicated in 1922, but the bronze plaque was stolen, the monument vandalized, and destroyed a few years later. It has since been rebuilt.

5. Lincoln's presence in Iowa was also prompted by his ownership of warrant deeds to two farms in the state, one of 40 acres in Tama County, and one of 120 acres in Crawford County. He obtained these for his service in the Black Hawk War of 1832, when the United States Army put down Chief Black Hawk's efforts to regain his people's lands, especially the wooded bottomlands of the Des Moines valley. Lincoln's service was brief and uneventful; from today's perspective, it would seem terribly at odds with his moralistic attitude towards slavery that he should accept a gift of land for having volunteered to participate in the destruction of the Black Hawks. Lincoln had been a volunteer captain of an all-volunteer force that got as far north as mid-Wisconsin before being disbanded, not having engaged any warriors, but, as Lincoln recalled, having been mercilessly attacked by mosquitoes. Also, Lincoln's horse was stolen, so he had to make his way back to Illinois as best he could.

6. On the development of high-yielding Krug corn, see John C. Hudson, *Making the Corn Belt* (Bloomington: Indiana University Press, pp. 163-165 and note 43.

7. Statistics on rural electrification as reported the Sioux City *Journal* on November 21, 1939 and the Des Moines *Register* on August 10, 1941, and February 8, 1942.

8. Joseph Frazier Wall, *Iowa: A Bicentennial History* (New York: Norton & Company, 1978), p. 187. Amos Currier's statement is from George S. May, "Iowa's Consolidated School," *Palimpsest* 37 (1956), p. 3.

9. Macmillan and Doubleday established separate departments for children's literature, patterned on British models and the Librarie Hachette in Paris, France that had pioneered the children's book market in the mid-nineteenth century. In Boston, the Bookshop for Boys and Girls began publishing and widely distributing the Horn Book Magazine, a catalogue of books recommended for children. Public libraries responded by setting aside special places for children's books.

10. The horn fly is the first to show up in the spring. Half the size of a housefly,

it makes up for its smallness by forming gangs-twenty or thirty clustered on the shoulders or backs of cattle in pastures and feedlots. While the horn fly tortures the top side of the cow, the giant heel flies attack the flanks and legs; they don't alight, they dart, at times terrifying the cattle into stampedes. And if the horn fly and heel fly aren't enough, the cow may be attacked during mid-summer by the horse fly, which doesn't discriminate and will even attack humans. It cuts a gash in the skin, through horsehide cowhide, or human hide, and sucks the flow of blood like a vampire bat. While stamping its feet and swishing its tail, the bleeding horse gets assaulted by the deadliest fly of them all, the bot fly, which hovers in front of the horse's nose (a horse cannot see what is in front of its nose because its eyes are the sides of its head), darts in and lays its eggs on the hairs of the horses' nose, lips, and chin. On hatching, the larvae make their way to the animal's stomach.

11. As reported in the Sioux City *Journal*, December 1, 1939. For the population drop, see the Sioux City *Journal*, April 24, 1941. This figure may be a bit exaggerated. The Iowa Farm Bureau federation annual report submitted to the state convention in Des Moines in 1937 revealed that the large banks and insurance companies owned about 20% of Iowa's farmland, having taken most of it over through foreclosures. Relatives of the tenant farmers owned about 23%, usually parents or grandparents. The largest ownership of tenant farms was by retired farmers, widows, and estates. Reported by the *Iowa Fall Citizen* and printed also in the Des Moines *Register*, February 6, 1937.

12. Sioux City *Journal*, February 26, 1933. Among other reports, this is summarized Wayne Girard, "The Farmers' Rebellion," *The Nation* (September 7, 1932), pp. 207-08.

13. Charlotte Hubbard Prescott, "An Iowa Foreclosure," *The Nation* (February 22, 1933), pp. 198-199.

14. Guest editorial by Max Duckworth. Sioux City *Tribune*, August 11, 1932. See also "Farmers and the Public Weal," Sioux City *Tribune*, August 16, 1932.

15. Transcription courtesy the Sioux City Public Museum. Sioux City's other newspaper, the *Journal*, also supported the farmers, but was less emphatic as it depended more on urban subscribers. On August 19, 1932, the *Journal* said that while public opinion may not approve of the farmers' strike, it must admit that the tillers of the soil have sufficient provocation for definite action in some form or another. For a general coverage see William Manchester, *The Glory and the Dream: A Narrative History of America 1932-1972* (Boston: Little, Brown, and Company, 1974). Most of these events, as reported by different participants and witnesses, and put into the news by different reporters, have contradictory details. I am not claiming accuracy in every case but assume that a summary of what was reported is a fair account of what went on. See "3 Tell of Seizing Le Mars Judge in 1933 Farm Revolt," in the "Iowa Farm Register" section of the Des Moines *Register*, April 26, 1953. Also the Sioux City *Journal*, February 26, 1933.

16. These quotations are from *The Literary Digest*, May 13, 1933. For the *New York Journal of Commerce* quote, see *Literary Digest* (September 10, 1932), p. 9.

17. Quoted in *The Nation* (September 7, 1932), p. 208.

18. This story of the milk truck driver being killed is as reported in Wall, *Iowa: A*

Bicentennial History, p. 178. Wall cites as his source an interview with Ed Clafkey, a Ford dealer from Akron, Iowa, conducted in July 1957, but does not say who conducted the interview or where the interview may be found. See also, "Agonizing Period of Farm Holiday Violence in Iowa Recalled," Sioux City *Journal*, February 26, 1963, and "The Farmer's War for Higher Prices," *Literary Digest* (September 10, 1932), p. 9.

19. The airport was at 4320, 41st Street in Leeds. On 17 October 1914, an Iowa farm boy Billy Robinson, from Grinnell, set a new flight record of 390 miles at an average speed of 80 miles per hour in a monoplane he had designed and built. A few years later, he plummeted to his death in a cornfield trying to set an altitude record of 17,000 feet. In 1935, the airport hanger and equipment was sold to North Sioux City's Rickenbacker Airfield.

20. See the statistics for 1939 published in the Des Moines *Register*, December 3, 1939, based on 12 Iowa counties and 123 cooperatives over the United States. Iowa led in most categories; 92.5% of Iowa farmwomen had an electric iron.

21. Butter manufacturers had managed to make it illegal for Margarine producers to color the margarine yellow, as it might then be sold as butter to the unwary. By keeping margarine white, like shortenings such as Crisco, the low price of margarine did not negatively impact the price of butter.

22. In the Sioux City Central High yearbook, *Maroon and White*, Esther's name is misspelled as "Anderson." She is listed as having been a member of the Friendship Club, of Hesperion, Hi-Tri, the Jay-Cees, Junior Chorus, International Relations Treasurer and Vice President, and Senior Chorus.

23. The golf course was called Meadow Grove. The end of the 1930s saw it refurbished with grass greens and nighttime lighting for the practice range. A good many women also played golf. My information is from *Leeds, A Pictorial History* (Leeds Community Club, 1991), p. 95.

24. As far as I know, the plan to create an isolated red-light district was not carried out. On April 15, 1913, the Sioux City *Journal*, reprinting a column for the Marshalltown *Times Republican*, reported that Sioux City had no segregated vice district and no recognized brothel, but a great many questionable hotels. While Pearl Street still exists, a 1994 tourist plan of Sioux City omits the Fourth Street area and modestly lists only two bars.

25. For more detail on Haddock, see John F. Schmidt, *A Historical Profile of Sioux City* (1983), pp. 123-25. First edition 1969. Available at the Sioux City Museum.

26. Davie Berman's life is told in the frank and beautifully written book by his daughter, Susan Berman, *Easy Street* (New York: Dial Press, 1981).

27. Berman, *Easy Street*, p. 111.

28. These statistics are given by Schmidt, *A Historical Profile of Sioux City*, p. 203.

29. In 1925-30, Iowa's population was about 60,000 German, 50,000 Scandinavian (15,000 were Danish), 11,000 English, 11,000 Austrian, 7,250 Irish, 4,500 Italian; the least represented were Hungarians at about 475.

30. Quoted in Jeffrey Ostler, *Prairie Populism* (Lawrence, Kansas: University of Kansas, 1993), p. 175. See also Frederick Jackson Turner, *The Frontier in American History*

(New York, 1920).

31. See Peter L. Petersen, "Language and Loyalty: Governor Harding and Iowa's Danish-Americans During World War I," *Annals of Iowa*, Vol. 42, No. 6 (Des Moines, Fall 1974), pp. 405-417. See also, "William Loyd Harding, "Iowa War Proclamations," *Iowa and the War*, No. 13 (July 1918), pp. 43-47; also I. A. Nichols, *Forty Years of Rural Journalism in Iowa* (Fort Dodge, Iowa, 1938).

32. Morningside College grew through changes and amalgamations out of the Northwestern German-English Normal School, and was taken over in 1864 by the Methodist Episcopal Church, "to educate young ladies and gentlemen to become teachers in German, English, of German-English schools, and to offer students an opportunity to obtain a thorough knowledge of the German language." German-speaking Methodists were the largest and most influential group of Iowa Methodists. See Timothy Orwig, *Morningside College, A Centennial History* (Sioux City: Morningside College Press, 1994), pp. 66-67, 88-90.

33. See T. P. Christensen, *A History of the Danes in Iowa* (Solvang, California, 1952), pp. 89-94; Beverly Larsen, "Danish Heritage," *The Iowan*, Vol. 18 (Summer 1970), pp. 10-14. Also, Stanley M. Toyne, *The Scandinavians in History* (London, 1948), pp. 266-267; Burt Wittrup, ed., *Elkhorn's First Fifty Years* (Elk Horn, 1966), p. 15; and J. M. McClintock, "Letter to the editor," Des Moines *Register*, July 6, 1918.

34. Peder Sorensen Vig, Letter to the editor, Des Moines *Register*, July 31, 1918.

35. Iowa Code, Sec. 689.10-13. For general information see Edward S. Allen, *Freedom in Iowa: The Role of the Iowa Civil Liberties Union* (Ames: Iowa State University Press, 1977). This law was eliminated by the legislature in 1977.

36. See Schmidt, *A Historic Profile of Sioux City*, p. 133.

37. The Grand Peavy was named after Frank H. Peavy, who made his fortune in Sioux City and was the leading contributor to the construction costs.

38. Orwig, *Morningside College*, pp. 85, 105.

39. Most of what I will say about Harley Andersen's musical career is from his hand-written notes, now in the possession of Betty Andersen, which were compiled by his daughter as the booklet *Music Memories*.

40. Quoted in Schmidt, *A Historical Profile of Sioux City*, pp. 103-04.

41. Esther Pauline and Pauline Esther were daughters of Russian-Jewish immigrants. After graduating from Central High, they attended Morningside College, founding there a gossip column for the Collegian Reporter, called "The Campus Rat" by "PE-EP." The Friedman's double wedding at Shaare Zion Synagogue was a big 1939 social event. Esther Lederer took the pen name, Ann Landers, in 1955 when she took over the advice column for the Chicago *Sun Times*, and Pauline Phillips began the "Dear Abby" column with the San Francisco *Chronicle* in 1956. Their columns appear in some twenty countries and reach 165 million people daily.